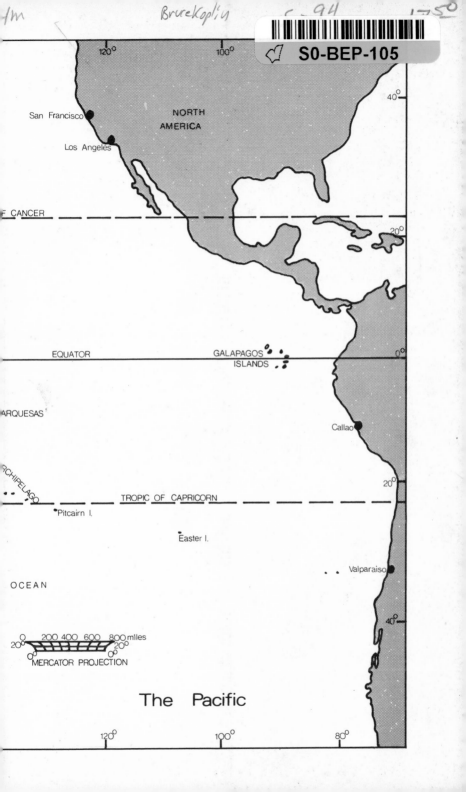

The Pacific

Grass Huts and Warehouses

To Greg and Harry

Grass Huts and Warehouses

Pacific Beach Communities of the
Nineteenth Century

Caroline Ralston

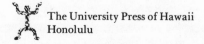

The University Press of Hawaii
Honolulu

Library of Congress Catalog Card Number 77-92406
ISBN 0-8248-0597-6

Simultaneously published by Australian National University Press,
Canberra

Manufactured in Australia

Printed by Southwood Press Pty Limited, 80 Chapel Street, Marrickville

Preface

Since World War II an increasing number of first-class Pacific history monographs have been published. This development of historical interest in the area, and the continuing emphasis that such history should be island-oriented, has been accompanied by a growing concern to move from the study of single islands or island groups towards more general comparative analyses. Koskinen, Morrell, Maude, Scarr and Pearson all focused their attention in at least one of their publications on wider areas of the Pacific using different types of incoming European agents, or the interest and involvement of an imperial power, as the organising centres for their work.[1] Maude's study of the Pacific beachcombers pointed out a further possible area for comparative analysis: the rise and development of the first beach communities.

Throughout the nineteenth century many visitors and expatriate residents in the Pacific referred to the aggregation of islanders and foreigners who lived in a variety of indigenous and Western style houses round the shorelines of the more frequented harbours as 'The Beach': hence the term 'beach communities'. Despite the fact that the five beach communities which developed in the Pacific in the first half of the nineteenth century appeared and evolved at different times, these proto-urban settlements had many characteristics in common, including their *raison d'être*, their combined island and foreign populations, and their problems of law and order, leadership and the maintenance of harmonious inter-racial relations. These and other similarities outweighed the differences in the beach communities and a comparative approach to the Pacific port towns proved valid since each settlement went through basically the same stages of development.

The attempt to compare the five beach communities, so diverse in location and whose development was not contemporaneous, gave rise to a problem of presentation — what structural framework would be most suitable? A comparative analysis of the beach communities for each developmental stage was finally decided upon as most appropriate since separate individual histories of the settlements with comparative summaries would have been cumbersome and would have masked the parallel development that did occur; in fact this would have constituted a partial withdrawal from the synoptic approach. Admittedly the method of presentation used forces the reader to jump across the Pacific both in place and in time, but I hope this becomes easier with practice.

The piecemeal beginnings of the beach communities were not difficult to document, but some explanation for the terminal dates chosen for each beach community should be given. In Kororareka, Papeete and Levuka in 1840, 1843 and 1874 respectively imperial intervention, either annexation or protection, marked without question the end of independent beach community life. The political and economic dominance of the expatriates was formally acknowledged while the islanders were forced to accept second-class, protected status. With the imposition of colonial rule these three ports became subservient to the dictates of European-oriented administrations and commercial interests. While Honolulu and Apia developed along very similar lines from beach communities to expatriate-dominated port towns, the Europeans' position was not recognised by official imperial intervention until many years later. Although Hawaii was not annexed until 1898, Honolulu was, by the mid 1840s, politically and economically in foreign control; *de facto* if not *de jure*. By 1843 the Hawaiian chiefs were committed to land and legal reforms and a form of parliamentary government, all of which innovations were manipulated to the expatriates' advantage. Similarly in Apia the Municipal Act of 1879 placed complete control of the town and the residents' affairs in European hands. Samoa was not annexed and divided by Germany and America until 1899, but by 1879 Apia had lost the significant characteristics of a beach community; the Samoans had neither power nor place in the port town, which became a foreign preserve, ruled over by the rival consuls of Britain, America and Germany.

This study of the first beach communities is a pioneer work which I trust will be refined and improved greatly by others over the years, as more specialist and comparative work is done. Perhaps inevitably it is not genuinely island-oriented. The size and emphasis of the whole project militated against independent island history in which European presence and influence would not be central. European documentation was all too readily and massively available, while island attitudes, feelings and ideas were not so prolifically recorded and proved time-consuming and difficult to find. More detailed trading and commercial histories and more genuinely island-oriented history would be at least two avenues through which a study of the beach communities could be expanded and improved. Limited in size, population and commercial activities the beach communities were no more than proto-urban aggregrations but three of them, Honolulu, Papeete and Apia, have become major Pacific commercial centres and this analysis of their origins and early growth provides at least in part the introductory framework for a general history of urban development in Oceania.

In the cause of readability notes have been kept to a minimum. The bibliography, however, contains a wide selection of the materials, both manuscript and printed, which were of significant use in writing this book. Any one wanting a referenced, fact-by-fact account is directed to my PhD. thesis, Pacific Beach Communities of the Nineteenth Century, in the Menzies Library of the Australian National University.

While working on this book I have received welcome assistance from more people than it will be possible for me to thank individually, but certain general and specific acknowledgments must be made. Field-work in the islands, an attractive proposition at any time, was enhanced by the expert assistance I received in several archives and libraries throughout the Pacific. In Honolulu my thanks are due to the staffs of the Archives of Hawaii, the Hawaiian Mission Children's Society, the Hawaiian Historical Society, the Bernice P. Bishop Museum and the University of Hawaii Library. In Suva Mr Selim Baksch assisted my research in the Central Archives of Fiji and the Western Pacific High Commission, now the National Archives of Fiji, while in Apia the staff of the Justice and Land departments helped my work greatly. In Wellington the staff of the Turnbull Library were also most co-operative. Finally in Australia I am grateful to the librarians of the National Library of Australia in Canberra and those of the Mitchell and Dixson libraries in Sydney who have throughout the seven years' gestation period continued to offer their justifiably renowned assistance.

For permission to use and quote from unpublished material and to reproduce pictures and photographs in their collections, I am grateful to the trustees of the Public Library of New South Wales and to the Hawaiian Mission Children's Society. The Peabody Museum, Salem, Massachusetts, owner of Stephen Reynolds's journals, kindly granted me permission to quote from them. To the Pegasus Press and the Hakluyt Society my thanks for their permission to reproduce maps 3 and 5 respectively in adapted forms. Access to records held in the Public Record Office, London, was made possible through the Australian Joint Copying Project (AJCP), directed by the National Library of Australia and the Public Library of New South Wales. Admiralty, Foreign Office and Colonial Office papers were read in the Mitchell and National Libraries on AJCP microfilms. I am also grateful to the editors of *The Journal of Pacific History* for their permission to republish in revised form as Chapter 8 my article, 'The Pattern of Race Relations in 19th Century Pacific Port Towns', from *JPH* 6 (1971), 39-59.

Several colleagues have been most generous with their time both in conversation and correspondence, in particular Professor Gavan Daws and Dr John Young. As a post-graduate student I greatly appreciated the opportunity to work in the Department of Pacific History at the Australian National University, the members of which offered expertise and time unstintingly. I remember with special gratitude the late Professor J. W. Davidson, who provided rigorous and stringent criticism for many of my ideas in their early stages. During the traumatic transition from thesis to book, Professor Torben Monberg of the University of Copenhagen offered me much encouragement and material support, while Professor John Smail of the University of Wisconsin, Madison, kindly but firmly pointed out that the rewriting could no longer be put off. Back in Australia I am grateful to Macquarie University for financial and clerical assistance to complete this project. And finally to Harry Maude, supervisor of my thesis and fount of continued advice, help and encouragement, my warmest thanks for such patience and enthusiasm. Clearly the advice and assistance I have received have been extensive and generous; however, responsibility for the interpretation and presentation of the following lies of course solely with me.   C.R.

Sydney, 1975

Abbreviations

Adm.	Admiralty Records held in the Public Record Office, London
AH	Archives of Hawaii
AJCP	Australian Joint Copying Project
BCS	British Consulate Samoa
BCT	British Consulate Tahiti
BPBM	Bernice P. Bishop Museum, Honolulu
CMS	Church Missionary Society
DL	Dixson Library, Sydney
DLNR	Department of Land and Natural Resources, Hawaii, Land Records
FO	Foreign Office Records held in the Public Record Office, London
FO and EX	Foreign Office and Executive, records in AH
HHS	Hawaiian Historical Society
HMCS	Hawaiian Mission Children's Society
HRA	*Historical Records of Australia*
HS	*Historical Studies: Australia and New Zealand*
JPH	*Journal of Pacific History*
JPS	*Journal of the Polynesian Society*
KC	Kuykendall Collection in UH
LCC	Land Claims Commission, Fiji (P — petition, R — report)
LMS	London Missionary Society
ML	Mitchell Library, Sydney
MMS	Methodist Missionary Society
NLA	National Library of Australia, Canberra
PMB	Pacific Manuscripts Bureau, Australian National University, Canberra
PMS	Peabody Museum, Salem
RNAS	Royal Navy Australian Station
UH	University of Hawaii, Library

USCD—   United States Consular Despatches
          A   Apia
          B. of I. Bay of Islands
          H   Honolulu
          L   Laucala (Fiji)
          T   Tahiti
USNR   United States Naval Records, Pacific Squadron
WTu   Turnbull Library, Wellington

Contents

Maps

Plates

one

Contact and Early Trade

Contact in the Pacific between islander and white was prolonged over a period of three centuries, during which time explorers discovered a number of islands, established satisfactory trading relations with some, and slowly increased the store of European knowledge about the Pacific. The kind of reception offered these first visitors was largely determined by certain cultural values and characteristics within the island societies, not all of which welcomed Europeans or their goods. It was not until the nineteenth century that sustained European trade and the development of beach communities in the islands began, the latter being heavily dependent on the former and also on the attitudes of the island hosts.

In Polynesia, the focus of this study, despite the dispersion and number of islands, culture and language were very similar. Politically the Polynesians were organised into hierarchical systems, which made it possible for a paramount chief to consolidate his authority over a numerous population inhabiting a comparatively large land area. This resulted in a wide network of loyalties and kinship relations and a relatively open political structure in which strangers of island origins were usually readily assimilated. Social and political styles of life in Micronesia had much in common with those of Polynesia, but limitations of land and population prevented the development of Micronesian chieftainship on the levels possible in Polynesia. By contrast in Melanesia, where a large number of isolated, culturally and linguistically distinct tribes developed, the small politically autonomous village units fostered a strong sense of group identity and treated any outsider as strange and almost always hostile. There was seldom a permanent superstructure of authority to encourage co-operation between the Melanesian 'big men', who won their positions by personal qualities and effort, and maintained only an unstable domination over their small communities. Clearly the reception of a stranger, island or white, would have been very different in Melanesia compared with either Polynesia or Micronesia.

From oral traditions, from European accounts of early post-contact times, and from the behaviour of the inhabitants on the Polynesian outlier islands, Rennell, Bellona, Tikopia and Kapinga-marangi, it is possible to establish a picture of the pre-contact patterns of Polynesian hospitality and receptivity. At no time had their world been a closed one. Islanders set out by canoe to find new homes or were swept away by sudden storms, and their reception and settlement on other inhabited islands were facilitated by the well developed social mechanisms in Polynesian culture for the assimilation of strangers: in particular adoption and marriage. Long before European contact, Tuamotuans were happily settled in Tahiti, and a regular link between the two groups was estab-lished. Similarly Fijians and Wallis islanders, who had been long resident in Savaii, were found living there peacefully when the first Europeans arrived. From the time of contact onwards the Europeans collected tales of the treatment of indigenous strangers arriving at the islands. While William Mariner was in Tonga between 1806 and 1808, the son and heir of the Tongan chief, Finau, returned from Samoa, where he had lived for five years and acquired two Samoan wives. A Tahitian woman arrived in Rarotonga after the explorers and first missionaries had landed on her native island, and thus was able to tell her hosts about the white men, their manufactured goods, and their new religion. The Rarotongans were greatly impressed by her stories and readily accepted her into their society. All these strangers, who are only a representative sample of a much larger group, were accepted into the social milieu of their hosts' community and assimilated without any major dislocation of the existing structure.[1]

Further from the Polynesian outlier islands, where until quite recently Polynesian communities still functioned along largely traditional lines, the treatment of incoming strangers has been well documented by anthropologists. Drifted canoes, which were ardently prayed for among the Rennellese, were believed to have been sent by the gods as gifts to particular individuals, whose duty it was to honour the visitors with food distribution rituals. Even castaways who behaved arrogantly were tolerated on Rennell and allowed to return home, which all but two arrivals seem to have done. Wives, usually of high rank, were offered to strangers on Kapingamarangi and Tikopia, and as a consequence present-day families trace their ancestry back to survivors from various drifted canoes. On Kapingamarangi a Gilbertese arrived whose cannibal habits were only apparent later, after a number of children had disappeared. Although the Kapingamarangi wanted to kill him he was eventually allowed to live on condition that he left the island.[2] From the legendary tales of Tikopia it is clear that a stranger was usually given a specific kinship title, land and ritual privileges.[3] The Bellonese have no traditions of assigning specific kinship roles to arriving strangers, who usually were called just 'friend'. Kinship terms were restricted exclusively to the Bellonese and Rennellese, but the bond of friendship was considered by the Bellonese almost as strong as kin ties — special friends had no secrets, and shared food and belongings without asking permission.

From the sources cited above, it would appear that hospitality was an established cultural characteristic of the Polynesians, but there is no reason to believe that this was so on islands where the necessities of life were only marginally supplied. On the coral atolls, for example, flotsam and jetsam were a major source of potentially useful materials, and were jealously sought after by all the inhabitants. While timber, pumice and other useful objects were highly coveted, the arrival of human migrants or drift voyagers was often a source of embarrassment. Thus oral traditions recorded by Edward Robarts in the early nineteenth century claim that the Marquesans landing on the Tuamotus were normally killed. Limited food, and frequently water supplies, combined with smaller, less elaborate political systems, conditioned the atoll dwellers' response to strangers who sometimes threatened their very existence.

On the high islands where, under normal conditions, considerations of available food and water did not influence the inhabitants' response to new arrivals, the Polynesians had evolved elaborate standards of hospitality of which their treatment of strangers formed a part. Material and sexual generosity and a willingness to accommodate newcomers were typical of Polynesian life in many areas. These characteristics could, however, be overridden if the islanders were threatened by famine or feared disease, but more frequently they were prompted to welcome strangers in their midst, and through their well established social mechanisms of adoption and marriage to assimilate them. Such traits augured well for the incoming European. But it cannot be assumed that the relative ease with which strangers of island origins were absorbed into another society, culturally similar to their own, would be possible in the case of a European of an entirely different racial and cultural background. The very appearance of a European amounted to a cultural shock for the Polynesians, who firmly believed that nothing lay beyond their island world. However, if the initial fear and suspicion on both sides could be overcome, Polynesian culture possessed the social values and attitudes, as well as the necessary institutions, to mediate the induction of alien individuals into it.

Balboa looked out across the Pacific in September 1513 but the honour of being the first European to sail upon it fell to Magellan in November 1520. From then until the end of the seventeenth century the Spanish, later succeeded by the Dutch, undertook sporadic exploratory voyages. At the beginning of the eighteenth century the majority of islands had still to be discovered by Europeans, but by its close the myth of the Great South Continent had finally been dispelled and all the major island groups of the Pacific were known to the Western world. Credit for this century of exploration belonged to the English; ultimately to Cook, whose three voyages of discovery between 1768 and 1779 left the Pacific a *mare cognito*. He had, however, been preceded by the Dutchman, Roggeveen, early in the eighteenth century, and later by Byron, Wallis, Carteret and the Frenchman Bougainville, all of whom sailed in the Pacific between 1761 and 1769. A number of small islands and many reefs remained to be discovered after Cook but by 1780 enough was known of the Pacific, its islands and resources, to tempt the first pioneer traders to hazard their ships and cargoes within its bounds.

Before the 1760s contact between the islanders and the Europeans was infrequent and largely superficial, except for Mendaña's disastrous second voyage. The northerly routes taken by the Spanish across the Pacific in both directions had kept them at a distance from most well populated islands, until in July 1595

Mendaña discovered the Marquesas. After a visit of eight or nine days at least 200 inhabitants had been killed, either by orders from Mendaña or casually by the soldier-settlers on board. Between September and November of the same year the inhabitants of Santa Cruz, where Mendaña attempted to establish a colony, suffered similar slaughter. With this exception, the trans-Pacific voyagers of the sixteenth and seventeenth centuries were primarily interested in crossing the ocean to the Asian markets as fast and as safely as possible.

But at the end of the Seven Years War Europeans again turned their thoughts to the Pacific and, as befits people from the Age of Reason, they were as much concerned with gathering exact knowledge about the Pacific, its people and resources, as with finding the Great South Continent, or new trade routes to Asia. Vessels stayed in the islands for longer periods. For all his Arcadian raptures, Bougainville only remained at Tahiti eleven days, but Wallis was there for over a month, and Cook on his first visit to Tahiti stayed almost exactly three months, while on his second visit to Tonga he remained two and a half months.[4]

Fresh supplies and rehabilitation of sick crew members were of first importance for all the explorers but they were also variously employed collecting botanical and zoological specimens, making astronomical observations and subjecting the island populations to a certain amount of haphazard anthropological investigation. Caution, however, dictated that the foreigners live strictly on board ship or in closely guarded camps ashore, so contact with the islanders was seldom sustained. Barter trade, which was well developed among the Polynesians, was usually brisk and easy, but it required a minimum of understanding between the two groups. Furthermore the explorers regulated bartering very closely in an attempt to ensure that sufficient fresh supplies and water were acquired before the islanders' desire for cheap manufactured articles was satiated. Until these necessities had been secured the ordinary sailors were forbidden to trade for curiosities, and their contact with island women was similarly curtailed as far as it was possible.

Before 1780 the only Europeans to have lived unprotected on the islands for any extended period were two Spanish Catholic priests left on Tahiti in 1774. Neither had the stamina or fortitude necessary for the task of evangelism and unfortunately they were too frightened of the Tahitians to establish any meaningful relationship with them. However, their interpreter Maximo Rodriquez spoke Tahitian well and gained the Tahitians' confidence.[5]

The balance of power and interest between the first European visitors and the islanders was delicate. Ostensibly the explorers were dependent on the island populations for food, water and women, but the islanders found that their ability to supply these wants did not give them licence to steal. Until fresh supplies had been loaded most Europeans were reluctant to display their superior military strength whatever the provocation, and many times the provocation was great. Any article lying unattached was subject to removal by a sleight of hand that the foreigners had to marvel at, however exasperated they became. Wallis, however, in 1767, was forced to repel the Tahitians' determined attempts to manipulate the contact situation to their own advantage and to acquire whatever European property they could. Only after two separate conflicts, during which about 100 Tahitians were killed, was Wallis able to convince them that military power lay in his hands. Both Bougainville and Cook, who visited in the following year, benefited from Wallis's demonstration of strength, which was not soon forgotten among the Tahitians. Whether the Europeans resorted to their cannons or not to regulate trade, there were still conflicting interests between the two groups. The foreigners' continued demands, not only for daily provisions but also for stock for the coming months at sea, put an enormous strain on an island's resources. However genuine their hospitality and desire for European goods, islanders at times faced the threat of famine if the foreigners did not sail away. The unexpected arrival of such numbers (sometimes as many as 200 men) was not something to which the Polynesians were accustomed. Previously, arrivals had been limited to, at most, the holding capacity of one or two canoes, except for the *ariori*, the company of chiefly persons who travelled throughout the Society Islands staging elaborate festivals for the god Oro, but their visits were anticipated and carefully planned for. The explorers found that the easy relations which were usually established in the first few days of contact often deteriorated if their sojourns were prolonged, and that their hosts became anxious to know when they would depart. Pressure on diminishing food supplies and acts of racist brutality by sailors and sometimes officers, made it increasingly difficult for even the most humanitarian captain or benign Polynesian host to keep the mounting tension at non-violent levels. Polynesians desired Western goods (some of them to the extent that they attempted to capture vessels when legitimate trading avenues closed) but when their own survival was at stake, they were glad to see the foreigners go. Despite the Europeans' seemingly miraculous powers the islanders were not overwhelmed by what the whites considered their superior civilisation. In 1802, while the Tahitians set a high value on such European goods as they found useful within the context of their own culture, they still considered their island and civilisation unsurpassed and liked to believe that the Europeans were dependent on them for food and women.[6]

The islanders had no opportunity to gain a rational insight into European culture, most aspects of which, beyond the foreigners' basic needs, were unintelligible to them. Chances for the Europeans to acquire some understanding of the island world were greater but their comprehension was limited by the brevity of their visits and the prejudices and beliefs they brought with them from the West. The superficial nature of this early contact, plus the inbuilt preconceptions many Europeans brought with them of the noble savage and an age of innocence, coloured their vision to such an extent that many described island life in terms of ideal Utopian societies. Chiefly tyranny, infanticide and human sacrifice failed to dispel their preconceived illusions. Not until the death of Cook, the massacre of La Pérouse's crew and the rise of militant evangelism did the image begin to fade.

The pattern of predominantly easy race relations established during this period cannot be considered as a norm which was later undermined by treachery on either or both sides. The generosity and hospitality of the majority of Polynesians were established cultural habits which persisted despite, or perhaps at times because of, their underlying fear and sometimes awe of the explorers. Mutual understanding was at a minimum, and later more intensive relations were to reveal, on both sides, attitudes, behaviour and systems of belief alien and often inexplicable in terms of the other culture. The novelty and the often festive atmosphere surrounding the early European visits inevitably gave way to suspicion and disappointment on more frequent and sustained contact. Total misunderstanding of motivation and intention caused tensions between the two races from the first contact, but even when this degenerated into violence and fatality, it was usually still possible to re-establish working relations once the Europeans had made clear their superior strength. More stable or intelligible contact was not possible, however, until the Europeans settled permanently in the islands. Through the explorers the islanders were made aware of the existence of an alien race utterly dissimilar to their own and were forced to make the first tentative accommodation to a society possessing other cultural values and procedures, but fundamental changes in island life did not occur until foreign traders and settlers appeared in the Pacific.

If one excludes the abortive expeditions of Mendaña and Quiros, the explorers were not intended or equipped to exploit the commercial resources of the islands, although of course they took careful note of any marketable product discovered. Further, far from encouraging would-be settlers, the captains used every means possible to prevent members of their crews from escaping ashore. The publication of the journals of Cook's three voyages to the Pacific, together with those of his forerunners, nevertheless revealed trading and whaling resources awaiting development, and the explorers' own experiences proved that the basic prerequisites for establishing commercial relations with some groups of islanders did exist. There was security, if one took certain minimum precautions, the islanders were familiar with exchange procedures, in many areas Western goods proved immediately acceptable and the islanders had surplus supplies to exchange for them. In Cook's journals there was evidence of seals on the north-west coast of America, timber in New Zealand, whales in many parts of the ocean and abundant supplies in Tahiti. This knowledge naturally led to the advent of commercial shipping, which brought not only trade goods but settlers to the islands.

One of the more immediate results of Cook's voyages was the establishment of a penal colony at Port Jackson. His very complete charting and descriptions of the east coast of Australia, combined with the knowledge of available provisions at Tahiti, provided the British government with a suitable dumping ground for its rapidly increasing surplus of convicts. Already at the earliest plan-ning stages when the colony was conceived as a penal settlement exclusively, the East India Company jealously insisted on its monopoly trading rights in eastern waters. Astute Company officials anticipated the time when ex-convicts or free settlers in the proposed colony would turn their eyes and resources to the commercial potential of the Pacific. Despite the Company's efforts to protect their trading empire from the encroachment of colonial vessels, the terms of Governor Phillip's and his successors' com-

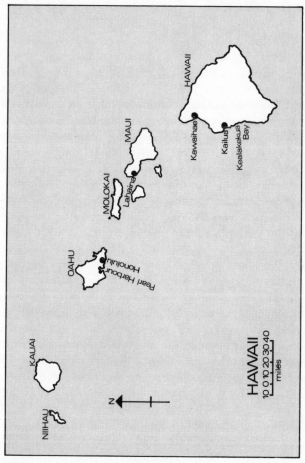

Map 2 Hawaii

missions put the islands of the south Pacific as far east as the Marquesas within the sphere of domestic trade for Port Jackson vessels.[7] Though colonial vessels were prohibited from trading to the north with China or the Asian mainland they were perfectly within their rights to roam the waters of the south Pacific and bring their cargoes to Sydney for sale, or re-shipment in Company bottoms. The colony was not slow to take advantage of these rights. In 1802, only fourteen years after the first convicts had been landed at Botany Bay, private colonial vessels were scouring the Pacific.

The first major domestic shipping interest was the salt pork trade with Tahiti, which was initiated and encouraged by Governor King in the early 1800s. After two successful government-sponsored trips to Tahiti, the trade was taken over by free enterprise in 1802. Between 1803 and 1807 only one pork cargo was collected but from 1807 until 1826 the trade supported an average of three cargoes a year. Profits, estimated at about 20 per cent per annum, were not great but there was a large degree of security and an established market. Pearls, discovered in the Tuamotus in 1803, and sandalwood first exported from the Marquesas in 1810, tempted Australian traders engaged in the Tahitian pork trade, but the risks from shipwreck or island hostility were high, and cargoes, which were liable for duty, could not be disposed of readily on the Sydney market. Despite its humbler profits the pork trade outlasted both the pearl and sandalwood ventures, which declined after 1817. Pearling was taken up again later by traders from Chilean ports but Marquesan sandalwood never regained its position as a major Pacific export.[8]

New Zealand, distant only 1500 miles from Australia, attracted a large number of colonial vessels from both New South Wales and Van Diemen's Land. Those engaged in whaling and sealing concentrated on the more southerly bays and waters of New Zealand and sailed directly to and fro across the Tasman sea, but ships working in the north of the North Island of New Zealand, especially at the Bay of Islands, were frequently involved in further Pacific trade at Tahiti or Fiji. The Bay of Islands lay on the most convenient route for sailing vessels leaving Sydney for the south Pacific. Thus between 1802 and 1827 several colonial vessels in northern New Zealand waters were refreshing and collecting

cargoes on their outward voyages to the islands north or north-
east. By 1810 eleven Sydney merchants had shipped cargoes,
principally seal skins, from New Zealand to Port Jackson. With
the decline of the seal trade, shipowners turned to timber and
flax. By 1816 sawyers were settled in northern New Zealand, and
prepared lumber was to be an important trade item for Australian
vessels until after New Zealand was annexed in 1840. The flax
trade was not so long-lived. A modest fifty-eight tons exported to
Sydney in 1826 had leapt to 1060 tons by 1831 when a Royal Navy
contract for cordage pushed the trade to its highest level. The
contract was not renewed and by 1836 only twenty-eight tons of
flax reached Sydney from New Zealand. Whale products dominated the New Zealand/Australian trade during the 1830s. Shipowners from New South Wales and Van Diemen's Land
established whaling stations in the South Island and along the
southern shores of the North Island of New Zealand. At one time
in the mid-1830s fifteen Sydney firms were operating twenty-two
whaling stations in New Zealand, and in 1839 one merchant,
Johnny Jones, had seven whaling establishments throughout New
Zealand and employed 280 men, which involved a capital outlay
of £15,000. By 1835 New Zealand products imported to Sydney
exceeded £113,000 in value.[9] Although Australian vessels virtually
monopolised the trans-Tasman trade, British and American ships
frequently called at the Bay of Islands, New Zealand's commercial
centre before annexation, but refitting and replenishing supplies
were their major activities. Attracted by more lucrative trades in
the Pacific, these vessels left the Australians to exploit the minor
products of both Tahiti and New Zealand.

News of stands of sandalwood growing on the south-west coast
of Vanua Levu, Fiji, reached Australian and American traders in
Port Jackson in 1804. Despite East India Company regulations
the Sydney shipowners showed no hesitation in fitting out vessels
to engage in this the first luxury trade that had become available
to them. At Fiji, Australian and American supercargoes competed
against each other to gain the favour of the Fijian chiefs who
controlled the sandalwood trees and the labour needed to fell and
transport the wood to the ships. Several captains became embroiled
in local politics in their attempts to complete their cargoes. But
once the holds were full the Americans had the advantage of a

direct north-west passage to Canton, while the Australian traders had to return to Sydney, pay duty on their cargoes and trans-ship them into Company vessels. Not all merchants were so obedient to the dictates of the mighty John Company, but if they flaunted regulations and sailed direct to China they faced crippling fines and sometimes were forbidden to unload their cargoes. Until 1810 the profits made in the sandalwood trade convinced the Australian merchants that the extra difficulties were worth it. Robert Campbell, one of Sydney's most successful merchants, estimated that his net profit on a six-month sandalwood venture to Fiji was well over 100 per cent—a very much more exciting return than the 20 per cent per annum available from the Tahitian pork trade. Between May 1808 and May 1809 at least six Australian vessels were employed in the Fijian sandalwood trade, but cargoes became increasingly difficult to collect, the quality of the wood deteriorated and the reactions of the Fijians became more and more difficult to predict. After 1810 the Australian merchants turned their interests elsewhere, leaving the Americans virtually to monopolise the final years of the sandalwood trade between 1810 and 1814. Later in the 1840s and 1850s New South Wales, freed from the East India Company restrictions since 1834, dominated the sandalwood trade in the New Hebrides and New Caledonia.[10] The colony's first economic probes into the Pacific were neither on a large scale nor highly profitable, except for the sandalwood trade, but they were responsible in part for introducing Western trading practices to the Pacific islands.

The establishment of New South Wales intensified European contact with the south Pacific and fostered particular trades that would otherwise have been ignored or pursued with less vigour. But even at this early stage of Pacific development Australian commerce was only a small part of the whole economic complex: the Americans dominated the lucrative luxury products and played a major role in the whaling industry. However, the presence of the struggling convict colony was responsible for tempting the first American vessels into the south Pacific. By 1796 American traders had found that speculative cargoes of spirits and provisions could be sold at great profit in Sydney, if the colony's need was such that the governor was forced to permit the sale. Cargoes for the China markets were then sought in the adjacent islands. Later,

American contact with Port Jackson diminished as the colony became self-supporting and the Americans established themselves in the islands, where they could refit and refresh without recourse to Sydney, and from whence they were free to trade direct with China with any cargo they could find that was marketable.[11]

Before American vessels were drawn to the south Pacific they had long been involved in the export of furs from the north-west coast of America across the north Pacific to Canton. British ships were first on the coast in 1785, but East India Company regulations and Spanish rivalry inhibited their activity and the Americans soon took over from them.[12] By 1790 the first major Pacific trade was well established with the indiscriminate slaughter of seals, which set a pattern for purely exploitative trading practices elsewhere in Oceania. Hawaii was incorporated as a supply and refitting centre on the fur trade route to China and became the first Pacific group to receive beachcombers from commercial shipping.

Sandalwood was recognised on these islands as early as 1790, but although the Winship brothers gained monopoly rights from Kamehameha I in 1812, the stands were not systematically exploited until after 1815. By that time the north-west coast seal population had been drastically reduced and the sandalwood trade from Fiji (1804-14) and the Marquesas (1810-16) had ceased, due to the rapid depletion of resources and the increasing hostility of the respective islanders. Both in Fiji and to a lesser extent in the Marquesas, the Americans had had to compete with Australian vessels, but in Hawaii they were able to monopolise the trade despite the grandiose ambitions of Georg Schäffer, a German-born doctor temporarily employed by the Russian American Company who, between 1815 and 1818, illegally attempted to create a sandalwood empire on Kauai for the Company. Kamehameha I, with the help of the American traders, quickly scotched that dream. Steadily the traders gained influence over the Hawaiians by offering them irresistible cargoes of crystal, silver, silks, satins, framehouses and luxury schooners in return for promissory notes on sandalwood, which was available in the mountainous regions of Kauai, Oahu and Hawaii. During Kamehameha I's rule sandalwood contracts were quickly completed and debts did not proliferate, but after his death in May 1819 his successor Liholiho,

Kamehameha II, was unable to enforce monopoly control over the trade, and a number of Hawaiian chiefs began to deal with the Americans on their own behalf. The boom lasted until 1823, by which time the prices were down on the glutted Canton market, the supply of sandalwood in Hawaii was greatly reduced, and the Hawaiians had become extremely reluctant to pay their debts.[13]

No single trade item was discovered by the Americans to take the place of the valuable fur and sandalwood cargoes collected between 1785 and the early 1820s, but a variety of products noted on previous voyages was used to fill their holds—primarily bêche-de-mer, but supplemented when possible by tortoise-shell, pearls, pearl-shell, edible birds' nests and coral moss. Fiji became the centre of the Pacific bêche-de-mer trade, which was controlled almost exclusively by Salem merchants. Bêche-de-mer fishing required closer contact with the Fijians than the earlier sandalwood trade had done, and vessels remained in the group for longer periods of time. Collection and curing depots had to be built on shore in several places, and Fijian labour was needed in great numbers to collect the bêche-de-mer, bring in the wood necessary to build the smoke-houses, storage pits and trade store, and to stoke the curing fires and help load the vessels with the filled casks. Several captains who made two or three voyages to Fiji became well known among the Fijians. One such captain, J.H. Eagleston, made five voyages through Fijian waters between 1830 and 1841, collected 4437 piculs (a picul weighs $133\frac{1}{2}$ lbs) of bêche-de-mer, for which total outfitting cost \$10,397 while the five cargoes sold for \$80,241. During the same period Eagleston also collected 4488 pounds of tortoise-shell at a cost of \$5700, which he sold for \$29,050. Not all ventures were so successful; one of the worst hazards was shipwreck. Two bêche-de-mer vessels went aground during the same night in March 1831. In later years, especially during the 1840s, the reefs were so denuded of bêche-de-mer that it was necessary for the ships to remain much longer in the group and to establish several more curing stations to complete their cargoes. However, during the periods of most intensive trading in Fiji between 1828-35 and 1842-50 an average of three ships per annum worked through the group and exported a total of approximately 1200 tons of cured bêche-de-mer.[14] Like Eagleston most captains collected tortoise-shell, pearl-shell and other products while waiting to take on their major cargo of bêche-de-mer.

None of the above-mentioned commodities, which were widely available throughout the Pacific was, however, the special monopoly of the bêche-de-mer traders. While the big Salem merchants concentrated their ships in the larger island groups, small, individually owned and operated American vessels, whose number greatly increased in the Pacific after 1815, scoured the less productive atoll islands searching for cargoes marketable in China. The majority of these vessels, however, had to be content to make several stops among the scattered remote islands, taking on small quantities of tortoise-shell, pearl-shell, coconut oil, coir and hemp, which were all disposed of in their home markets, rather than in China. The English-born Trainer was one of these owner-operator trading captains, who spent much of his life in speculative voyages along the western coasts of North and South America and into the Pacific. In 1835 he left San Francisco in a well armed brig for a Pacific cruise, particularly to the Gilberts, which he had visited before, to collect bêche-de-mer, tortoise-shell, sandalwood and dye woods. In fact when he arrived there, only tortoise-shell and a very little bêche-de-mer were available. On his return voyage he called in at Tahiti to pick up a quantity of arrowroot and pearl-shell which he had ordered previously. After a voyage of about six months he had a complete cargo which he sold to good advantage in Valparaiso. From Kusaie in the Eastern Carolines, the whaling bark *Eureka* sailed on 6 July 1852 for Hong Kong not with a cargo of whale oil, which she had been unable to procure, but loaded with sandalwood, bêche-de-mer and tortoise-shell.[15] The smaller islands with fewer resources did not experience the frequent contact and disrupting pressures which characterised the sandalwood trade in Hawaii, Fiji and the Marquesas, or the bêche-de-mer trade in Fiji. But through the 'ragamuffin' traders, who took on board bits and pieces of cargo wherever they could be obtained in the Pacific, they were drawn into the Western commercial world and recognised the advantages of stockpiling their non-perishable marketable commodities ready to sell to the first passing trader, in exchange for increasingly acceptable foreign goods.

Whaling was the only economic activity in the Pacific which sustained a high profit level for a considerable length of time. By

the late eighteenth century, when Cook's journals were first published, the Atlantic whaling grounds had been fished out. The
first whaler into the Pacific in 1789 was the British ship, *Amelia,*
whose captain and first mate were both Nantucket men. News of
her successful voyage reached New England in 1791 and the same
year five American ships left to work the new grounds. Five British
whalers, after conveying convicts and supplies to New South Wales,
were in the Pacific at the same time. Tension between the East
India Company and British whalers was apparent from the beginning and by 1806 the British had left the field largely to the
Americans. Australian shipowners lacked the capital and experience
to venture into deep sea whaling on a big scale but they were
heavily involved in bay whaling and sealing from shore bases off
the southern coasts of Australia, Tasmania and New Zealand.
During the first two decades of the nineteenth century whaling
activities were concentrated on the western coasts of North and
South America and the eastern coast of Australia, but with the
discovery of the Japanese and equatorial whaling grounds in the
early 1820s, whaling vessels were drawn into the midst of the island
world and were eager to find places to refresh and refit there. In
the northern Pacific Honolulu became the unchallenged centre for
the whaling industry, while in the south whaling captains could
choose between Papeete, Kororareka, Apia, the southern islands of
Fiji, or the Marquesas to refresh and refit at, depending on which
was most convenient. Despite their seeming aimlessness whalers did
not roam casually round the Pacific, but worked through the
different whaling grounds systematically according to the migration
patterns of the whales, and their arrival at different port towns
could be estimated fairly accurately. The heyday of Pacific whaling
lasted from 1835 to 1850, but serious decline in the industry was
not perceptible until the mid 1850s and major recession occurred
only with the American civil war.[16]

During the first two decades of the nineteenth century island
products were shipped almost exclusively to the western Pacific
ports of China and Australia, or beyond to India, Britain or New
England. After 1825 some trade connections between the Pacific
islands and the west coast of South America were established, but
these were never to challenge the supremacy of the western ports.
The major trade was set up between Valparaiso and Tahiti in the

late 1820s, the principal cargoes being Tuamotuan pearls and pearl-shell, which had been discovered as early as 1803. Australian vessels had collected several cargoes of Tuamotuan pearl-shell between 1803 and 1817, but the high risks involved and the lack of official backing forced them to withdraw and the find was left for almost a decade before merchants based in Valparaiso and later Papeete commenced full-scale operations. Jacques-Antoine Moerenhout, a Belgian merchant from Valparaiso, fitted out his first pearling expedition to the Tuamotus in Papeete in 1829. After a most successful beginning Moerenhout continued in the trade throughout the 1830s and employed a large number of Tahitians and Europeans in Papeete to build vessels, staff his warehouses and pearling expeditions, and to work on his agricultural experiments. In 1828 a considerable quantity of arrowroot was exported from Papeete to Valparaiso and from that date island products were shipped from Papeete by the pearl merchants and 'ragamuffin' traders like Captain Trainer, to the south American coast.[71]

Coconut oil was first collected in commercial quantities for the Western market in Tahiti under missionary influence in 1818 (the price for a copy of the Gospel according to St Luke was ten gallons of coconut oil), but it was many years before it became a major Pacific export. By the early 1840s new techniques had been perfected for using coconut oil in the manufacture of soap and candles, and its consequent increase in value made the trade more attractive. Companies based in Sydney and Tahiti shipped coconut oil from Samoa, the Society Islands, Fiji and many of the smaller groups, especially the Gilberts. During the 1840s and 1850s whaling captains, who were aware of the increased value of coconut oil, would stop at the islands to land casks and trade goods to exchange for coconut oil and would return one or two weeks later after whaling in the adjacent waters. Later, bêche-de-mer traders who experienced difficulty completing their cargoes also collected coconut oil. For the islanders, most of whom had made coconut oil for their own uses since time immemorial, this trade provided easy access to the European goods they coveted. In 1857 the German Godeffroy company sent their agent, August Unshelm, who had been watching the growing value of Pacific exports from his office in Valparaiso, to establish a depot in Apia. By 1870 the company virtually monopolised the central Pacific coconut oil trade, through their agencies in Samoa, Tonga, the Lau Islands, Tokelaus, Gilberts and Ellice, Marshalls, Carolines, New Guinea, Niue, Futuna and Wallis Islands. In the early 1870s the company experimented with the making of copra (dried kernels of coconut) and began shipping it instead of coconut oil, which was soon superseded.[18]

The dominant characteristic of trading activity in the Pacific before 1870 was the fluctuation in economic importance of individual exports. One commodity was usually exploited at a time until its exhaustion or local hostility made it impossible to pursue the trade; only then were less valuable cargoes considered. However carefully merchants tried to conceal the discovery of a seal rookery or a stand of sandalwood the news soon leaked out, and a rush ensued. Nursing and baby seals were slaughtered, sandalwood trees felled and bêche-de-mer stripped from the reefs without thought of future cargoes. Depletion of resources was frequently coupled with glutted markets and low prices. Bêche-de-mer was recognised in Fiji by the earliest sandalwood traders, but it was ignored in favour of the more lucrative product until 1813, when Captain Robson, experiencing difficulty in procuring sandalwood, shipped the first sun-cured bêche-de-mer cargo. Later, when the Americans had learnt the smoke-drying method, which made large shipments possible, the Fijian reefs were fished until profitable bêche-de-mer cargoes could no longer be collected. The traders then took on mixed cargoes of any marketable Fijian product available, chiefly coconut oil.

In many trades there was an element of secrecy, great competitiveness between rival traders and a gamble with both fluctuating markets and the possibility of a hostile reception from the islanders, but behind it all lay the lure of great fortunes to be made. The first participants in a new trade might make a killing, but for the majority profits were hard-earned in the Pacific and the strain exacting. Those who came deluded by stories of instant cargoes easily collected and unprecedented turnovers in Canton often found the prospective cargo widely scattered and of inferior quality, the islanders suspicious, and the market once they finally reached Canton overstocked; not to mention the general hazards of sailing in poorly charted waters, sometimes among cannibals. Whaling products commanded a steady, high profit margin but it was not always possible to procure a full cargo even after as much as four years working on the grounds. Further, the conditions of employment were rigorous in the extreme and the wages infinitesimal for the men who served on the ships.

During the first half of the nineteenth century the proto-industrial societies of America and Australia exploited Pacific resources, and the profits were accumulated as working capital for new manufacturing industries. British merchant shipping was never absent from the Pacific during this period but most vessels were loaded with manufactured goods, or Indian opium, and did not need to scour the islands for marketable cargoes to sell in China. The British-China trade complex was more secure and profitable than any enterprise the islands could offer to English merchants. So it was predominantly Americans and Australians who drew the Pacific islands into the Western economic sphere, and provided the commercial shipping that was the basic prerequisite for the beachcomber boom, and later the economic stimulus for the development of the first beach communities.

two

The Beachcombers

The first Europeans to make any significant impact on the islanders
in terms of inter-racial understanding and the advance of European
interests and technology were the beachcombers. Before them the
explorers had established brief contacts in the islands, but intelligible associations and dealings between the two races were only
possible with the arrival of the beachcombers who, as less tran-
sitory visitors, were able to assume recognised roles in island society.
The *Oxford English Dictionary*'s definition of a beachcomber: 'a
settler on the islands of the Pacific living by pearl fishing, etc.,
and often less reputable means', covers superficially the nineteenth
century Pacific beachcombers, although the term 'settler' gives
greater permanence to their periods of residence than was usually
the case. In anthropological terms a beachcomber can be identified
as one of a number of transculturites, who, being temporarily or
permanently detached from one group, enters the web of social
relations that constitutes another society and comes under the
influence of its customs, ideas and values to a greater or lesser
extent. The uniqueness of the beachcombers' position among the
early white immigrants to the Pacific lay in their complete dependence on island hospitality and goodwill for their livelihood and
security. Those who were prepared to remain any length of time
in the islands inevitably found their skills and loyalties adapted to
the interests and activities of their hosts. If a beachcomber lived
among islanders who had had little or no contact with foreigners
and who were unaware of the value of iron, muskets and similar
goods, his presence in such a society was in no significant way a
catalyst for change. But once islanders recognised the value of
foreign goods and were eager to learn more about foreign skills
and knowledge, then a beachcomber settled amongst them could
play a very important interpretive and teaching role. It is these

economic and social roles and the relationships the beachcombers established with the islanders that were to facilitate the later development of beach communities and influence the pattern of race relations.[1]

Since Magellan the Pacific has tempted men to desert and settle, but they were only able to do so in any numbers when the first traders and whalers began to frequent the area, discipline on their vessels being customarily less strict than that enforced by the explorers. From on board ship most Pacific islands looked attractive, but once contact was established, the Melanesians did not prove so hospitable or eager to accommodate foreigners in their societies as the Polynesians or Micronesians. Sailors who were forced to impose themselves on the Melanesians through shipwreck or marooning found that life was dangerous and disease-ridden if indeed they succeeded in existing at all. Some Europeans did survive in New Guinea, New Britain, New Ireland and parts of the Solomons but those who later wrote of their experiences revealed none of the sympathy or affection for their hosts which is clearly perceptible in most beachcomber accounts from Polynesia and Micronesia. From the accounts of the beachcombers Leonard Shaw and John Renton, who survived lengthy stays on different Melanesian islands, it is clear that neither found his hosts very congenial.[2] With reason, Polynesia and Micronesia became the favoured beachcombing haunts.

Beachcombers appeared with the first Pacific trader and their period of influence in each island group varied according to trading patterns and the advent of other Europeans seeking more permanent settlement. The English and American vessels plying the north-west coast of America for furs in the 1780s brought the first beachcombers to Hawaii, where they and many later arrivals enjoyed security and some status until the second decade of the nineteenth century. During this period beachcomber numbers fluctuated continually. The maximum figure was probably about 150 throughout the whole Hawaiian group, but of this number few would have remained for more than three or four months. In the south Pacific the Tahitian pork trade, the Fijian and Marquesan sandalwood trades, the Fijian bêche-de-mer trade, and the New Zealand seal, timber and flax trades were responsible for conveying many potential beachcombers to the islands. In Tahiti beachcombing conditions were most congenial between 1790 and about 1808. Land and women were available to foreigners who participated in Pomare I and Pomare II's wars, and as long as a beachcomber had no great political or economic ambitions, living conditions were usually pleasant. After 1808 Pomare II's military strength was successfully challenged by rival Tahitian clans who

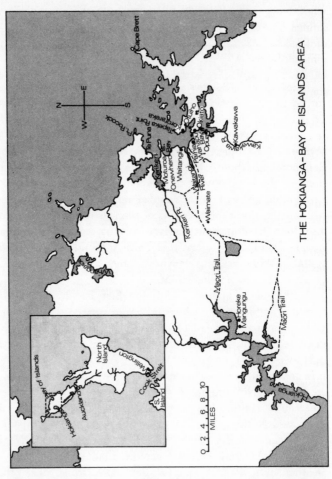

Map 3 The Hokianga-Bay of Islands area (with inset of New Zealand). Adapted from Lawrence M. Rogers *The Early Journals of Henry Williams,* Christchurch, 1961.

forced the chief and his followers to flee from Tahiti. Subsequent wars and the eventual triumphal return of the newly converted Pomare with the missionaries to Tahiti marked the end of beachcomber influence. At the height of their influence, beachcombers on Tahiti probably totalled not more than thirty-five. South of the Bay of Islands, in New Zealand, pakeha-maori, as the Europeans who lived with the Maori tribes were called, enjoyed great influence from the mid 1820s until annexation in 1840. In the Bay of Islands itself, where Europeans were more numerous and shipping more frequent, the pakeha-maori had lost much of his status by the mid 1830s. Constant shipping between New Zealand and the convict colonies of New South Wales and Van Diemen's Land was largely responsible for the high estimated total of about 150 pakeha-maori who settled in New Zealand, a significant percentage of whom were convicts or ex-convicts.[3]

In Fiji, where the missionaries did not arrive until 1836 and had little influence before the 1850s, there were two distinct periods of beachcomber settlement and status. Between 1804 and 1815 many sailors associated with the sandalwood trade deserted ships and allied themselves with Fijian tribes. During the lull in European shipping to Fiji between 1815 and 1822 these men were almost completely annihilated by the continual wars in which they became heavily involved. After 1822 until the late 1830s the bêche-de-mer trade encouraged many beachcombers to settle in the area, where they retained much influence until the 1850s. The total number of beachcombers in Fiji during the second period of settlement was about fifty. Samoa, which was avoided by traders and whalers for many years after the massacre of La Pérouse's crew in 1787, was frequented by beachcombers from about 1820 until the late 1830s, when the missionaries, permanent traders and consuls arrived. Beachcombers are known to have been in Samoa before 1820 but it was not until that date that any significant number arrived — the first two parties of them being convicts. Since Samoa was not part of any major trading complex during the early decades of the nineteenth century, the total number of beachcombers to settle there was not great, probably never being more than thirty. Beachcombing did not end once other foreigners had settled permanently in the major island groups, but rather its participants either changed their occupation or moved away from the centres where the newly arrived Europeans congregated.

Common sailors were the basic element in beachcomber populations; some of them intentional residents, who had deserted or been put ashore with their captain's permission, others enforced visitors who had been castaway, kidnapped by the islanders or marooned by a commander. To many of these men, subjected to cramped, insanitary shipboard conditions, often subordinated to inhumane masters and with little prospect of comfort or influence at home, life in the islands offered irresistible attractions. But of the hundreds who landed on the islands, few stayed longer than six months; incoming vessels usually found as many men ready to re-embark as there were wanting to leave. Disillusionment with island life was, in fact, rapid among most Europeans.

> Here, I at first thought, my dreams of island felicity were to be realized . . . But this could not continue. The gloss of novelty wore off in a few weeks, and disclosed the bareness and poverty of savage life, even in its most inviting forms. I grew weary of lying all day long in the shade, or lounging on the mats of the great house, or bathing in the bright waters. I soon found that the quietude of Samoan life was but apparent. Petty feuds and open hostilities disturbed this small world.[4]

The sailors who did adapt to this kind of life and who were prepared to remain for several years, usually had little education and even less love for Western society and its standards. This latter was presumably one hundred per cent true for the convicts, who would have had no ambition whatsoever to return to the 'civilised' world. The desire to change penal servitude for life in the islands drove convicts to steal boats from Port Jackson, Norfolk Island and the Derwent, to stowaway, and to desert from ships to which they had been assigned. Of the total beachcomber population in the Pacific about 20 per cent were convicts, the majority of whom were concentrated in New Zealand.

Early in the nineteenth century alarmist reports emanated from Sir Joseph Banks and certain New South Wales officials about the numbers of dissolute and criminal men in the islands and their fatal influence upon the inhabitants. Unquestionably the beachcombers as a group taught the islanders how to distil alcohol from a variety of native products, joined in wars armed with muskets, and some were excessively quarrelsome, but they were very seldom in control of the situation. Their very aggressiveness worked against them since they frequently murdered one another or were killed by exasperated chiefs long before they had caused any major harm. Not all beachcombers of common sailor and convict origins were the desperate, degraded characters some naval captains and officials delighted in describing. Several of them were literate, among them those who left invaluable records of their island experience, the majority of which, except the New Zealand items, Maude has listed and annotated. The crew of the wrecked vessel *Glide,* marooned on the south-east coast of Vanua Levu, Fiji, in March 1831, spent some of their time parsing passages out of Pope's *Essay on Man,* hardly a pastime that would corrupt the Fijians.[5]

A handful of better educated men, including a ship's surgeon, Stevens, a linguist, Davenport, an Anglican clergyman, Howell, an LMS missionary, Vason, and an East India Company captain, McCluer, also dabbled in beachcomber life in the Pacific, but not one of them remained in the islands long. Howell stayed in Hawaii only a year and McCluer, despite all his protestations of philanthropic zeal, was back in Macao within fifteen months of landing on the Palaus. Even the well educated William Mariner, who was a susceptible youth of fifteen when he was left in Tonga after the capture of the *Port au Prince* in 1806, stayed only two years and then returned to England.[6]

In established contact areas in Polynesia and Micronesia an incoming white could be fairly sure that his arrival would cause little disturbance, but at isolated islands little visited by Europeans, or on atolls with limited resources, a friendly reception was not guaranteed. On many islands the goods and sometimes persons of new arrivals were controlled by strictly observed regulations; thus stripping of clothing and removal of property occurred frequently, and sometimes even murder. In Fiji, the borderland between Polynesia and Melanesia, to be shipwrecked and arrive on shore with 'the salt water in one's eyes' almost inevitably resulted in death. In other parts of Polynesia and Micronesia, however, if a foreigner refrained from claiming ownership of his salvaged property, his subsequent acceptance was greatly facilitated. In time the islanders lost interest in many of the goods they had appropriated — the Tahitians played ducks and drakes with the dollars rescued from the wreck of the *Matilda* in 1792 — and items essential for escape, compasses, sextants and even boats could often be recovered. When the crew of the wrecked *Minerva* expressed their desire to send part of their number for help, their hosts, the Vatoans, returned their boat, sextant and compass, and supplied them with food for the voyage.[7]

On several islands ceremonies to prevent the introduction of any new disease and for adoption immediately followed a newcomer's arrival. In 1853 Captain Pease of the *Planter,* one of the first Europeans to appear off Nanumea in the Ellice group, was rigorously subjected to washing and propitious ceremonies before he was even allowed to step ashore:

Their manner of receiving strangers is most tedious and ceremonious but at the same time much of it is amusing and attractive. The stranger is required to stop at the water's edge five or six hours when the King and all head chiefs are engaged in religious ceremonies and consultations to intercede with their deities that the stranger may prove good friends, that no calamities may come upon their people in consequence of their strange arrival and to consult respecting the reception to be given and hospitality to be extended to the stranger during his stay on the island.[8]

In contrast, both the mate and the steward of the *Planter,* who were South Sea Islanders, were welcomed into the community without such elaborate ceremony. Later in 1862 a missionary on Nanumea recorded that all new arrivals were tabued until they had been subjected to a purification ceremony, which took almost a whole day. On Niue in the 1840s a marooned sailor was given a canoe, a paddle and some food and sent away by the islanders, who feared disease. He hid one night in an isolated cave on the island and the following morning had the extreme good fortune to paddle out and find another European vessel near the island. In 1853 on Tongareva in the Northern Cook Islands, the survivors of the shipwrecked *Chatham* were put through a process of adoption, which involved religious ceremonies, fresh water bathing and a long period of wailing and cutting of skin among the islanders.

Only later did they learn that by this ritual each of them had become the chosen 'child' of a particular chief.[9]

Apart from the earliest arrivals in some localities few islanders believed that Europeans were supernatural beings, but they were accepted into Polynesian and Micronesian communities as possible sources of new goods and skills, and in some societies as status symbols. Frequently the duration of a foreigner's welcome was pragmatically determined by the amount of property or the usefulness of the skills, if any, that he brought with him. Without either, his prestige rapidly diminished. The fate of a number of beachcombers in Tahiti in 1803 was typical of other parts of the Pacific:

> The condition of these men was by no means enviable; they complained very heavily, and with great reason, of the royal family; who after having tempted them to desert their ship for the sake of their property, had left them when become poor, to shift for themselves. They were now in the most abject state, differing little from the natives.[10]

While most chiefs recognised the value of skilled Europeans and were prepared to foster them, commoners often resented a foreigner's rapid and unorthodox assumption of status and influence. Kamehameha I, anxious to attract resident Europeans to Hawaii, gave wives and certain land rights to those he felt would be of long-term use to him, soon after their arrival. The crippled Archibald Campbell, however, who had been encouraged to settle in Honolulu by one of Kamehameha's wives in 1809, found the Hawaiians very lax in feeding and tending him during Kamehameha's absences. In Tonga in 1807, William Mariner found that even with chief Finau's protection: 'His life was still not only uncomfortable, but often exposed to many dangers, or, at best, he suffered many insults from the wantonness and malevolence of the lower orders.'[11] Throughout Polynesia and Micronesia commoners were likely to tease and harass new arrivals, who found it in their interests to remain close to a chief. This was particularly true for ordinary sailors and convicts, since the islanders were adept at distinguishing differences in rank and ability among foreigners and treating them accordingly. High rank, however, did not always protect one.

The priests composed a definite class of islanders instinctively hostile to incoming foreigners. If accepted into the community, a foreigner's very presence undermined the priests' power. They escaped unscathed from flagrant abuse of the tabu system, which should have resulted in great misfortune, disease or death. During a tabu period immediately before a funeral ceremony, Mariner inadvertently sneezed, an ill-omened occurrence in Tongan custom, liable to severe punishment. Protected by the high chief Finau, Mariner, however, was not punished and no later disaster befell him. James O'Connell and George Kennan on Ponape in 1830 knowingly ate sacred eels. When the bones were found the Ponapeans had little difficulty in ascribing the guilt, since not one of them would have dared do such a thing, but no judgment was passed, and neither foreigner later regretted the act. The impunity with which Europeans broke these tabus forced the islanders to recognise at least that Europeans were controlled by different gods, if not that their own gods were powerless. Clearly the priests had a vested interest in protecting their spiritual domain and keeping such influences at as great a distance as possible. On Tubuai in 1789 the religious men confronted by the *Bounty* mutineers:

> became jealous of us with respect to their religious authority to which they saw that we not only refused to take notice of but even ridiculed, for this reason they used all the Means in their power to keep the Chiefs from making Friends, thinking perhaps if we staid in the Island, their Consequence would be lessen'd.[12]

In Fiji the fate of the *Glide's* crew, who had been shipwrecked in 1831, was debated between the chief and the priest of the tribe in whose hands they had fallen. The chief's argument, that they could mend and use the new equipment acquired, prevailed over the priest's hostile demands that they be killed.[13]

An incoming foreigner had only his skills and perhaps some property to balance against this instinctive suspicion and distrust of the priests and commoners, but such was the Polynesians' and Micronesians' desire for foreign goods and knowledge that usually a beachcomber, however ill-trained in Western techniques, was able to gain approval and a position in an island community for a time at least. Highly acceptable to the islanders was the man who could handle and fix guns. They were not slow to learn these skills themselves but during the first decade after the introduction of muskets and cannon into the different island groups Europeans were essential for such services. The political and military importance of the introduction of guns into the island world and of the role the beachcombers plus their new equipment played in the rise of island kingdoms, will not be discussed here, since it more properly belongs in a study of island political development. Suffice it to say that during the early years of European contact a complex of island and European factors resulted in the unification of Hawaii, Tahiti and Tonga and the partial unification of Fiji. During the process the beachcombers were co-opted into island wars and often found their greatest influence derived from their limited military and tactical knowledge, while the success of one chief over another made it necessary for some of them to change their allegiance and places of settlement. Whether a chief was actually engaged in military aggrandisement or not a foreigner with a repair kit and a taste for fighting was always welcome. The beachcomber Diaper, for example, was warmly received in the 1840s among any Fijian tribe, with his box containing: 'a hammer, pincers, one or two files, screw-driver, together with some old leather, salt, bone, etc., for putting fire into the hammers of flintlock muskets, besides a bag full of scissors, mainsprings, feather-springs, hammer-springs, dogs, tumblers, plates, etc.'. As an individual Diaper was not highly respected among the Fijians, some of whom 'would say I was a leper, or like one, while others would contradict, by saying I resembled a pig with all the hair scorched off'.[14] Not surprisingly Diaper was thought most presumptuous for aspiring to a chief's daughter, who was considered far beyond his station. But he was able to force the Fijians to concede to his wishes by refusing to mend their guns. Charles Savage at Bau, Fiji, in the first and second decades of the nineteenth century, gained much status and respect through his prowess with a musket and his tactical skills. John Young and Isaac Davis rose to positions of great power and trust under Kamehameha I in Hawaii because of the skill and fidelity with which they led his army and navy. On Tahiti in 1803 Peter Haggerstein, a Swede, finally forced Pomare I to make good his promises of land by threatening to transfer his loyalties to another tribe. Pomare had no alternative but to agree since Haggerstein was one of the mainstays of his army.[15]

In times of hostility all beachcombers were likely to be called out to war, but they assumed equally if not more important roles in the economic sphere during daily life. The Tahitian pork trade revealed the organising talent of beachcombers Connor, Pulpit and Haggerstein, all three of whom were employed by the captains of the *Venus* and *Norfolk* in 1802. In 1803 Haggerstein took over the management of the trade for Captain Turnbull of the *Margaret*. He was responsible for buying hogs from all parts of Tahiti and transporting them to the harbour where the killing and salting operations were in progress. Through the sale of pigs, a large assortment of European goods reached the Tahitian population, whether they remained in the hands of the commoners who raised the hogs or were accumulated in the houses of the chiefs. Tahitians near the harbours frequented by the pork traders witnessed the organisation and skills needed to cure a cargo of pork and load it, and the nature of economic transactions between Europeans. With this knowledge, they were able in later years to conduct the trade themselves without the help of middle men. No islander needed encouragement to sell provisions, but the beachcombers often acted as overseers of the trade, helping them to get a fair price. Some of the more energetic foreigners cultivated potatoes, melons and other plants new to the islanders, who soon copied them, once they saw how acceptable these supplies were to foreign crews.

In the sandalwood, bêche-de-mer, and timber and flax trades beachcombers played similar roles — keeping an eye on trading transactions, and organising and controlling island labour when it was needed. From the island of Bau Charles Savage took parties of Fijians and beachcombers to the sandalwood areas of south-west Vanua Levu where they hired themselves out to the waiting vessels, and later returned to Bau with the trade goods they had been given in payment. The autocratic Hawaiian chiefs were fully capable of organising their own labour to cut and transport sandalwood, but Kamehameha I, at least, looked to John Young for advice concerning the justice of contracts made and the quality of the goods offered by the American traders. Later in Fiji, the beachcombers David Whippy, an American sailor who arrived in 1825, and William Cary, sole survivor of the *Oeno* crew, were in charge of the local organisation of the bêche-de-mer trade. Through them beachcomber pilots and interpreters were made available to the Salem traders if needed, and the Fijians were hired to collect the 'fish', as it was called, and to help at the curing establishments. In New Zealand in 1820, a Hindu Bengali who had been living with the Maori of the Bay of Islands for ten years, helped the *Dromedary* to take on a cargo of timber. He remembered scarcely any English, despite which fact his help was invaluable.[16]

Trade was not the only focus of beachcomber activity. Without their help in this sphere the islanders might have been more susceptible to unfair practices, but European goods would still have found their way into island societies. Of great importance was the beachcombers' ability to demonstrate the use of the more complicated tools and muskets appearing in the community, to refashion and resharpen iron implements, scissors and axes, and to mend broken equipment. Western methods of boat building revealed a variety of new skills to the islanders. The Tahitians were most interested in the boat the *Bounty* mutineers built in 1789, but they felt the process was too slow. Kamehameha I, who built a fleet of small Western style vessels to transport his army around Hawaii, appointed the English carpenter Boyd and other beachcombers responsible for its upkeep, and for building new vessels. Thomas Hunt, a follower of the Hawaiian chief, Kalanimoku, was always available to fit out and work his chief's small ships. He was also hired as an ordinary seaman on several voyages to the north-west coast, the proceeds from which were shared with his protector.[17] David Whippy and his companions at Levuka, Ovalau, were skilled ships' carpenters.

A blacksmith with a makeshift forge was never short of work refashioning scrap iron into knives, nails, and other articles, or sharpening axes. Leonard Shaw, on Kilinailau in 1830, probably owed his life to the fact that the inhabitants needed someone to fashion knives from all the iron they had plundered from the ship. Similarly James Magoun, sole survivor of the massacre of the *Fawn's* crew in Fiji in 1830, made himself, as he had hoped, indispensable, by constructing a forge in which he cleaned and repaired the equipment salvaged from the wrecked vessel. On Hawaii Island in 1794 a Hawaiian was found making charcoal under a beachcomber's direction, to sell to ships' forges.[18] Archibald Campbell introduced yet another new skill into Oahu in 1809, when, having repaired the sails for Kamehameha I's fleet, he set about to make a loom and weave new canvas. Not all new techniques attracted the islanders, but the majority had immediate appeal and the islanders were not slow to acquire them. By 1809 the Hawaiians near Honolulu had learnt several new trades and manned the forge without European supervision, a state of affairs which some beachcombers greatly deprecated, fearing that their period of usefulness would be shortened. Kamehameha's carpenter refused to help Campbell make his loom because he believed the Hawaiians would soon learn to make cloth and then European vessels would cease to visit. William Mariner claimed that the beachcombers refused on principle to teach the Tongans too many skills. Even Isaac Davis, who lived happily in Hawaii for over twenty years, and who was well integrated into the society, argued that the Hawaiians should be taught nothing that made them independent of whites. Such conservatism was, by 1810, already too late in Hawaii and became so in the other islands in subsequent decades. The beachcombers' part-island sons were nearly always taught their father's trade so even the most jealous artisan left his skill on the island in one way or another. Finally it should be pointed out that all this activity did not tax the beachcombers too greatly; none of them, however great a trader or artisan, was overworked. The majority idled their days away in a haze of native toddy or imported liquor for which they may have worked for a few hours. While the heavy drinkers were rarely the ones who rose to positions of prestige in island communities, their lives differed only in degree from the most influential.

With regard to European development, another important function the beachcombers performed was the interpretation of the incoming civilisation to the island people. New products, plants and skills were assimilated with the help of the beachcombers, but the Polynesians and Micronesians still had no conception of the world beyond the islands, the power and economic systems of Western nations or the empirical knowledge they had accumulated. On Tonga Mariner attempted to explain to Finau the nature of money, the function of the pulse and its relation to disease and passion, the general laws of the solar system and its effect on tide, and he taught him to use a compass. Lamont spent much of his time among the Tongarevans telling them of Western inventions. Undoubtedly the islanders received some highly garbled answers to their constant questions, and frequently such lectures were considered amusing entertainment on both sides. Vason on Tonga was much respected and esteemed once he had learnt the language because he could: 'amuse them with tales and descriptions of European customs, inventions, and events'.[19] Similarly on Ponape O'Connell and Keenan found:

> Not the least interesting among our occupations and amusements on the islands was conversation with the natives, and watching the avidity with which they swallowed whatever we told them, and the dexterity with which they applied the information thus gained to the improvement of their arts.[20]

Notwithstanding the limitations of the knowledge the islanders gained, by the end of the beachcomber era they understood the function of money, although most of their trade was still based on barter and they realised to a limited extent what importance Europeans put on individual ownership of property.

In Samoa, where conventional trading opportunities were not numerous during the early decades of the nineteenth century, the beachcombers found an unexpected market for the white man's god and the practices necessary for worshipping him. Early in the 1830s the Samoans received news of the new religion and, determined to enjoy the superior benefits of the white man's god, they turned to their beachcombers for explanation and guidance. These unlikely propagators of Christianity improvised their own churches and ceremonies; some genuinely attempted to reproduce what they remembered of Christianity, but for most the opportunity to set themselves up in a position of power and plenty was irresistible. When the LMS missionary John Williams returned to Samoa in 1832 he found many 'sailor religions' and other unorthodox creeds flourishing, the most successful of which was organised by Siovili, a Samoan who had lived briefly in newly converted Tahiti and been intimate with members of the visionary *Mamaia* sect who combined Christian and traditional Tahitian beliefs into a new millenarian cult.[21] The sailor priests inevitably lost out to the missionaries once the latter were permanently settled in Samoa, but while these quasi-Christian religions lasted, they were yet another example of the islanders' attempts to accommodate themselves, with beachcomber help, to their rapidly changing world.

Beachcombers were not, however, only valued for the new knowledge or skills they made available; some found a livelihood and status by adapting their talents to traditional island roles. John Danford, long settled in the mountains of Viti Levu, Fiji, was asked to officiate on calling the gods before the *yagona* ceremonies, since he was accredited with knowing the names of more gods than most Fijians did. The narration of tales from *The Arabian Nights* earned him two fat pigs. Jobs of great tabu significance were often performed by Europeans for the chiefs, whose persons and personal belongings were sacrosanct to their own people. Thomas Wright, formerly servant to the Reverend Walter Lawry on Tongatapu, remained on the island after the missionary left, and was responsible for shaving several of the chiefs. Similarly Thomas Sam was remuneratively employed as spittoon carrier for Kamehameha I.[22]

Patterns of beachcomber settlement changed according to political and economic pressures throughout the period of their influence. Brought to the islands by different trade and whaling vessels, they tended at first to settle with separate chiefs among whose tribes they hoped, as individuals, to enjoy some status. Together, beachcombers were prone to rivalry and fighting among themselves, which made them open to stealing and trickery from their hosts. However, such was the desire to have a resident foreigner that the chiefs rarely allowed them to live together, but shared them out among themselves. Eight sailors who had been stranded on Vatoa Island, Fiji, in 1829, were picked up by the chief of Lakeba when he came to collect tribute from the Vatoans, and taken to his township. There they were divided up among the petty chiefs. Similarly four deserters who landed on Abemama in the Gilbert Islands were distributed among the subsidiary chiefs by the High Chief, who kept only one for himself.[23] Strain on a single village's resources would also lead to a dispersion of sailors over an island, while in some cases when the island as a whole was too small to sustain an influx of castaways, the newcomers were generously assisted in their attempts to leave. Convicts and deserters arriving in the islands sought solitary inaccessible retreats in their efforts to escape later detection.

In Hawaii beachcombers at first conformed to this pattern of scattered settlement, living with chiefs throughout the group, but once Kamehameha I began his conquest of the islands they were rapidly drawn into his sphere of patronage. After the defeat of Oahu in 1795, the American Oliver Holmes, and several other foreigners, who had previously been allied with Kalanikupule and his lesser chiefs, found that security and status were available only from Kamahameha. In Fiji Charles Savage, fighting for the Bauan chief, Naulivoi, between 1808 and 1813, attracted the other scattered beachcombers to his chief, since it was not safe to live

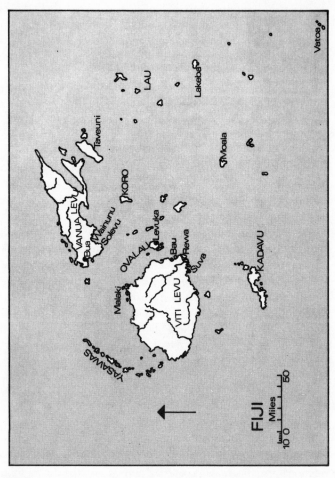

Map 4 Fiji

among his enemies. Again in Fiji in the late 1820s David Whippy
and William Cary, although they had been boyhood friends in
New England, were content to live separately and to associate
themselves with different chiefs until the arrival of the bêche-de-
mer traders made it to their economic advantage to settle together
at Levuka.[24] In Samoa and New Zealand beachcombers settled
individually among the different tribes and did not move into
white aggregations until the arrival of permanent traders or missionaries undermined their influence and forced them to seek new
employment. In the southern parts of New Zealand this happened
only after annexation. On Tahiti prolonged civil wars and the subsequent triumph of the missionaries led beachcombers to move into
Papeete or leave the island entirely.

The degree of integration into a Polynesian or Micronesian
society achieved by a beachcomber was conditional upon a number of factors: age, previous attitude towards the islanders, length
of residence, motivational considerations and the nature of the
roles he performed. Much integration was dictated by expedience.
Completely dependent on their hosts, beachcombers had to adopt
new habits and acquiesce to the demands of the chiefs. Many
Europeans, however, identified themselves with their new environment more closely than was strictly necessary. After his first two
years in Hawaii John Young had associated himself so fully with
Hawaiian patterns of life that in later years he rarely even visited
the growing town of Honolulu. To a lesser extent men like David
Whippy and Edward Robarts became champions of their island
hosts for several years before reverting to European standards.

In the interests of European development the ideal degree of
integration was for a beachcomber to become a mediator — someone with sufficient knowledge of both cultures in the contact situation to be able to interpret one to the other. Such a person held
a recognised position in an island community but was not a
de jure member of it. Beachcombers like Robarts in the Marquesas,
Whippy and his companion Cary in Fiji, Young and Davis in
Hawaii, Haggerstein in Tahiti, James Read and Thomas Wright
in Tonga and many others enjoyed such a position. They mediated
between the islanders and incoming foreigners, oversaw trading
relations, organised work parties and attempted to familiarise the
islanders with new Western goods and techniques. They were

1. Kororareka, Bay of Islands, New Zealand, 1836. Frontispiece in J. S. Polack. *New Zealand: Being a narrative of travels* . . . Reproduced by permission of the Mitchell Library, Sydney.

2. British Consulate, Tahiti, 1826. William Smyth Sketch book on board H.M.S. *Blossom*. Reproduced by permission of the Mitchell Library, Sydney.

happy to promote the Europeans' trade but usually they had no desire to leave their island homes. Complete and permanent integration in an island society minimised a beachcomber's influence, but few Europeans, it seems, were capable of total transculturisation. The majority of beachcombers submitted, under protest, to enforced tattooing, took part in island wars as a duty to their hosts, and accepted island wives with commendable good grace. Tattooing physically identified them as members of the tribe, while participation in local hostilities guaranteed their loyalty and an island wife gave them a social position in the community and a good opportunity to learn the language quickly. But none of these things inhibited their roles as interpreters of one culture to the other. On the contrary, active involvement in island affairs gave a beachcomber the opportunity to question island values and beliefs, even if he did so only by his attitude. Few beachcombers would countenance the cannibal feasts which usually followed a successful battle among the Marquesans, Maori, Fijians and Tongans. Some just absented themselves for the duration of the feast but others openly condemned the practice and tried to convince the chiefs of the evils involved. Savage, Whippy and Twyning at different periods in Fiji publicly denounced it, as did John Marman in New Zealand, and Edward Robarts among the Marquesans.[25] Little notice was taken of them but their temerity was not punished, and through them the islanders became aware of the instinctive European reaction to cannibalism. The Maori quickly learnt that in their contacts with Europeans it was wisest to deny any charge of cannibalism, and to isolate themselves carefully from white settlers before indulging in human flesh.

The duality of attitude apparent in some beachcombers towards their island hosts and incoming foreigners underlines the peculiar ambiguity of their position. Robarts protected the Marquesans from sailors' swindles and pleaded with the captains of vessels not to punish them when they were caught stealing, but on the other hand he cautioned Krusenstern: 'not to place any confidence in these islanders; to be always on our guard, and, when any of them offended us, to shoot them immediately'.[26] Further, he believed that it was his divine duty to stay in the Marquesas for the benefit of European shipping. Similarly O'Connell and Keenan were finally most eager to leave Ponape but, when the captain on whose vessel they departed became involved in a fracas with the Ponapeans, neither O'Connell nor Keenan would fire at their one-time hosts. Other beachcombers readily identified with their foster civilisation but still felt that their part-island offspring should be protected from the pervasive pagan influence surrounding them. James Read, wrecked on the Tongan Islands in 1820, twice left the group to satisfy a whim, but both times he came back and by 1830 had no intention of ever returning to Western civilisation. However, he devoted much of his life to the education of his three part-Tongan children, whom he sheltered from certain aspects of island life.[27] Such reservations helped to prepare the islanders for the attitudes and demands of the Europeans who followed the beachcombers.

A European who was capable of the degree of adaptation on which the islanders insisted and at the same time of acting as a mediator, often assumed a position of great influence and prestige. The protection and patronage of a chief enabled him to become a teacher and sometimes policy-maker, thus enjoying an authoritative position in island society. There are no recorded instances, however, of a foreigner becoming a paramount chief. Those who claimed that they were given chiefly status were in fact accepted into chiefly ranks as one among many, over whom there was always an ultimate authority. John Young and Isaac Davis, who both acted as governors at different times in the Hawaiian Islands, were always subordinate to Kamehameha I. Charles Washington on the Palau Islands, who attained considerable prominence in local affairs, was only ranked as sixth chief. No islander would have accepted as head and embodiment of his social, political, economic and religious cosmos, a man who was not liable to its tabu system, which was the case with most Europeans. Vason, for example, was able to assist in a Tongan war by setting fire to a sacred burial ground, an act no Tongan could have performed. On Oahu in 1809 Campbell described the strict respect paid to tabu regulations: 'White people were not required to pay these honours, though scrupulously exacted from the natives'.[28] Thus a beachcomber who had some influence could suggest or demonstrate new ways of doing things and could act as a focus for change, but always under the guidance of an established paramount chief.

During their period of influence a beachcomber, regardless of his status, made some impact on his host's daily life and accepted beliefs, while those with ambition were usually able to achieve some power. It was seldom, however, that a beachcomber remained the only representative of Western culture for long. Newly arrived traders and missionaries who wanted to settle in the islands reacted in different ways to the European residents already established, but both were to undermine the latter's position. Ship-bound traders, fearing plots on their property, vessels and even persons, were wary of unknown beachcombers who, it was believed, could entice their chiefs and people to acts of plunder and at times murder, if they were so inclined. The whites scattered round Viti Levu were justly notorious for such activities. Exasperated by the frequent desertions of his crew, who were enticed to settle ashore by unscrupulous beachcombers, the bêche-de-mer captain, Eagleston, wrote to Whippy and a friend: 'I think it would be a good thing for you two to give all this gang a lecture and see if they will not reform and if they do not they will soon be wanted for enticing people to leave ships . . .'.[29] A brisk 'talking to' was hardly likely to change these men, as Eagleston presumably well knew, but there was nothing else he could do except threaten naval intervention. Many beachcombers, aware of the light in which the rest of the world held them, supplied themselves with certificates from ships' captains who had found them reliable pilots and interpreters. For a few years the more stable beachcombers worked with the itinerant traders but once traders became permanent residents they enjoyed many advantages over their one-time partners or rivals, and had little cause to fear them.

To the missionaries a beachcomber was, without question, a renegade, profligate and godless. Such opinions, however, did not prevent them from accepting beachcomber help when needed. On arrival in Tahiti in 1797, the LMS missionaries asked Peter Haggerstein to use his influence and knowledge of Tahitian on their behalf with Pomare I. Through him land was made available, and when the LMS ship *Duff* continued her voyage to the Marquesas and Tonga, he went as pilot and interpreter. Despite this assistance and many other services, the missionaries refused to baptise his Tahitian mistress and then marry them as he requested.[30] In Tonga and Fiji the missionaries were similarly forced to accept beachcomber help to interpret their wishes to the chiefs, but few of them found it possible to change their stereotype conception of the beachcomber as a class. David Whippy in Fiji was perhaps the only one whose worth most missionaries who met him would openly allow.

The advent of traders and missionaries with supplies of foreign goods, and with new methods for obtaining access to the white man's god, marked the end of beachcomber predominance. Some stayed in remoter areas of the large island groups, while others moved further westward to the less frequented islands of Rotuma, Nauru and Ponape. Matthew Hunkin and Henry Gibbons in Samoa tided over the period between beachcombing and village trading by becoming missionary assistants, but few could emulate them.[31] Whippy and Cary in Levuka, and the foreigners who had followed Kamehameha I to Waikiki, Oahu, in 1804, had already moved out of the beachcomber milieu and were capable of, and willing to become, members of beach communities. No beachcomber had the means to prevent the islanders from turning to the missionaries and traders for explanations of the outside world and for the supply of the increasing number of Western goods that had by now been assimilated into their culture.

During the beachcombers' period of usefulness and influence, however, a tenable and easy relationship was established between themselves and the islanders. The killing of foreigners was usually due to differences or misunderstandings about concepts of behaviour, which had not yet been linked to doctrines of race. To quote two instances among several, all but Cary of the *Oeno* crew were massacred on Vatoa Island, Fiji, when they disputed the right of the visiting Ono chief and his people to appropriate their property. Similarly in New Zealand Rutherford's companion was killed because the chief's mother died after eating potatoes peeled with the companion's knife, which had been previously used by a slave. Rutherford pleaded for his friend's life, but the owner of the knife, who had been so careless as to let it fall into the hands of a slave, and then use it to prepare food for the chiefs, was held fully responsible for the death. The body was later buried, however, not eaten.[32] Generally the beachcombers were hospitably and generously treated, their idiosyncrasies and ignorance were tolerated, while their skills and property were duly respected.

The beachcombers were the only group of foreigners who settled in the Pacific in the nineteenth century to articulate a sensitive and well informed appreciation of the islanders. Although back in 'civilisation' a beachcomber's expression of his experience was inhibited by Western attitudes and values, there still remains throughout the extant beachcomber records a commonly expressed feeling of affection and respect for the islanders. The capacity and adaptability of the Polynesians drew acclaim from many of them. Campbell was impressed with the progress of the Hawaiians, while Morrison in Tahiti maintained that: 'The Ingenuity of these people is highly Conspicuous in evry article of their Manufacture . . . Their only pride is Cleanlyness and Generosity for which they are remarkable, and I may say that they have no equals in these points'.[33] Twyning's praise of the treatment which he and his fellow sailors received from the Vatoans in 1829 was less fulsome than most, but it emphasised the mutual tensions and difficulties to be overcome before a tenable islander/beachcomber relationship could be established, and recognised the consequent generosity of the islanders.[34] Even a man like the missionary Vason, who returned to England and sorely repented his lapse from grace in the islands, still wrote of Tonga and the people with a depth of attachment and understanding that no discreet reserve could hide. Whatever effect Western prejudices might have had on the writing of beachcomber memoirs, in practice on the islands the majority of beachcombers and their hosts were able to create and maintain remarkably friendly and mutually beneficial relations.

In the light of this, and given the fact that these first European settlers were insignificant in terms of numbers, and dependent on island chiefs for their survival, it is hard to substantiate the theory of Europe's 'Fatal Impact' in the persons of the beachcombers and later arrivals on the islands. European guns and personnel were used for Polynesian and Micronesian goals, while traders in bêche-de-mer, sandalwood and other island products found themselves dependent on the islanders to collect a cargo. Thus sandalwood traders in Fiji could not avoid involvement in the military affairs of the chief of Bua. Similarly, the widespread European fears of the bad influence that the beachcombers could, and in some cases did exert, totally ignored the independence of action and decision which all chiefs could exercise. It cannot be denied that a number of beachcombers in the different island groups taught the islanders how to distil alcohol, indulged in prolonged drinking bouts, treated island women poorly and were not averse to cheating their island hosts when the opportunity arose, but the chiefs had some control over them, if they wished. In 1845 the foreigners at Viwa, Fiji: 'became so uproarious and dangerous that the chiefs commanded some of the natives to tie them, which was done, and they were kept in that situation till they became sober'.[35] William Stevenson, ex-convict from New South Wales, living on Oahu in 1809, became so alcoholic that Kamehameha I deprived him of his still.[36] Further, there is at least one recorded case of the islanders corrupting Europeans. In 1811 the captain of a north-west coast vessel in Honolulu harbour found that:

> The natives surrounded the ship in great numbers with hundreds of canoes, offering us their goods, in the shape of eatables and the rude manufactures of the island, in exchange for merchandise; but as they had also brought intoxicating liquors in gourds, some of the crew got drunk; the Captain was, consequently, obliged to suspend the trade, and forbade any one to traffic with the Islanders except through the first mate.[37]

Whether influential advisers or drunken sots, the beachcombers were largely instrumental in the early processes of island acculturation. Once Magellan had entered the Pacific, the advance of the West was inevitable. The beachcombers made no conscious attempt to change island life, but their frequent refusal to countenance cannibalism and ritual killing, their unpunished violation of the tabu system and the superiority of some of their skills and property helped to accustom the islanders to the demands and behaviour of more stable European groups, who came later. Outstanding beachcombers like Young, Davis, Whippy and Robarts acted with responsibility towards their adopted people, introduced new ideas and skills among them, and explained many aspects of the incoming civilisation. Few foreigners visiting the islands at the time recognised the worth of such men, but Turnbull in Hawaii in 1803 was an exception. He wrote of their 'good conduct and character' and then continued:

> Fortunately, however, for these enterprising people [the Hawaiians], they have now resident among them several Europeans and Anglo-Americans, men of ability and knowledge; such

as Mr. Young, Mr. Davis, Captain Stewart, etc., etc. For twelve or fourteen years before our visit, these gentlemen employed themselves successfully in instructing the natives, . . . in many useful arts.[38]

The beachcomber role was not peculiar to the Pacific. Among the American Indians, the Aborigines in Australia and among certain African tribes, during the early stages of Western penetration in each area, individual Europeans were assimilated and became mediators and interpreters between the cultures involved. Before the pressures of Western penetration became inescapable beachcombers and islanders created a similar pattern in the Pacific. The equilibrium, however, was not permanent. With the arrival of Europeans, convinced of the superiority of their own culture and determined to change island society in their own interests, the balance of power was irrevocably upset. To the beachcombers' credit was the establishment of egalitarian race relations and the islanders' growing understanding of Western habits and methods, which were to help them cope to a certain extent with the surge of missionaries, traders, consuls and naval personnel who followed, demanding religious, economic, social and political change.

three

The First Pacific Beach Communities

The traditional cultures of the Pacific islands were essentially rural. There was no function for urban aggregations and indeed no economic structure that could sustain them. Most people were settled in household groups or hamlets along the beaches, in valleys leading to the sea, and in Melanesia in the more mountainous areas beyond. These settlement groups were focused upon, but not crowded about, ceremonial centres or the dwellings of leading persons. Despite their preference for dispersed rural living the Polynesians and Micronesians, at least, were not socially isolated. They travelled within island groups, and even beyond, as shown by the enclaves of settlers from other islands. Large gatherings of people did occur under special circumstances. Threatened with war, the Fijians of Bua Bay built a fort to protect themselves and their newly acquired European goods from the depredations of envious neighbouring tribes, but it did not subsequently become a permanent place of residence. Like the hill forts of Rapa, *pa,* built by the Maori, were of a more lasting contruction, but the residents worked outside the settlements and were accustomed to erect grass huts when engaged in long fishing or hunting expeditions. In eastern Polynesia the only settlements resembling villages were those concentrated round such exceptionally rich resources as the fish-filled Lake Maeva on Huahine. Pre-contact aggregations throughout the Pacific usually owed their existence to defence needs, an exceptionally plentiful food resource or to a hierarchical social structure causing concentrations of people round the court of an important chief.[1] The important distinction between these villages and later proto-urban aggregations was that in few cases were the former established for purely commercial reasons or in places necessarily suited to trade. In Melanesia central market places were maintained, often on small islets, to which the mountain people could bring their goods to exchange for the products of the coast dwellers. These villages were first and foremost concerned with trade, but they are found almost exclusively in Melanesia and Fiji.

One basic factor that militated against concentrated settlement was logistical: the need for people to live within reasonable distance of their food supplies. Several additional circumstances were also involved. While in many parts of the Pacific the islanders conducted elaborate and extensive trading operations, none of these transactions required any large *entrepôt* centre. Between Oahu and Kauai, in the Hawaiian group, considerable trade developed, the former exchanging *tapa,* the production of which it excelled at, for Kauaian canoes, spears and paddles. On Tahiti different chiefs controlled particular trading spheres — that between Tahiti and Mehetia was monopolised by the chief of Taiarapu who in the 1790s sent newly acquired European goods to Mehetia in exchange for island products including stools, pillows, matting, pearls and provisions. From Mehetia, trading expeditions were launched as far as the Tuamotus. Similarly the trade between Tahiti and Tetiaroa was monopolised by the Tu family. In the western Pacific, trade between Fiji, Tonga and Samoa was well established. The Tongans sailed to Fiji to collect sandalwood, pottery, canoes, timber and red birds' feathers. The last were re-exchanged in Samoa for fine woven mats, which were important in Tongan ceremonials. Within Fiji the production of many speciality goods was strictly localised and the artisans depended on trade to acquire regular provisions.[2] All these transactions were regulated through kinship ties or long established trading relations. Goods were collected together under the guidance of a chief and loaded onto canoes. No permanent storage or harbour facilities were needed and at the other end of the trading voyage where the bartering was carried out, similar conditions prevailed. In Fiji, the traditional exchange of goods between different villages or islands involved elaborate preparations. The host tribe built a receiving house to accommodate the visiting traders, but in keeping with trade elsewhere in the Pacific this was only a temporary structure.

Hostilities among the islanders were conducted on a principle of raid, plunder and withdrawal which made administrative centres for subduing and controlling a defeated people unnecessary. Pacific conquerors loaded their canoes with movable trophies and other plunder, and, after razing or otherwise destroying their enemies' houses and food supply, returned to their own districts or islands. Tribute might be exacted in succeeding years but no formal daily control was imposed. In none of the islands was the political structure so elaborate as to require more than rudimentary urban centres. Even the courts of the Polynesian chiefs were small in scale and often itinerant. Lastly, the Micronesian and Polynesian traveller who could rely on the wide inter- and intra-island ramifications of his particular kinship group was never in need of accommodation such as would normally be provided in town areas.[3]

The early explorers, traders and beachcombers had no occasion, and usually no power, to change the existing patterns of settlement. Trade for supplies was conducted from the ships' decks or tiny outposts on shore, while none of the first commercial ventures in the Pacific — the provisioning of fur traders in Hawaii, the Tahitian pork trade or the sandalwood trade in Fiji and later in the Marquesas — necessitated the development of proto-urban communities. Further, the beachcomber found all his needs well catered for with one of the island chiefs and his people. But when the earliest exploited products no longer guaranteed profitable margins, new commodities and trade patterns were instituted that demanded and stimulated the growth of port towns. Harbours with related onshore storage and informational facilities within the Pacific basin became necessary adjuncts to the development of the sandalwood trade in Hawaii, the bêche-de-mer trade in Fiji and the general provisioning trade to whalers. The major ports on the Pacific periphery, Sydney, Manila, Canton and Valparaiso, which had serviced the various trading ventures of the early nineteenth century, could no longer meet the immediate and multifarious needs of the new island trade complexes. The greater periods of time spent in the islands collecting cargoes and the discovery of the new mid-Pacific equatorial and Japanese whaling grounds remote from the peripheral refitting centres made a number of island bases essential, for although the marketable resources of the Pacific were not inconsiderable they were scattered across the ocean, from sandalwood in Hawaii to flax and timber in New Zealand. As early as 1818 the naval captain Alexander M'Konochie claimed that: 'The Pacific Ocean is of such immense extent, it is hardly possible that any one point should be susceptible of general application to all its branches of trade'.[4]

Granted that ports were necessary in the region, their location and number were largely determined by geographic and economic factors, and the range of choice open to European traders was restricted to a few harbour locations in the major archipelagos that alone constituted potentially viable trading areas. The factors determining trade (that is the availability of exportable products) also stimulated and determined the choice of a port's location, and vice versa. Thus the growth of sandalwood in Hawaii and the group's commanding position on the north Pacific trade routes, the growth of timber and flax in New Zealand, and the presence of bêche-de-mer on the reefs of Viti and Vanua Levu, Fiji, and of seals and whales in many areas of the Pacific, all interacted with geographic factors in determining the location of the five major Pacific island ports established in the first half of the nineteenth century. The location of a port within an island group was largely determined by the navigational needs of sailing vessels up to 1000 tons. Suitable harbours needed to have good anchorage of no great depth, open approaches largely free from reefs, and ease of entry and exit with the wind in various quarters. Access to the harbours by land was not important, since everywhere the sea was the main avenue of transportation whether by ship or canoe. The interdependence between trade and port location, plus the fact that only certain harbours were suitable for European shipping in each potential trading area, imposed severe limitations on the number of new centres. Alexander Spoehr, while discussing twentieth-century port towns, wrote: 'As these Pacific towns and small centers have changed from being *creations of necessity,* or for the convenience of administering metropolitan nations, to an ethnically integral part of the Pacific scene, they have become a focal point . . .'[5] Given the resources available and the presence of Europeans in the Pacific with trading propensities, Honolulu, Papeete, Kororareka, Levuka and Apia were 'creations of necessity' to make possible the development of the new trades. In contrast, Noumea, Honiara, Suva and Auckland were port towns established later, primarily for colonial administrative purposes.

The limitation of beach communities to Polynesia and Fiji was determined to a great extent by geographic fragmentation in

Micronesia and ethnic fragmentation in Melanesia. No island in Micronesia could provide an economic hinterland sufficient to support an independent beach community. The town of Agana, on Guam in the Marianas, did grow into a sizeable Pacific port under the auspices of Spanish rule but it was one of Belshaw's 'colonial-parasitic' towns, not a typical beach community.[6] At Koror in the Palau Islands the development of a beach community was pro-hibited by the chiefs in power. Similarly on Ponape, the more numerous foreigners were divided among the various tribes. Only on Kusaie in the Carolines did a beach community appear for a short time during the height of whaling activity on the equatorial grounds. But its size and significance were severely restricted by the scarcity of provisioning resources, difficulties of egress from the harbour and the unpredictability of the islanders' attitude to foreigners.[7] In Melanesia the inhabitants' deep-seated suspicion of strangers and the widespread debilitating diseases were inimical to the aggregation of small numbers of foreigners which marked the beginnings of beach communities in Polynesia and Fiji.

The first major marketable product to attract traders to Mela-nesia was sandalwood, found in the New Hebrides and New Caledonia. The short-lived trading stations set up by the Australian entrepreneurs Paddon and Towns during the 1840s and 1850s were, however, very different in structure and origins from the island ports to the east. Each depot was the deliberate creation of either Paddon or Towns, on one of whom every white inhabitant was dependent. They did not evolve spontaneously through the volun-tary co-operation of a few independent settlers, with the tacit agreement of the local chief.

In Polynesia and Fiji, where a number of beachcombers had been integrated into island society from the earliest years of the nineteenth century, Honolulu, Papeete, Kororareka, Levuka and Apia grew up with the new trades. A variety of factors drew pre-viously isolated beachcombers into these port areas. The deserters and castaways who had become disillusioned with island life after the first careless rapture found them convenient centres for seek-ing passages on incoming vessels. Once ships began to appear with some regularity in the island groups, other beachcombers were quick to recognise the profitable use to which they could put their skills and special knowledge, particularly in piloting and interpret-

ing. Hope of economic gain and independence from chiefly hospitality and its obligations drew some of them to the harbours
frequented by European shipping. Here, removed from daily involvement in island life, they enjoyed the psychological satisfaction
of participating in Western economic practices and of identifying
themselves with other Europeans. The money and goods earned by
the foreigners in these new pursuits provided the means to support
their island women and part-island offspring. These small multi-
racial groups, plus the agents left by the incoming vessels, were the
first inhabitants of the beach communities. The logistic problem,
which had impeded the development of aggregations in traditional
cultures, was overcome in the early beach communities by the
islanders' desire for European goods. Supplies were brought in from
an extensive radius round each centre to be bartered for axes,
cloth or whatever took the islanders' fancy.

Honolulu's early growth was largely due to internal political
factors. After the defeat of Kalanikupule, ruling chief of Oahu, in
1795, the beachcombers on that island gravitated towards the
victor Kamehameha I, the only chief south of Kauai from whom
land, wives and positions of influence were now available. At this
time Honolulu, which had been discovered by Europeans in 1792
or early 1793, was already used as one of the supply centres for the
north-west coast fur trade. Between 1795 and 1804, Honolulu
competed with Kealakekua Bay in Hawaii Island for the fur
traders' custom, but in 1804 when Kamehameha moved his fleet
and army back to Oahu, Honolulu became the focus of European
population and trade for the whole Hawaiian group. Kamehameha's desire to unite the entire Hawaiian group under his own
rule was the basic reason why he returned to Waikiki in 1804.
After his victory on Oahu in 1795 he had remained for a time at
Waikiki preparing an attack against Kauai, which was by then the
only major island in the group not under his control. But rebellion
on Hawaii Island forced him to return there before a successful
attempt could be made. While resident on Hawaii between 1796
and 1803, Kamehameha built up his fleet of European vessels,
replenished his supply of foreign guns, ammunition and equipment, and made very attractive, and often successful propositions
to skilled artisans and visiting sailors in an attempt to entice them
ashore and into his service. In 1803 Kamehameha left Hawaii

confident that all sparks of resistance were quenched on the island, and that John Young, the English beachcomber-settler who had proved his military prowess and loyalty throughout the wars of the 1790s, would govern effectively. With all his naval and military power, he sailed first to Lahaina and later to Waikiki, where his attempt against Kauai was again thwarted, this time by a foreign-introduced disease which swept Oahu in 1804.[8] Since Kamehameha was determined to conquer Kauai, Oahu was the logical base from which to launch an attack, and Honolulu the only harbour which could accommodate his European ships. Although no further attempt was made to conquer Kauai by force, Kamehameha remained on Oahu until 1812.

For a few years after 1804 Honolulu continued to compete with Kealakekua Bay but foreign captains became increasingly aware of Honolulu's advantages — its deep water harbour, good shelter and facilities for hoving down and repairing vessels. By 1812 Honolulu's predominance as the major port for foreign shipping was assured, and Kamehameha I's return to Hawaii Island in the same year had little effect on Honolulu's foreign inhabitants, who were by then profitably engaged in commerce and no longer in need of his patronage or protection. However, after 1812, captains engaged in the fur trade and later the sandalwood trade generally stopped first at Kailua on Hawaii Island to visit Kamehameha and to take on board one of his official messengers who sailed with the vessel to Honolulu and made sure that Kamehameha's instructions were carried out.[9]

The systematic exploitation of the sandalwood trade after 1816 was to sustain and increase Honolulu's development. While the sandalwood trader in Fiji had worked the limited wooded areas in south-west Vanua Levu from his ship, his counterpart in Hawaii a few years later found sandalwood growing on Kauai, Oahu and Hawaii Islands. Such dispersion required depots and agents in many places and one central harbour through which European ships could collect their cargoes and distribute trade goods. Only Honolulu had the facilities. Capital and goods from the sandalwood traders accumulated in the small port town and later when the Hawaiians' debts became difficult to collect, some agents previously scattered throughout the group were forced to settle in Honolulu in pursuit of defaulting Hawaiian chiefs. Thomas Brown, an agent for Marshall and Wildes, one of the two major New England sandalwood companies, wrote to his employers to explain his change of residence: 'The King of Atooi [Kauai] is now living on Woahoo [Oahu] with his new wife which has induced me to give up our establishment there'.[10] As an export sandalwood was soon exhausted but by that time Honolulu was so securely estab-

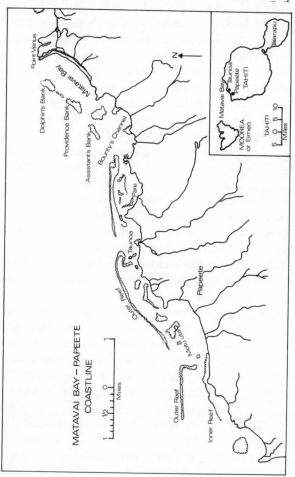

Map 5 Matavai Bay-Papeete coastline (with inset of Tahiti). Adapted from John Davies, *The History of the Tahitian Mission 1799-1830,* Cambridge, 1961.

lished that later economic development in Hawaii continued to depend on it.

In Tahiti the several anchorages available between Matavai Bay and Papeete were among the first known to Europeans and were later found to provide the best protection to foreign shipping throughout the Society Islands. For a number of years the explorers and traders took on supplies and refitted along this coast and it was not until almost fifty years after Tahiti's discovery that Papeete became the major port, in the late 1820s. Tahiti's lack of exportable resources, except hogs and other island products which were picked up along the coast wherever they were available, was largely responsible for this late development of a major port. The increased number of whaling vessels in the area in the 1820s, and more particularly the decision of Valparaiso traders in 1827 to use Papeete as an organising and storage centre for the Tuamotuan pearl-shell trade, marked the beginning of the port's rise to predominance. The harbour of Papeete had the advantages of double entry passages and protection against almost all weather except a hurricane from the islet of Motuuta and the barrier reef. Few beachcombers were numbered among the town's earliest inhabitants. During the civil wars of 1808 to 1815 they left the main island of Tahiti and in 1813 the missionary, William Henry, reported to Governor Macquarie that there were no foreigners on Tahiti other than the mission people. However, from reports of missionaries on the Leeward Islands, it is clear that a number of beachcombers had not moved far. How many returned to Tahiti after 1815 is difficult to ascertain. A pilot called Williams who was referred to in mission records in 1809 as being at Huahine appears at Matavai Bay in 1820, but it is not definite that it is the same man.[11] No reference has been found to persons who had been beachcombers in Tahiti living in Papeete once it was recognised as the major port. The new settlers in the 1820s were of missionary descent, like Samuel P. Henry and George Bicknell, or newly arrived in the Pacific, like Thomas Ebrill. These men and others who arrived in visiting foreign vessels were encouraged to settle in Papeete by Pomare II, who was eager to build up his own fleet and establish trading connections throughout the south Pacific. Later in the decade men of capital arrived from Valparaiso, and Papeete's position as the major port for foreign shipping in the

3. Queen Pomare's house, Papeete, 1835. Sketch by Conrad Martens. Reproduced by permission of Mr P. M. Smyth.

4. View of Levuka, Ovalau, Fiji Island. From a photograph by F. H. Dufty in the *Illustrated Sydney News and New South Wales Agriculturalist and Grazier*, 14 November 1874. Reproduced by permission of the Mitchell Library, Sydney.

Society Islands was assured.

Harbours suitable for sailing vessels were not lacking in the larger islands of New Zealand, but in the northern parts of the North Island where most European activity, except bay whaling, was concentrated, Kororareka had decided advantages over the other two possible port locations, Hokianga on the west coast and Whangaroa on the east coast. The former was exposed and a sandbar made entry difficult, but despite this, Hokianga became the centre of the timber trade and supported a viable community of sawyers and lumbermen throughout the 1820s and 1830s. Whangaroa, which European vessels shunned for many years after the massacre of almost the entire crew of the *Boyd* by Maori in 1809, did not have the shelter or good anchorage to compete with Kororareka, which was less than 50 miles further south, in the Bay of Islands, and which Captain Cook had highly recommended in his journals as a protected anchorage. This endorsement by Cook, plus the presence of the CMS missionaries after 1814, resulted in the Bay of Islands becoming the focus of European trade and settlement. In the late 1820s the flax and timber traders used it as a refitting and supply centre, although the products they sought were collected in areas beyond the Bay of Islands. It was not until the early 1830s, when the number of American whalers in the southern Pacific Ocean greatly increased, that Kororareka became an important whaling rendezvous port, where oil could be trans-shipped or exported, supplies bought and repairs made. Some pakeha-maori visited the town but most preferred to remain with their tribes where their livelihood was guaranteed through the flax and/or timber trades. Thus Kororareka's population in its early years consisted largely of sailors, convicts and ex-convicts and a few retired whaling captains. This early aggregation of foreigners was only possible through the good offices of the Maori chief Whareumu (King George) who in the 1820s finally persuaded himself that such a collection of Europeans would be an asset. Without his support, the foreigners would have been even more vulnerable to attack, especially from the powerful Ngapuhi tribe, and as it was, Whareumu was not always able to protect them from depredation.[12]

During the days of the sandalwood trade in Fiji, the incoming vessels anchored where best they could along the sandalwood coast of Vanua Levu, but no harbour facilities or aggregation of foreigners developed. It was not until the bêche-de-mer trade, which kept a number of men and vessels working through the group for several months, that a centre for information concerning the movement of ships, and a depot for mail, pilots, interpreters and skilled ships' carpenters became necessary. There were a number of possible harbour sites available in Fiji among which Levuka on the small island of Ovalau just east of Viti Levu owed its supremacy over Lomaloma, Galoa, Savusavu and Suva to its geographical centrality, the advantage of its two passages through the reef making it possible to enter and leave with the wind in almost any direction, and its relative isolation from Fijian political pressures. Galoa on Kadavu monopolised the supply trade to whalers. However, since whaling vessels were not numerous in this part of the Pacific, it never became a major whaling centre, as did Kororareka and Honolulu, and it could not compete in importance with Levuka.

At Levuka, as in New Zealand and Hawaii, a friendly chief, here Tui Levuka, encouraged and protected the first settlers. David Whippy tired of beachcomber life within a year of his arrival in Fiji and retreated to Levuka where he hoped to be uninvolved in the hostilities which so frequently convulsed Fiji. Before this Whippy had been allied with Tanoa, the chief of Bau, and it seems highly likely that Tanoa allowed him to retire to Levuka, over which he had recently gained suzerainty, so that they could monopolise the benefits from the itinerant ships that called there. By April 1826 two other foreigners had joined Whippy in Levuka. Of the two, one was a Manilaman from a Spanish ship, whose crew had mutinied in January 1824; the other is believed to have been Patrick Connel, a beachcomber from the 1808-15 sandalwood days. Very few beachcombers survived the hiatus of European shipping between 1815 and 1822, and none besides Connel is known to have moved into Levuka. William Cary visited Levuka in April 1826, but as he was still enjoying Fijian life and the protection of different chiefs he did not remain. However, more than a year later Whippy invited him to return and join him in piloting and interpreting for the Salem bêche-de-mer traders, an offer Cary could not resist. For their services to the ship *Clay* in 1828 Whippy and Cary were paid a boat, a keg of powder, two muskets and several small articles. After that, whenever Cary was not employed on the vessels, it was to his economic advantage to live in Levuka, available for employment by the next arrivals. During the first period of concentrated bêche-de-mer fishing, 1828-35, Levuka grew very slowly, since the handful of residents was largely employed away from the township on board the vessels or in the bêche-de-mer smoking and collecting depots. The second major period of bêche-de-mer trading, 1842-50, was more important for the development of Levuka, which became a shipbuilding centre and attracted a number of new settlers.[13] Most deserters and castaways who arrived in Fiji after about 1828 found life in Levuka more attractive and secure than with a chief and his people.

Finally in Samoa, Apia and Pago Pago were the only two harbours to offer sailing vessels good anchorage and shelter. The latter was the more extensive and protected of the two but the limited supply potential of the small island of Tutuila made Apia more suitable. Like Papeete and Kororareka, Apia lacked any large-scale marketable resources other than provisions, and was dependent on the supply trade to whalers for its early growth. Later the export of coconut oil and copra was to prove the mainstay of Apia's development. The first whaler known to have entered Apia harbour in 1836 found the LMS missionaries already there. In fact the presence of the missionaries, who were the first foreigners to settle in Apia in June 1836, proved to whalers and traders that the harbour was safe to use. Several resident traders followed the missionaries and set up provisioning and repair centres for the increasing number of whalers that frequented the port. The movement of beachcomber into beach community here is poorly documented. The high percentage of convicts among the original beachcombers certainly lessened the numbers eligible for such a transfer. Of the others, Matthew Hunkin and Henry Gibbons on Tutuila became missionary assistants and later village traders. A number of beachcombers moved into Apia seeking protection or guns to sell to the Samoans during the 1848 civil war. Only one beachcomber, however, is recorded as becoming a permanent resident in the beach community. He had lived on the eastern end of Savaii for several years when the LMS missionary John Williams met him there in 1830. By 1855 he had settled in

Apia and become involved in its political intrigues.[14] From respectable missionary beginnings in 1836, Apia grew slowly, until by 1850 it was recognised as an important supply and trade centre.

Geographic and economic factors have been emphasised as the major determinants in the location of the first beach communities, but human decisions and attitudes were also of undeniable importance. Without the co-operation, or at least tolerance, of the islanders the likelihood that the early proto-port towns would have foundered on local intrigue is very high. In 1851 on the Gilbert Islands of Abemama, Kuria and Aranuka, the ruling chief Tem Baiteke had all the resident foreigners, who were engaged in the coconut oil trade, killed. Exasperated by their continual disturbances Baiteke had decided to rid himself of these nuisances, and in the future to conduct all trade through his own officers. He thus flatly refused to allow the development of a foreign enclave on his islands. On Niue not one foreigner was allowed to remain. Under missionary guidance the chiefs of Rarotonga passed a number of laws to retard European settlement and the development of beach communities in particular—foreigners were not allowed to alienate land or marry Rarotongan women, and their trading activities were carefully regulated.[15]

In sharp contrast to these reactions, Kahehameha I, Pomare I and II, Whareumu and Tui Levuka were well aware of the advantages accruing from European trade and skills, and were prepared to encourage foreigners to settle in their territories. Gifts of land and island wives were offered to visiting craftsmen and sailors to induce them to stay. At different periods all these chiefs courted the possibility of attacks from neighbouring tribes jealous of the foreign trade goods flowing into them. Tanoa, to whom Tui Levuka was subordinate, greatly angered many leading Fijian chiefs in 1834 when he refused to allow them to plunder two foreign vessels beleaguered off the island of Ovalau, but to him the goodwill of the foreigners was more important.[16] Despite such hazards Kamehameha, Pomare II, Whareumu and Tui Levuka, in co-operation with Tanoa, persevered and under their auspices Honolulu, Papeete, Kororareka, and Levuka had their beginnings. Kamehameha I and Pomare II clearly benefited from the association. On the other hand Whareumu died in 1828 before Kororareka had become a thriving community, but his early encouragement had given the foreigners the foothold they needed. Finally it is difficult to gauge whether Tui Levuka prospered from his alliance with Levuka but certainly Tanoa and later Cakobau did.

The beach communities of Honolulu, Papeete, Kororareka, Levuka and Apia were not just subsidiary branches of the major ports on the Pacific periphery; they were also linked with a much wider complex of world trade. Levuka and Honolulu looked to New England companies engaged in the China trade for much of their early working capital. Later Honolulu, Apia, Kororareka and Papeete owed their development to New England whaling companies. Valparaiso was a second and important source of capital for Papeete. Sydney had extensive commercial links with Kororareka, Papeete, Levuka and Apia, all of which except Kororareka were strengthened by the expansion of the coconut oil trade in the 1840s. Trade routes across the Pacific incorporated island and peripheral ports with several major ports beyond the Pacific basin in a combined exploitation of resources.

None of the sites of the new island ports had enjoyed any great importance in pre-European times. A centre to the islanders was a place of ceremonial or military significance; canoes could be pulled up on any sandy stretch of beach, and trade in Polynesia and Micronesia required no special harbour facilities. European requirements for a town in the Pacific were very different. Ease of access and egress for their vessels, good anchorage, shelter, adequate onshore storage facilities, supplies and protection, and proximity to trading and whaling routes, all had to be considered. It was factors such as these, of concern only to Europeans, which determined the situation of the ports, and not those which had conferred locational importance to particular sites in the island cultures. In the Society Islands, before the advent of Europeans, Raiatea and Huahine were more significant in terms of culture and religion than Tahiti, and of the foreign-created town a chiefly Tahitian remarked: 'No native Tradition or dignity was associated with Papeete which grew into consequence only on account of its harbour'.[17] The chief exaggerated a little—the area where Papeete later developed and the adjoining islet of Motuuta, were used as a watering place in pre-European times and as an *ariori* meeting ground, but both activities were occasional only. As the organising focus of economic and political affairs, Papeete owed its existence

and development to the Europeans, and the Tahitians were forced
to recognise that it was the major source of European goods and
Western advancement. In 1827 Pomare IV, who had been brought
up in the town, settled there permanently and the quasi-parliamentary body proclaimed it the seat of the Tahitian monarchy.[18]

Similarly Hawaii Island had been a more important ceremonial
centre than Oahu. The sandy beach at Waikiki had attracted
great canoes, which brought the chiefs to holiday there, but none
had settled on the dry plains round the harbour of Honolulu just
to the north. Kamehameha I lived in Honolulu itself for only two
or three years, 1809 to 1812. However, in September 1820, little
over a year after his death, the chiefs in council at Kailua, Hawaii
Island, decided that henceforth Oahu should be the principal
residence of the royal entourage. At this time it was considered of
commercial importance only, Lahaina on Maui being the site of
the royal home and government meetings from 1820 to 1845.
Honolulu was formally proclaimed the capital city in 1850. After
the 1820 decree Kamehameha II moved first to Lahaina, and then
to Honolulu, arriving in February 1821. Both he and his successor
Kauikeaouli, Kamehameha III, preferred the relative peace of
Lahaina, to which they escaped as often as possible, but the growing foreign population and their incessant demands forced them
to spend increasingly long months in Honolulu.[19] Kororareka was
the site of a small Maori *pa*, but Whareumu, chief and protector
of the district, was just one warrior chief among many and the
area had no particular significance for Whareumu's tribe or the
Maori culture in general. At no time in its short existence did
Kororareka enjoy any political importance among the highly
independent Maori chiefs, who seldom frequented the town even
for economic transactions, preferring to work on their own or
through their pakeha-maori.

In Samoa and Fiji the islands on which the Europeans chose to
settle had not been of outstanding traditional importance. Savaii
in Samoa took precedence over Upolu, as did Bau and many other
places over Ovalau in Fiji. The area later to be incorporated into
Apia had been the site of three Samoan villages in pre-European
times; none of them, however, of any particular significance. In
1868 the Samoan chiefs and orators agreed to the formation of a
central government with its headquarters at Mulinuu, the narrow

promontory bounding Apia harbour on the west. From then on Apia was considered the Samoans' political capital.[20] Cakobau recognised the usefulness of Levuka and his dependence upon it as a source of European trade goods, especially guns and ammunition, only after he had banished its inhabitants to Solevu in 1844. Captain J. E. Erskine reported in 1849 that Cakobau had soon relented and tried to coax the foreigners back to Ovalau, but for reasons of their own they refused to go until early 1849.[21] Later,

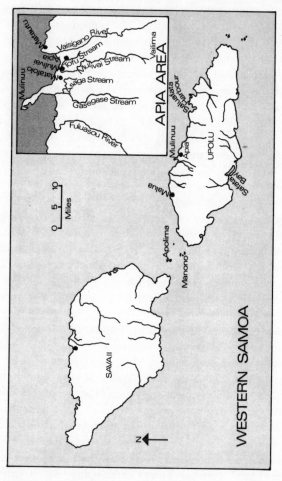

Map 6 Western Samoa (with inset of Apia)

although Cakobau never moved his permanent residence from Bau, he did allow himself to be crowned at Levuka and permit a series of quasi-parliamentary governments to work from there.

Two distinct functions were characteristic of island ports: one, the draining of local products (especially sandalwood, bêche-de-mer and coconut oil) from the hinterland to outside markets and two, the supply trade to whalers and other traders who were not basically interested in hinterland products as items of cargo. The two were not mutually exclusive: whalers after 1840 were willing to take on coconut oil while they provisioned or to leave barrels on the islands while they hunted on the whaling grounds nearby. Nor was a port confined to only one operation: Papeete served both Valparaiso and Sydney traders (who bought up coconut oil, pearl-shell and other island products) as well as American whalers. Honolulu began its commercial life as one of several supply and refitting centres in Hawaii for the fur traders. Later it thrived on the export of sandalwood, only to return to the supply and repair trade with the rise of the whaling industry.

Whatever their initial function the island ports slowly developed their commercial operations by expanding their economic hinterlands as well as the products they dealt with and the services they provided. Honolulu's hinterland was restricted to the Hawaiian group but from its strategic position it grew to dominate the north Pacific trade routes. As an *entrepôt* between China and the Americas, and in the path of whalers to and from the Japanese grounds, the lack of internal resources after the decline of the sandalwood trade had little effect on its growth. The products of the Society Islands did not attract big companies from the outside world, but Samuel P. Henry and Thomas Ebrill, under Pomare II's patronage, established themselves in the early 1820s as small island traders conveying sinnet, pork, arrowroot, coconut oil and other products to the New South Wales market. Under their auspices Tahiti gradually became the centre of the whole Society Islands trade. Later Tuamotuan pearls attracted merchants from Valparaiso to the eastern Pacific, to the benefit of Papeete, the only port in the region suitably equipped to serve the trade. Taiohae Bay, on Nukuhiva in the Marquesas, had the basic potential to make a good port for European shipping, but it could never overcome the advantages which the Matavai Bay-Papeete area enjoyed from its early discovery and subsequent use. Tuamotuan and Marquesan resources were therefore channelled through Papeete, later to be joined by Austral and Cook Islands products. Avarua, the only anchorage of Rarotonga in the Cook Islands, could not admit large ships across the reef. Furthermore the LMS missionaries stationed on the island looked to Tahiti as their base, which reinforced the geographic factors determining Papeete's predominance. Thus by mid century Papeete monopolised the south-east Pacific trade in pearls, pearl-shell and lesser island products.

After 1820 the Bay of Islands was little used by the timber and flax traders. Some, however, called into Kororareka for provisions, but their major cargo items were not channelled through that port, nor were the trades organised from there. Kororareka owed its major development to the supply trade to whalers, who began to frequent the port in large numbers only after 1830. Provisions were channelled through Kororareka from all round the Bay of Islands, and from north and south of it. Any products not sold to the whalers or other vessels were exported to New South Wales and Van Diemen's Land. Despite its rapid growth Kororareka was unable to diversify its services or exports and its complete dependence on the supply trade was partly responsible for the town's demise soon after annexation. Auckland became the centre of commercial and political activity, while Kororareka was closed as a free port. Levuka's hinterland encompassed the whole Fijian archipelago from which bêche-de-mer, tortoise-shell, birds' nests and some food products were collected. With the decline of the bêche-de-mer trade after 1850, Levuka was dependent on a motley trade of island products from all areas, including pigs and yams. The gold rushes to western America and south-eastern Australia gave rise to a transient provision trade which helped the Levuka merchants to tide over a thin period — 800 pigs were sent to California in 1851 and 80,000 yams and 200 pigs to Sydney in 1853.[22] The hiatus in systematic commercial activity in Fiji eased in the late 1850s with the expansion of the coconut oil trade, but Levuka did not recover from the recession until the 1860s and the arrival of new settlers to exploit the cotton boom.

The Samoan Islands which constituted Apia's hinterland were little exploited during the port's early economic development, based as it was on the supply trade to whalers. Small quantities of coconut oil were exported, but the islands' oil-exporting capacity was not fully recognised until August Unshelm established an agency for the Hamburg-based Godeffroy company in Apia in 1857. At the centre of an area with a high potential for coconut oil production, and unclaimed by any Western power, Samoa was an eminently suitable place for the Germans to move into. By 1870 the Godeffroy company had agents stationed throughout the central Pacific — in fact, 'they had an agent in every productive island inhabited by natives sufficiently well-disposed to permit a white man to reside among them'.[23] Apia became the centre of the Godeffroy Pacific empire with an island hinterland spread over a wide area of the mid-Pacific basin.

With the exception of Apia and Levuka, which vied against each other over the exploitation of the Lau Islands, competition between the port towns of the different island groups was non-existent. Alexander Spoehr has claimed that this lack of competition, which continued into the twentieth century, is due to the distance between port town locations, but to this must be added the fact that the resources of the outer islands that each town virtually monopolised were, and still are, too meagre to support any rival port.[24] The vulnerability of five major ports to competition did not, however, prevent the appearance of port towns subsidiary to them in adjacent but less developed economic areas, such as Avarua in the Cook Islands, Nuku'alofa in Tonga, Loma-loma in the Lau Islands, Hokianga on the west coast of northern New Zealand and Lahaina on Maui, Hawaii, to name only five. These aggregates, which were usually never fully self-sufficient or independent, tended to augment rather than diminish trade through the major ports. The small town of Avarua was supplying as many as 100 whaling ships in the 1850s, but they were forced to remain outside the reef. Provisions were taken out by canoe and small boat while any ship needing refitting facilities had to go to Tahiti. On shore the missionary-inspired laws greatly retarded foreign settlement. Tahiti, and later in the 1880s Auckland, handled the bulk of the Cook Island exports and imports, and Avarua never became a major island port. In Tonga, the growth of Nuku'alofa was similarly retarded by prohibitive land-holding laws and a lack of marketable resources. However, with the development of the coconut oil and later copra trade it was drawn into Apia's sphere of influence, once the Godeffroy company set up collection depots throughout the group.[25]

The settlements dispersed along the Hokianga River on the west coast of the northern tip of New Zealand did enjoy a largely independent existence as the centre of the timber industry. The overall population, which was in many respects more stable than that of Kororareka, grew slowly from about 40 in 1827 to over 200 in 1840.[26] There was, however, no concentrated port town, and Kororareka, which was only 30 miles away by foot, was in no way threatened by the timber trade, in which it had no interest. In fact a number of timber vessels still called in at the latter port for provisions. Ships not engaged in the timber trade would not risk the hazards of the Hokianga entrance, when Kororareka was so close and so much more readily accessible. Lomaloma on Vanua Balavu in the Lau group was not the only port to test Levuka's predominance. Port Kinnaird, south-west of Levuka on Ovalau, which was William T. Pritchard's projected base to supersede Levuka, never constituted a serious challenge, since it was handicapped with a difficult down-wind entrance and a late start in 1859-60. Lomaloma, however, did at times challenge Levuka as an economic and even political centre. The worldly Tongan chief, Ma'afu, who established his control over the Lau Islands during the late 1850s and early 1860s, co-operated with the increasing number of European cotton planters, and offered them greater security than Cakobau was ever able to provide on Viti or Vanua Levu or the adjacent islands. For a number of years cotton planters preferred Lau to the larger islands, and Lomaloma grew with their interest. But there was little of a permanent nature either in Lomaloma's origins or later development — its beginnings were closely linked with the Apia-dominated coconut oil trade. A Godeffroy agency had been established there by William Hennings in 1858, and the later sudden expansion of cotton plantations soon proved a flash-in-the-pan enterprise. By 1874 Lomaloma's future was already uncertain, but it was listed as a port of entry under the new British administration and it continued to function until 1882, when Suva was proclaimed the capital, and it was finally closed. Earlier in the century Galoa harbour, Kadavu Island, monopolised the supply trade to whalers who approached the

Fijian group but did not penetrate the hazardous archipelago
further than this easily accessible island. Between 1869 and 1877
its peripheral location was the basic factor in its selection as Fiji's
port for the trans-Pacific steamers, but this did little damage to
Levuka's position since all goods, passengers and mail were ferried
direct to Ovalau.[27]

Only in Hawaii did a minor port rival and even attract a greater
number of ships than the recognised major port. With better

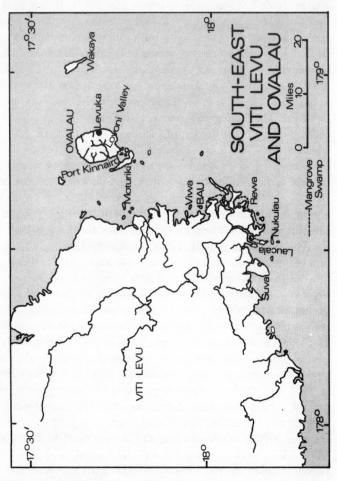

Map 7 South-east Viti Levu and Ovalau

harbour and supply facilities than Lahaina on Maui, Honolulu was visited by a greater number of whaling vessels between 1820 and 1830, but during the following decade cheaper supply prices at the open roadstead of Lahaina brought the number of ships at each place to a par. The 1840s saw twice as many ships at Lahaina as at Honolulu, which re-established its pre-eminence only in the early 1850s. Two reasons for this sudden reversal of positions have been suggested: one, that Lahaina was the first to offer supplies of white potato, far more popular with sailors than the sweet potato available at Honolulu; and two, that after the death of the devout Christian, chief Hoapili, Governor of Maui, his successors let the prohibition laws lapse which soon led to a proliferation of grog shops and prostitution. Since many whaling captains from New England ports sailed under strict temperance regulations, perhaps the second reason should be given less weight, although degrees of strictness among temperance captains and the control they exercised over their crews differed greatly. However, the majority of them preferred the cheaper prices at Lahaina and there were other captains and sailors who willingly availed themselves of the more liberal entertainments offered there. Commercialised vice was never totally extirpated from Honolulu, but its grog shops were limited by the number of liquor licences available and periodic temperance drives had far-reaching influence for short intervals. The potato boom was over in Lahaina by the mid 1850s and with prostitution and the sale of alcohol flourishing in Honolulu, the *status quo* was re-established.[28]

Neither Avarua, Hokianga, Lomaloma, Galoa nor Nuku'alofa was able to compete directly with the parent port. Lahaina successfully challenged Honolulu for over a decade, but only as the result of a combination of fortuitous historical factors, which proved transient. It seems clear that during the nineteenth century the resources available in Polynesia, Micronesia and Fiji could not support more than five major European ports, and that of these Levuka's position during the 1850s was tenuous. Late in the 1850s the Godeffroy company revealed its interest in Fiji by establishing coconut oil depots in the Lau archipelago, and had W. T. Pritchard not appeared as British consul in 1858 and re-awakened outside interest, it may have been possible for Apia, through the Godeffroy company, to have established its economic hegemony over the whole group. The subsequent cotton boom, followed by the more permanent success of the sugar industry, re-established Fiji as an economically viable region, able to support its own major port.

Once the island ports were established there was a mutual relationship between trade and population growth. Honolulu, on the cross-roads of the north Pacific, grew most rapidly. From 1820 onwards its foreign population was never less than 100, while in Papeete, Kororareka, Apia and Levuka for comparable periods in their development 50 was a maximum figure. Carpenters, coopers, blacksmiths, boatbuilders, merchants and storekeepers, grog sellers, boarding-house keepers, and frequently a tailor, bootmaker and butcher, were the core of these early beach community populations. For some beachcombers the movement into a proto-port town was a relatively easy process of re-identification with fellow Europeans and frequently the resumption of jobs for which they had been trained in earlier life. The social and sexual attractions of island life which they had more recently enjoyed were continued in the ports. For the islanders, however, the rise of the first port towns was a crucial development in their relationship with foreigners. In the earlier beachcomber period the onus of assimilation and the assumption of new codes of behaviour had fallen heavily on the Europeans, if they wanted to survive and be accepted, but in the new proto-urban environment, the pendulum began to swing in the opposite direction. With the sense of security and self-assurance that results from greater numbers, the expatriates slowly imposed their ways upon the islanders, who had to adopt European methods and work habits to succeed in a beach community. Forces of cultural change emanated from the new centres in the form of Western goods, ideas and economic life. For many years there was no compulsion upon the islanders to become involved in the new foreign communities. But the very presence of the port towns underlined the intensification of European and American interest in the Pacific — their desire to control and exploit its economic resources, which inevitably led to greater and more sustained demands on many other aspects of island life.

four

Early Beach Community
Development

Since none of the beach communities developed contemporaneously, the term 'early' necessarily refers to different periods of time in each port town. The towns least frequented by foreign shipping evolved more slowly and retained the features of the 'early' period longer, while the aspects considered characteristic of early development did not always appear in each beach community in their entirety. However, certain patterns of growth continually reoccurred throughout the beach communities, giving them a basic common identity.

Between 1804 and 1820 Honolulu grew from one of several small supply places to the major port of the Hawaiian group. By the latter date Kamehameha I was dead, the whaling trade was just beginning, and within the ensuing year the first contingent of missionaries and the first United States commercial agent were to arrive in the town. For the early Honolulu residents the style of life was to change markedly after 1820. Similarly in Papeete the leisurely tempo of commerce and social activity during its early years (1815-27) was altered by the arrival of the Valparaiso traders in 1827-8 and the rapid expansion of the whaling industry during the early 1830s. Within Kororareka's short life span as an independent beach community, approximately 1824 to 1840, it is not easy to discern a distinct early and later period. Perhaps the most significant change occurred in the mid 1830s when a stream of settlers, believing that British annexation was imminent, flowed into Kororareka and the Bay of Islands area. At the same time the number of whaling vessels frequenting the port had greatly increased.

The character of Levuka, or one should more strictly say of its residents, since the site of the Levuka township did not enjoy continuous occupation by foreigners due to their enforced exile,

changed dramatically in the early 1850s. Before this date the
foreigners had lived together fairly harmoniously under the leadership of David Whippy, and had sought to settle their affairs with
the Fijians without interference from consuls or visiting naval
captains. After 1852, however, the Levuka men allied themselves
closely with the representatives of the great powers, demanded
compensation from the Fijians for every misadventure, and quite
clearly threw in their lot with the Western world and its ambitions
which previously they appeared to have largely repudiated. The
multiplicity of small provisioning and ship chandlery merchants
who competed vigorously for the patronage of whaling vessels
during Apia's early years (1841-56), faced reduced profits and even
closure in the mid 1850s due to the recession in the whaling
industry. In 1857 the Godeffroy company established itself in
Apia in the person of August Unshelm, under whose guidance it
soon outstripped all the other companies in the town and grew into
one of the largest mercantile establishments in the south Pacific.
Changes in commercial life were reflected in the makeup of Apia's
population, which acquired a number of more respectable citizens
in the late 1850s. In all the early beach communities there was a
movement away from small independent economic enterprises,
and in Honolulu and Levuka away from island/foreign co-operation, towards greater foreign dominated commercial activities and
increasing identification with the Western powers.

Only the roughest estimates can be made of the size of foreign
populations in beach communities at any time before colonial rule
was established. A passing observer had no means of distinguishing
temporary visitors — shipwrecked sailors and crews from vessels in
the harbour — from the more permanent residents, and frequently
they gave foreign population figures for the whole island or group
rather than just the town area. The following figures given by
visitors to the early beach communities must therefore be taken
as guidelines only. Archibald Campbell claimed that Honolulu's
foreign population in 1809 was about sixty but he commented later
that it had decreased markedly before his departure in February
1810. By the early 1820s the foreign population in Honolulu was
well over one hundred. During Papeete's early growth its foreign
population was rarely, if ever, distinguished from the total foreign
population on Tahiti. In 1824 Kotzebue claimed that there were

5. Butcher's shop, Levuka, Fiji, Christmas 1874. From H. J. Hoare, *My Journal of H.M.S. Dido . . .* Reproduced by permission of the Mitchell Library, Sydney.

6. Levuka from the south, 1873. From Scrapbook of Australasian Illustrations. Reproduced by permission of the Mitchell Library, Sydney.

twenty foreigners on the whole island. At the Bay of Islands, New Zealand, the missionaries constituted the major part of the foreign population for several years, but by 1827 their adult numbers were matched by about forty non-missionary Europeans who were living in the area, the majority at Kororareka, which henceforward became the centre of foreign population. The number of foreigners in Levuka fluctuated considerably. In 1842 the missionaries believed there were about twenty at Solevu between 1844 and 1848 records consistently estimated the foreign population at thirty, while later, back in Levuka in 1849, Captain Erskine claimed that there were only fourteen or fifteen. Dysentery and fever had killed a number of them in Solevu in 1848. By 1852 their numbers had increased to about fifty. Apia, the last beach community to be established, grew slowly throughout the 1840s and also had a foreign population of about fifty in the mid 1850s.[1]

In the early beach communities, these small pockets of expatriates lived in varying degrees of association with the island people. Freed from the more immediate demands of chiefly domination, and with no assistance or control forthcoming from home governments, the foreigners had to rely on their own skills and ingenuity to maintain good relations with the islanders and to establish profitable trading links with Western shipping. The resultant organisation of beach community life was a combination of Western economic practices with island social and sexual *mores*. Patterns of conduct usually had no more sanction than the tacit agreement of the group at the time, but on two occasions a leader appeared on the beach capable of enforcing a more definite code of laws and of regulating society with the consent of the majority. All 'codes' or behavioural patterns, however, were constantly being modified, since the contacts established within these racially mixed communities, and between the communities and visiting shipping, tended to stimulate economic advancement and social change. Since the beach communities were beyond the fringe of Western control, the problem of maintaining a semblance of law and order was accentuated by the lack of any agency that the foreigners were willing to recognise for enforcing justice, which, in the circumstances, had to be supplied in partial and *de facto* forms by the residents themselves or by an accepted leader, be he islander or foreigner. The presence of missionaries and consuls in the early towns had a decided influence on the patterns of leadership that evolved and the attitudes foreigners assumed towards their island hosts.*

Neither consul nor missionary appeared in Honolulu between 1804 and 1820. The foreign traders, artisans and loafers on the beach had to deal directly with Kamehameha I or his appointed governors, on whose goodwill their lives and security of property depended. The LMS missionaries arrived in Tahiti in March 1797, long before Papeete showed any signs of becoming a European centre. But even between 1815 and 1828 they had little influence over the resident foreigners in Papeete, which during this period slowly established its precedence over the other harbours of the Matavai Bay-Papeete coastline. Although a mission station was established in Papeete in 1818, its success was limited and by 1823 conditions were so uncongenial that the incumbent, William Crook, was forced to leave his dwindling congregation to the temptations of the grog sellers, both foreign and Tahitian, some of them ex-members of his church.[2] George Pritchard recommenced mission work at Papeete in 1825 but he had little influence over the foreigners until he changed his missionary role for a consular one in the late 1830s. Yet despite the fact that consular representatives did not arrive in Papeete until the mid 1830s and that the missionaries had little influence over the foreign residents, the clergy had considerable power over the Tahitian chiefs, through whom they introduced legislation and regulated Tahitian society as strictly as possible. This control prevented any non-missionary foreigner from gaining an ascendancy with the chiefs, which in turn left the small aggregate of foreigners at Papeete without a leader. However, with so few foreign settlers and so little commercial activity, the lack of community leadership in Papeete during the early years created no major difficulties. The Tahitian chiefs kept what order and laws they thought necessary and sought missionary advice only if foreigners' demands or threats became insistent, which in fact rarely happened.

Missionaries were also the first permanent expatriate settlers in the Bay of Islands, but while they gained some influence in time

* Throughout the nineteenth century many American representatives in the Pacific were appointed as commercial agents not consuls. I have, however, used 'consul' as a term when discussing both British and American agents.

over a number of Maori chiefs, the latter were too independent to be united into one political entity. The foreigners who arrived later were able to find Maori chiefs who were not aligned with the missionaries, and who were happy to encourage their settlement. Kororareka was always, both physically and consciously, completely separated from the mission station at Paihia just across the bay, and the two foreign groups established distinct spheres of influence. James Busby, British Resident, arrived in New Zealand in 1833, took one look at the Kororareka residents and settled at Waitangi where he was even more isolated from the foreigners than the mission. An American consular representative was not appointed until 1838. Despite this lack of interference from the outside, no foreigner revealed any ambition towards leadership within the Kororareka community and the chief, Whareumu, while nominally their protector, was unable to prevent the depredations of the Ngapuhi in 1827, and showed no desire to organise or regulate their daily lives.

J. B. Williams, who was appointed United States commercial agent for Fiji in 1844, reached the group in 1846, but he refused to settle in Levuka until 1858, when the arrival of W. T. Pritchard, the first British consul in the town, made his presence there essential. Between 1846 and 1858 Williams lived at Rewa, Viti Levu, where almost all his time was spent conducting his own private business. The Wesleyan missionaries settled in the group as early as 1836 but a permanent station at Levuka was not established until 1852 and then by John Binner, who was not a trained minister but a schoolmaster greatly interested in trade and land buying. The Roman Catholics who had preceded the Wesleyan missionaries in Levuka by a year devoted their energies to saving the Fijians from Protestantism, leaving the foreigners to their own devices. Between 1825 and the early 1850s, therefore, neither consuls nor missionaries interfered with the Levuka residents' organisation of society or their relations with the Fijians.

In Apia the LMS missionaries were the first settlers in the area in 1836 and the non-missionary foreigners who followed in their wake found consuls soon settled amongst them. In 1839 W. C. Cunningham was appointed acting vice-consul for Great Britain by George Pritchard, who was then British consul at Tahiti. The appointment was never ratified in London and Cunningham left

Apia in 1841, but J. C. Williams, who had been appointed United States commercial agent by Lieutenant Wilkes, commander of the United States exploring expedition in 1839, remained in the area. George Pritchard became the first official British consul in Samoa in 1845, by which time the foreign population was not more than thirty. From the beginning of settlement at Apia, therefore, both missionaries and consuls were present, competing for influence and control over the Samoans and the foreign residents. Among the Samoans the volatile nature of the problem of political unity or the recognition of a predominant chief made it impossible for any one chief to establish his hegemony over the Samoan people, let alone exercise undisputed control over the foreign settlers. In these circumstances any crisis or issue of general importance divided the foreigners in town into rival factions; sometimes national, sometimes occupational. These divisions were usually neither lasting nor exclusive but there was one antagonism that did remain constant. Good relations existed between individual Samoans and foreigners, but as a group the expatriates, especially the consuls, were jealous of the resident Samoan chiefs' reluctance to sell land, their control over their people's social and economic activities and their constant efforts to thwart foreign expansion. Captain Fremantle was in Apia during the height of a very troubled period, 1854-6, and commented on the consuls' antagonistic attitude:

> The inclination to browbeat the natives is participated in by the Consular Agents who, being all engaged in traffic, have (on this point only) a fellow feeling. Even Mr. Pritchard and Mr. Van Camp will make common cause to obtain an advantage over the Samoan, though they could hardly be trusted in the same room together to discuss a matter in which their happened to be any rivalry between themselves.[3]

At no time did the Apia residents, with a British and American representative in their midst, feel compelled to suit their habits or style of life to Samoan standards. Always they fostered the hope that external assistance would arrive to undermine the chiefs' power over their people and to enforce foreign demands.

From the above it is clear that there were few circumstances in which an individual, either islander or foreigner, could establish himself as a leader. In fact throughout the history of the beach communities it happened only twice, in Honolulu and Levuka, and in both towns during periods when neither missionary nor consul was present. Between 1782 and 1810 Kamehameha I extended his traditional chiefly powers to include all the Hawaiians and foreign residents. The latter were encouraged to settle in the islands, especially at Honolulu, but none enjoyed any special privileges; land-holding and the building of permanent houses were carefully restricted, as they were for the Hawaiians themselves, while the establishment of segregated expatriate areas was prohibited. The unquestioned nature of Kamehameha's authority made it possible for him to impose a monopoly on the pork trade to shipping and, later, on the more lucrative sandalwood trade.[4] Although fond of alcohol he limited its production and consumption as far as it was in his power:

> Old Tameameha not only forbid the distilling of it, but that no *native* should be allowed to have any in possession, and that old ruler was one whose orders were respected & that law was in force at Oahu until the last of 1820 or the beginning of 1821 — in 1817 & 1818 to my knowledge one of the constant crys of Oahu was Tabu ka lama, Tabu ka wiwi*.[5]

By 1817 Kamehameha had returned to Hawaii Island, where he lived the remaining years of his life, but he maintained his control over the multi-racial population at Honolulu through his governors. Oliver Holmes, who had lived on Oahu since 1796, was the first to be appointed after Kamehameha's return to Hawaii in 1812, but the Hawaiian chief, Kalanimoku, took over the position in 1817, only to relinquish it to the chief Boki the following year. Orders brought by messengers from Kamehameha were executed by these men, who exiled undesirable foreigners, regulated the residents' activities, collected taxes and protected the special royal trading monopolies. Experienced traders in the islands knew the wisdom and advantage of seeking Kamehameha's 'permission-to-enter' and protection at Hawaii before proceeding to Honolulu harbour. From the diary which the merchant, James Hunnewell, kept in Honolulu for the years 1817-18 it is evident that economic pursuits were

---

* *lama* — rum, *wiwi* — rickety, literal translation. *Wiwi* may have referred to drunken behaviour or it may have been a variant of whisky — *wekeke* or *waikeke*.

profitable and life as a whole secure and even dull.[6]

It is difficult to appraise Kamehameha I, the source of this security and good government. Conflicting reports are as numerous as the foreigners who made them. However, there can be no doubt that Kamehameha was a shrewd politician and economist who was wary of any challenge to his position and had no intention of relinquishing his power either to foreigners or to his subordinate chiefs. Traditional and conservative in most things, Kamehameha used Western goods, skills and personnel to obtain his chief ambition, the unification of Hawaii under his own rule, but having accomplished that he sought no further social or political change. Some Europeans accused him of greed and overweening power, but it should be pointed out that the majority of these foreigners revealed little aptitude for dealing with island authority, usually showing the king no respect or deference. Nearly all the critics had been thwarted in their missions to the islands. Thus the disgruntled German adventurer Schäffer, who in 1816 had found Kamehameha I very much better informed and less gullible than he had expected, described Kamehameha's methods as follows: 'Only the king trades, and every foreign ship must first come to him on the island of Hawaii and allow itself to be plundered by him before receiving permission to enter the harbor of Oahu'.[7] On the other hand the sandalwood trader, Peter Corney, who was much liked by the Hawaiians, believed the customary visit to Kamehameha on Hawaii worked very much to his advantage. Kamehameha died before either missionaries or consuls appeared in Hawaii, but despite his well developed sense of sovereignty it is doubtful whether he would have been able to maintain his position for any length of time against their insidious and sustained influence. Certainly neither Liholiho, Kamehameha II, nor Kauikeaouli, Kamehameha III, was to have much success.

While in Honolulu the foreigners' activities were controlled by a Hawaiian, in Levuka it was the expatriate David Whippy who for a period of about twelve years, from 1840 to 1852, maintained an effective leadership — to the extent that he was able to persuade his fellow residents and the Fijians in contact with the town to formulate their own laws and establish an *ad hoc* body to enforce them. In 1838, Dumont d'Urville had seen no sign of leadership among the foreigners at Levuka whom he believed hated one another mutually. But in Fiji in 1840 Lieutenant Wilkes met the reprobate Patrick Connel who:

> had lived much at Rewa, and until lately had been a resident at Levuka, but had, in consequence of his intrigues, been expelled by the white residents, to the island of Ambatiki. It appeared that they had unanimously come to the conclusion that if he did not remove, they would be obliged to put him to death for their own safety.[8]

Clearly in the intervening two years between d'Urville's and Wilkes's visits the Levuka men had joined together and agreed upon a few basic rules, one of which was that they would harbour no one in their midst who was involved in Fijian politics. Wilkes approved of the Levuka men's 'general deportment and good conduct', and particularly of their leader Whippy. In fact he considered them the best disposed community that he met anywhere in the Pacific. Several bêche-de-mer captains, including Eagleston, owed the continued safety of their vessels to Whippy's timely warnings of planned Fijian attacks. Captain Bureaux of *L'Aimable Josephine* ignored his advice and lost vessel, crew and his own life.[9]

A crude system of justice was practised by the Levuka settlers, who in March 1842 took it upon themselves to catch the murderers of James Carter — a Hawaiian and a Fijian — and after careful inquiry, hanged them. In 1849, after a period in exile, Whippy and his companions were still able to command respect, this time from Captain Erskine who commented that: 'He [Whippy] is a man of excellent character, and has succeeded by his good example in giving a tone of order and true respectability to the community'.[10] In fact good reports concerning the 'honest and upright' David Whippy were written by such diverse people (the missionaries, American and English naval commanders, trading captains and even the wife of one of them, and the English settler, later to become colonial official, J. B. Thurston, all wrote appreciatively of him) that one is tempted to believe that whatever his virtues he was certainly adept at presenting an image of himself well suited to please his current visitor. This is a little unfair — Whippy was unquestionably concerned to improve living conditions in Levuka and to protect certain of the Fijians' interests, but a remark from the Reverend James Calvert in 1861 reveals the dexterity with which Whippy handled his different colleagues. 'I was pleased to see Mr. Whippy who has felt compelled to leave Ovalau, because of the great changes there, since the opening of public houses.'[11] From 1849 onwards, liquor had been available in Levuka, but Whippy did not feel compelled to leave until 1858, suspiciously soon after a devastating fire and the arrival of the consuls Pritchard and Williams, who took over control of the town. One person Whippy did not impress was the newly appointed American commercial agent J. B. Williams, who claimed in the mid 1840s that Whippy did not command 'proper respect' among the Fijians. Such a remark, however, was symptomatic of Williams's inability to establish good relations with the Fijians, something which Whippy was able to maintain, whatever respect he commanded. There is insufficient data on which to base an analysis of Whippy's character and motivations, but it cannot be denied that his standing with the Fijians, among whom he was accepted as chiefly messenger and interpreter, combined with his steadying influence over the Levuka settlers and his loyalty to foreign shipping, made it possible for him to work in the interests of both races, and to keep relations between them on an easy level.[12]

The maintenance and acceptance of such leadership as exercised by Kamehameha I and David Whippy was, however, exceptional. In Papeete, Kororareka and Apia neither local authorities nor foreigners were able or willing to create a working liaison through which to control the various activities of the newly established port centres. During the early years in Papeete foreign numbers were too small to make the problem acute and the missionaries were always available to advise the Tahitian chiefs if they were needed. Conditions were similar in Kororareka, although sometimes a captain of a trading or whaling vessel in the port could be prevailed upon to take the necessary steps to stop some blatant miscarriage of justice, as the foreign settlers saw it. In Apia the number of foreign residents certainly warranted some form of recognised leadership but the town was so riven with dissension, national and occupational factions, and rival spheres of missionary and consular influence that no one could gain acceptance from all sections, although one attempt at combined leadership was partially successful. In no town did it prove possible to maintain a person in a position of leadership once missionaries and consuls had arrived. Thus in Honolulu no one appeared to fill Kamehameha's place after his death, which was so quickly followed by the advent of American missionaries and an American commercial agent. In Levuka Whippy gradually became involved in the American residents' claims for compensation, and later removed himself from the town completely. As in Honolulu no one could assume the position he voluntarily vacated.

Virtually all foreign residents in the beach communities had to participate in some form of economic activity, however sporadic. Fortunately no trade or business pursuit required a regular weekly, much less daily, work pattern. Even men engaged in the more substantial commercial enterprises, such as the sandalwood trade in Hawaii, enjoyed long periods of inactivity. A partner of the New England company of Marshall and Wildes, which traded in China, maintained that in Honolulu at the end of the sandalwood era: 'Most of the agents at the Sandwich Islands divide the 24 hours into three parts, Drinking, Gambling, and Sleeping'.[13] The date or the hour of the day was of little significance; only the appearance of a ship on the horizon was likely to galvanise the foreigners into action. Once she had sailed again, life quickly reverted to its old ways, each man doing as little or as much as he felt inclined. Standards of regular hard work in vogue in the Western world had no place in the Pacific ports.

While major development in the beach communities depended on the different marketable resources of the respective island groups, and on their proximity to trading and whaling routes, certain basic skills and economic activities requiring a minimum of capital were found in every town. Piloting vessels was one job for which the foreign residents would compete. Many were ex-sailors and once they were familiar with the harbour and the hazards of the surrounding islands, navigating foreign vessels new to the area was a pleasant and easy way to earn a few dollars or a small quantity of trade goods. Dumont d'Urville, in Fiji in October 1838, found that: 'all the Europeans I met were provided with certificates', and competed for the job of piloting.[14] The Englishmen, John Young, Isaac Davis and John Harbottle, who had all settled in the Hawaiian Islands before 1795, acted as pilots among the Hawaiian group and particularly into Honolulu harbour. For length of service Alexander Adams was to out-do them all. Although he did not start as a pilot until 1816, he was still active in Honolulu harbour in the mid 1840s when the Hawaiian government was induced to dismiss him on Lieutenant Wilkes's complaint that he was drunk on duty, a not infrequent occurrence. Jonas Coe, pilot at Apia, was dismissed from his post under very similar circumstances in 1864, but the loss of employment affected him little, since almost immediately after he was appointed United States commercial agent.[15]

As whaling and trading expanded throughout the Pacific an increasing number of expatriates and islanders were employed growing and purveying fresh supplies. Even the consuls J. C. Williams and George Pritchard in Apia engaged in such activities, and were not averse to using their official positions to protect their businesses. In March 1846 they issued a joint communiqué warning ships not to use the harbour of Fagaloo, situated on the north-east coast of Upolu. The unscrupulousness of the foreigners settled there was the reason given, but might they not also have been concerned over the trade they were losing from Apia harbour?[16] Francisco de Paula Marin, a Spaniard who had been resident in Hawaii since the early 1790s, finally settled on Oahu, where he engaged in a most lucrative supply trade, importing and cultivating exotic fruits and vegetables, and raising goats, rabbits and other animals, which were most welcome to crews weary of salt provisions. Throughout his life he maintained a large correspondence with American sandalwood captains and the Spanish Roman Catholic priests in California to whom he sent requests for seeds and saplings of any new or different plant so that he could experiment with them. Oliver Holmes and Harbottle also added purveying to their other occupations. The Hawaiians were similarly aware of the profits to be made in the trade but their attempts to participate were often blocked by the chiefs, in particular by Kamehameha I, who frequently enforced a monopoly on the sale of all native produce. Pigs were only supplied through Kamehameha or his appointed governors, and in June 1815 an order was issued that no one but Holmes, Marin and Queen Kaahumanu was allowed to kill goats. About 1818 Pomare II tried to establish a similar royal monopoly on Tahitian trade by claiming an exclusive right to purchase all island produce.[17] In the Bay of Islands the Maori controlled a large proportion of the provision trade.

Grog victuallers, stocked with raw alcohol bought or received as payment for services from incoming vessels, or with even more lethal brews distilled from local products, had little difficulty finding ready customers among the visiting sailors and resident foreigners. For the islanders alcohol was an acquired taste but one to which the Hawaiians were all too well adapted by the second decade of the nineteenth century. Kamehameha I did everything in his power to limit the consumption of alcohol in Honolulu, but while no permanent grog shops were set up, there always appeared to be plenty of spirits available on the beach. By the following decade, the 1820s, the Tahitians had become similarly addicted. In 1822 the LMS missionary, Crook, wrote glowing reports of how he envisaged the future Papeete: 'We hope to succeed in building a town in regular order with a square in the centre formed by the Chapel, school house, Mission house and workshop'.[18] Fourteen months later a rash of shanty grog shops had sprung up in the town, heavily patronised by both Tahitians and foreigners. Crook found the situation so disturbing that he was forced to leave. The Maori revealed little interest in alcohol until the mid 1830s, but it was readily available to the foreign residents from the ships in the Bay and from the grog shops that appeared in Kororareka after 1830.

In Apia between 1838 and 1850 the chiefs and missionaries together tried to maintain strict prohibition, but in the early 1850s a plethora of grog shops appeared, reminiscent of Papeete's development in the 1820s. George Pritchard, British consul and ex-LMS missionary, was responsible for breaking the prohibition by importing several large cargoes of spirits and turning the British consulate into a pot shop. Captain Home, who returned to Apia in 1852, found the place 'much less civilized' than on his previous visit in 1844, when the prohibition had still been in effect. In 1852:

The place called the Consulate is of a description quite unfit for a respectable Englishman to live in or for the English Flag to fly in front of. Although the sale of spirits is contrary to the law of Samoa established by the Chiefs, yet of the few houses which compose the town of Apia, I have reason to believe that nearly everyone of them deals in that article; no vigilance could keep the people sober who were engaged in watering.[19]

The same year the Reverend William Mills complained that there were more than twelve grog shops within less than a half mile either side of his house, and that at a time when the foreign population in Apia did not exceed sixty. In Papeete and Apia it should be remembered that the grog shops supplied the crews of whalers as well as the local population, although in Apia the 'local' population did not include the Samoans, who were never to become seriously addicted. The early development of Levuka is marked by a pronounced lack of alcohol. Neither on the cargo inventories for the bêche-de-mer vessels nor on the lists of goods offered to the Levuka residents for services rendered does the article occur. Dumont d'Urville in 1838 took advantage of the dry state of Levuka to give all his men leave ashore, and the town appears to have stayed dry until 1849 after which date the usual victuallers were always in evidence.[20] At no time did the Fijians become major consumers.

During this period of early development island women most frequently received goods rather than money for their favours. Any money they did earn on board ship or in the groggeries and dancehalls was spent almost entirely in the shops of the small traders. In Honolulu, later in its development, these traders expected to net a large proportion of their incomes during the biannual whaling visits to the port. Prostitution in Apia and Papeete was prohibited by the missionaries and religiously minded chiefs, but except for very brief periods their attempt were singularly ineffective and the women's 'illegal' earnings were spent in the same way as in Honolulu. At the Bay of Islands the CMS missionaries' position was so unstable, even in 1830, that any attempt on their part to stop the time-honoured custom of Maori women staying on board the vessels in the harbour would have jeopardised the tenuous security they had achieved.[21] In Levuka there was too little shipping for the profession to become an important source of wealth.

Carpentering, coopering, blacksmithing, and other skilled trades connected with shipping were widely patronised and small busi-

nesses could be set up with little financial backing. Archibald
Campbell described the number of foreign artisans working at
different tasks in Honolulu for Kamehameha I in 1809-10. Brick-
layers, joiners, carpenters, masons and blacksmiths were employed
as well as a number of men tending and enlarging Kamehameha's
fleet. At the time the *Lelia Byrd,* a 175-ton vessel acquired by
Kamehameha in 1805, was anchored in the bay for repairs. In the
second decade of the nineteenth century these men were in-
ceasingly absorbed into the sandalwood trade, repairing and refitting vessels used in the islands and on the north-west coast. In
1816 John Young was in Honolulu supervising the building of a
stone fort. Among his many accomplishments, Marin was also a
stonemason who was employed by Kamehameha, Kalanimoku and
Boki to build them lasting Western style houses.[22] In the other
ports chiefly patronage did not encourage or support such a diver-
sity of mechanical skills, but services among themselves and for
incoming vessels kept many foreigners employed. Shipbuilding and
carpentering occupied a number of settlers in Levuka, where
Whippy set up a partnership with the later arrivals, William
Simpson and William Cusick. Between 1831 and 1836 Gilbert
Mair, who ran one of the leading refitting and ship-chandlery
businesses at Wahapu, just south of Kororareka, employed about
fifteen mechanics in his shipyard. Whaling vessels formed the bulk
of his custom.[23]

Although these trades, which made up the economic substrata of
the beach communities, were in constant demand throughout the
nineteenth century, few participants in them worked consistently
enough to accumulate any great wealth. However, by 1856 Whippy
had saved enough money to send his second son Samuel to school
in Sydney, while Jonas Coe; pilot and trader in Apia since his
arrival in 1845, was similarly able to afford to send several of his
children to school in New South Wales and California. Harry
Zupplien, an eccentric Dutch boarding-house keeper and grog
seller, who arrived in Honolulu about 1813 with nothing, was a
well established merchant and hotelier in later years with enough
ready cash, which he kept buried in the back yard, to lend the
Hawaiian government $1000 at a moment's notice in 1839. John
Colcord did not arrive in Honolulu until 1821 but he was employed
as a blacksmith before he set up his own mercantile establishment.

In 1844 he returned to the United States, which he had left as a penniless sailor more than twenty years earlier, worth an estimated $20,000. The only person to make a large fortune in these artisan trades was James Robinson who arrived in Honolulu, a destitute, shipwrecked sailor in 1822. He established a shipyard and was in possession of several hotels and stores when he died there in 1876 worth half a million dollars.[24] Both he and Colcord expanded from small workshops where they had been self-employed to large mercantile establishments where they employed and organised the skills of several mechanics and clerks. This kind of development was, however, only possible in Honolulu, which attracted the greatest volume of trade of any of the Pacific port towns.

The prosperity of the beach communities and their development were, however, ultimately dependent on the more substantial commercial enterprises which brought capital to the islands, stimulated economic growth and supported the individual service trades that were at all times subsidiary to them. Honolulu received its first large influx of capital from the sandalwood trade, which flourished from 1816 to about 1822. The first cargoes of sandalwood were exported from the islands in 1812 by Captains Nathan and Jonathon Winship and Captain W. H. Davis, who signed a monopoly contract for Hawaiian sandalwood with Kamehameha I. The Anglo-American war soon put a stop to this new trade and it was not recommenced until 1815 when three Boston companies, J. and T. H. Perkins, S. G. Perkins and Co., and Bryant and Sturgis sent a ship to the Pacific to load copper at Valparaiso and sandalwood at either the Ingraham Islands or Hawaii for the Canton market. The captain found that sandalwood grew in abundance on the Hawaiian Islands but he did not have a vessel available for sale and Kamehameha would consider nothing else in exchange for wood. The New York merchant John Jacob Astor was quickly informed of Hawaiian wants and had two suitable vessels sent to the islands in 1816 where he had no trouble selling them for sandalwood. The trade flourished and soon all these companies plus the Boston firm of Marshall and Wildes were competing to supply Kamehameha I and his chiefs with the vessels and other goods they so keenly sought. In 1817 James Hunnewell from Charlestown, Massachusetts and an agent for Bryant and Sturgis, became the first resident sandalwood trader in Honolulu.

He remained less than ten months but other merchants followed him. William French, an agent for Marshall and Wildes, was established in Honolulu for six months in 1819.[25] Most of the semi-permanent traders in Honolulu at this time were agents for the Boston or New York companies and the bulk of the profits they made were enjoyed by their employers, but ultimately many of them became permanent, independent merchants in Honolulu. Such men had sound financial backing and large warehouses full of European goods for disposal in the islands. Labour was required to build these factory-type establishments, with their accompanying wharves, and clerks, storekeepers and mechanics were needed to staff them. Sandalwood vessels had to be manned, provisioned and repaired. Money and/or goods were therefore distributed through several sectors of the community, both Hawaiian and foreign.

Although the sandalwood traders were the major source of capital in the town, they were carefully controlled by Kamehameha I, and had to submit to the orders of his governors and to respect all tabus. On 15 January 1818 James Hunnewell recorded in his diary: 'The principal chiefs left here [Honolulu] in the Columbia. We have had no business, as it is tabooed till their return'.[26] The death of a chief or any other customary tabu period also left the traders without customers or an incoming supply of sandalwood. Despite these temporary inconveniences the trade remained highly profitable until the early 1820s, and it was the chiefs who made it so. Between March and November 1819 Kamehameha I, his successor Liholiho, and the chiefs, parted with $61,600 worth of sandalwood for a variety of foreign goods that ranged from a brig to guns and ammunition, playing cards, shirts, Chinese umbrellas and yards and yards of cloth.[27] In 1819 the first whaling vessels called at Honolulu, forerunners of the rush of whalers *en route* to the Japanese ground, so the port's development and permanence were guaranteed even when the sandalwood trade collapsed early in the 1820s.

Early development in Papeete enjoyed no such impetus from large mercantile traders. The first settlers, Henry, Ebrill and Bicknell, who had no financial backing, were employed by Pomare II in the early 1820s sailing vessels between Tahiti and Port Jackson, and they also organised their own sugar plantation in the

islands. After Pomare II's death in December 1821, Bicknell concentrated entirely on sugar, while Henry and Ebrill took part in a
number of commercial ventures, collecting coconut oil, pork, sinnet
and arrowroot throughout the Society Islands from chiefs and other
traders, and exporting more exotic goods from distant groups. By
1825 Solomon Levey, an emancipist merchant in New South Wales,
had an establishment in Tahiti connected with Ebrill and Henry
and employed two brigs of 140 tons to collect various island products. Over £5000 was invested in the business. The same year
Levey joined forces with Daniel Cooper, who was also financially
interested in Henry's enterprises. However, although Henry and
Ebrill were based in Papeete during this early period, they collected
their cargoes from a number of islands in the south-east Pacific
and often shipped them direct to Sydney. While no rival port
centre was established, Papeete still benefited little from this trade,
and since the Tahitians' demands for European goods were limited
to cloth and hardware, no mercantile company could be tempted
to set up an agency for such a small market.[28] By the early 1820s
the Hawaiian chiefs were buying fabrics, spirits and hardware, not
to mention cut glass, expensive dinner services, billiard tables, frame
houses and sailing vessels, all of which helped to stimulate American
enterprise. But few desires for Westernised styles of life disturbed
the scene at Papeete, where the handful of foreign residents, excluding Henry, Bicknell and Ebrill, survived on piloting fees and a
small supply trade. In 1824 there was only one forge on the island
and 'even the foreigners established here carry on no kind of
mechanical trade'.[29]

The provision trade to whalers formed the economic basis of
Kororareka's development. While extensive repairs were usually
carried out at one or other of the large shipyards a little farther
south of Kororareka, it was from the latter town that water and
refreshments were taken on board, and to it or Pomare's notorious
pa at Otuihu that sailors resorted when on shore leave. By the mid
1830s the Kororareka area offered extensive ship-chandlery and
refitting facilities. The large establishments, which had a rather
feudal air about them, included Gilbert Mair's shipyard set up in
1831 at Wahapu Bay, J. R. Clendon and S. Stephenson who commenced at Okiato in 1832, and Captain J. Wright who established
himself near Mair at Wahapu Bay also in 1832. None of these

7. Lynch law in Samoa, 1877. From *The Australasian Sketcher*, 16 March 1878. Reproduced by permission of the Mitchell Library, Sydney.

8. View of the port of Honolulu, Hawaii. From Louis Choris, *Voyage Pittoresque autour du Monde*, Paris, 1822. Reproduced by permission of the Mitchell Library, Sydney.

places was further than 3 miles from Kororareka by sea. During 1834 ninety-one vessels, sixty-seven of them whalers, anchored in the southern part of the Bay of Islands, near Kororareka, which by that time could offer a wide variety of ships' provisions plus the full range of entertainments expected ashore.[30]

Bêche-de-mer, which was thickly distributed on the reefs of south-east Vanua Levu and the islands of the Koro sea, attracted a number of capital investors to Fiji and was the basis of Levuka's development from the 1820s to the early 1850s. Salem traders first collected it in large quantities in 1819, but it was not until the smoke-drying technique of curing the 'fish' was taught to the Americans in 1827, by the crew who had mutinied from a Spanish ship that the trade became fully established and expanded rapidly. After 1828 it was possible for a newly arrived bêche-de-mer vessel to find Levuka deserted, all its residents being employed by ships in the group, as pilots, interpreters and agents between the Fijians and the traders. They also helped to repair vessels. Eagleston's ship, the *Peru*, was caulked by two Levuka carpenters in December 1832. Despite this activity the township's gain from the first intensive exploitation of bêche-de-mer from 1827 to 1835 was slight in terms of capital acquired. In 1834 David Whippy and 'his comrades' were paid the following for the help they had rendered Joseph Winn of the *Emerald* in collecting a full cargo: 1 musket, 1 keg of powder, 2 pieces of dungaree, a piece of lead, some beads, some vermillion, 2 whales' teeth, a looking glass and also 1 barrel of beef and some bread 'for a taste'.[31] The number of comrades with whom Whippy had to share this bounty is not known, but clearly no one had made a fortune over the transaction, except perhaps Winn. However, during this period Levuka was at least recognised by the Salem traders as the centre of foreign population and source of skilled help in Fiji. By 1835 the serious depopulation of 'fish' on the reefs led to a lull in the trade, which lasted from 1835 to 1842. Only Captain Eagleston and the Sydney ship *Sir David Ogilby* visited the group for bêche-de-mer in the intervening years.

The second major trading period, 1842-50, was more directly important for the Levuka residents and the development of the town. On no reef was the bêche-de-mer as prolific as it had been previously; many more fishing establishments had to be set up and the time required to collect a full cargo was much longer. The Levuka men, who had increased in numbers by the 1840s through shipwreck and desertions, were hired to work on the boats and ashore. Some set up their own curing stations and sold the produce to the big traders. At Levuka itself the shipbuilding company, Whippy, Simpson and Cusick, built small vessels which were then hired out to the traders as tenders to scour the outer islands for bêche-de-mer, tortoise-shell and supplies of food. Eagleston, who in 1834 was the first to use a boat built in Levuka, wrote to his employer, S. C. Phillips, about her:

> I mentioned to you before leaving home of the whites residing at these Ilds. ᵇaving a small vessel under way [on the slips] and that I should employ her if possible. She will be ready to launch on my return from Otahitie and if I can obtain masts for her I shall put her in commission, and while she is under my orders she will answer to the name of opposition. Sails I shall make for her out of some of the Ship's old ones. I think of putting Mr Litch as skipper of her, and some of the owners as pilots.[32]

After 1842 shipbuilding increased rapidly and continued even when the settlers went into exile at Solevu. The missionaries in Fiji also relied on the Levuka men for transport between their stations and to build them small schooners. On 14 October 1848 the Reverend R. B. Lyth recorded in his journal that Simpson and Miller had come over from Solevu in order to make arrangements with him about a new craft. On 8 June 1849 the schooner was delivered from Ovalau and payment was settled soon after. Missionaries' trips between stations in Levuka craft cost an average of £10 per fortnight. However, in comparison with the bêche-de-mer traders, mission contributions to Levuka finance were small. Late in 1849 the bêche-de-mer trader Thomas Dunn congratulated himself that he had been able to hire a tender from Whippy and Company for only $70 a month — $20 cheaper than his rival Captain Wallis paid for the vessel earlier in the same year. But he found that the Levuka men were not lacking in business sense. Aware of the competition between Sydney and Salem traders for tortoise-shell, they had collected over 2000 pounds of it throughout the group and demanded high prices. Dunn had hoped to carry off the whole lot but when he came to settle with them, he found that they wanted none of the trade goods he had to offer. Clearly by 1850 the Levuka men were in a commanding position, no longer satisfied with the meagre trade goods they had accepted in 1834.[33] Unfortunately for them 1850 marked the end of the large-scale bêche-de-mer trade, which was followed by a heterogeneous and small profit traffic in provisions and other products. A whole decade was to pass before Levuka was again a thriving centre of economic activity.

In Apia the supply trade to whalers attracted a number of small mercantile companies to the beach community. The first trading store was probably that of W. C. Cunningham, set up in Apia in 1839. More permanent establishments appeared in the 1840s, including J. C. Williams in 1841, George Pritchard in 1845-6, W. C. Turnbull at about the same time, and William Yandall between 1845 and 1850. In 1846 a cut-rate store was opened in Apia by the Société Française de l'Océanie, a French organisation dedicated to planting Roman Catholic missions and trading stores throughout the Pacific. Arson razed the first French building in 1847 and the second was totally destroyed by a gale in 1850. The company did not survive these two disasters, much to the relief of its British rivals. All these outfits were basically dependent on the provision trade to whalers. Some coconut oil was collected and sold to Sydney vessels but this was only of secondary importance. In 1846, seventy-two whalers and other vessels anchored in Apia and the numbers greatly increased in the following decade. Mercantile companies and grog shops expanded with the trade, but by 1856 the number of settlers involved in the whaling complex exceeded the demand for these services, and a decline in the whaling industry in the central Pacific at this time was, consequently, felt acutely. This was intensified by the fact that the Samoans' demands for European goods were spasmodic and then only for cheap items of cloth and hardware. Increased competition between rival companies forced several to close; Pritchard and Company in 1855, William Yandall was financially broken by the late 1850s and the large Tahitian-based Hort company collapsed in 1862. The last's demise was strongly influenced by the growing Godeffroy company, which was established in Apia in 1857 and rapidly grew into a position in which it challenged and overwhelmed the smaller companies.[34] Too many merchants had believed that a quick fortune could be made in Apia, whose early growth was in fact characterised by instability, debt and foreclosure.

Few of these early settlers had any desire to own large tracts of land, but there was a widespread and vital need for small areas suitable for housing, stores and workshops. Except in Apia such parcels of land were usually acquired from the islanders without difficulty. However, ignorant of European systems of land tenure, the donor conceived that he was giving the right of temporary usufruct, not any form of freehold ownership. As a rule the land belonged to a foreigner during his lifetime only; he could not sell it nor could his wife or children inherit it after his death. Some foreigners acquired land through their island wives but the same restrictions obtained, except of course that the woman retained her customary rights to it after her husband's death or departure. Foreigners who left the islands had no claim to land given them during their residence.

In Hawaii Kamehameha I rewarded the services of several foreigners with land grants. In time many of these allotments came to be considered foreign property and those who settled permanently in the islands, or their descendants, claimed them before the Land Commission in the late 1840s, and were granted freehold titles. Among the foreigners who received land at this time were the pilot Adams, the hotelier Zupplien and the worthy ship-builder James Robinson. Further, the descendants of Isaac Davis, John Young, Francisco de Paula Marin and Oliver Holmes received land given to their fathers earlier in the century. Although this was a natural consequence of the controlling power which the foreigners exercised in the Hawaiian government by the late 1840s, plus the fact that the Hawaiians had by then become accustomed to considering these lands as foreign property, it was a sequel which Kamehameha I, when he distributed the land, had never intended. During the early years even well established and respected settlers such as Marin, Davis and Young paid rents for their land and clearly understood that they held it under the authority of Kamehameha or one of his chiefs. At all times foreigners who were granted land were expected to behave properly according to Hawaiian lights. The chiefess, Kekauonohi, explained to the Land Commission the terms under which she had given land to John White in 1826: 'It was not given to be his forever but given as land is always given by the Chiefs to foreigners: that is as long as they behave well and live uprightly'. E. R. Butler paid Kamehameha I $100 in cash for land which was allotted to him near Honolulu in 1813. Five years later Joseph Thomas paid the chief Keaumoku $100 in cash and goods for five or six acres at Wailua. Neither of them, however, received deeds for their property and their security of tenure was not absolute. Leases for short-term residents were always most precarious, and as late as the 1830s they could be thrown off their temporary holdings at the whim of the chiefs.[35] Kamehameha's general concern that the foreigners might come to wield undue influence in Hawaiian affairs led him to restrict freehold land ownership and to forbid most of the foreigners to build permanent houses or warehouses. The law was waived for Marin, who was allowed to build himself a substantial stone house in 1810, but only after he had completed one for the king. Schäffer complained bitterly in 1816 that Kamehameha: 'refused to let me build a stone warehouse on the island of Oahu for the Russian factory, as previously agreed, but offered me his own warehouse, which he could always supervise'.[36] It is impossible to know whether Schäffer had misunderstood earlier discussions. Certainly Kamehameha I's later stand seems characteristic. As one of the older foreign residents testified in the late 1840s: 'in those days [the first two decades of the nineteenth century] no one thought of erecting houses without consulting a chief'.[37]

Among the early settlers in Fiji the holding of land under casual verbal arrangements had much in common with the usage of their island hosts. No records or evidence have survived of any land sales in Levuka before 1838, although foreigners had been resident there for over twelve years. During this early period they presumably held land by usufruct only and made no attempt to claim individual freehold ownership. Deeds of sales for 1838 and later were lost in the fires which periodically swept Levuka after 1841. But it appears from evidence collected for the Land Claims Commission in the 1880s that, as a rule, land was only formally divided and given to individual owners during this period to settle a debt or a dispute, or for a foreigner who expressly demanded it. In the late 1830s the bêche-de-mer captain, John Eagleston, bought a number of small land lots near Levuka from the Fijians, presumably in the belief that they would be a good investment. However, his failure to return to Fiji after his last trading voyage in 1841 and thus to make good his initial claims left the Fijian vendors in the happy position of being able to sell the same land again to later foreign arrivals. Casual arrangements had their advantages. Lydia Connor, former widow of the ships' carpenter William Cusick, explained how her first husband came into possession of half an acre on the edge of Levuka-Vakaviti: 'First of all it was given in a friendly way afterwards property was given and the soil was given actually. There was a deed made out at that time'.[38] Usually land was held by extended family groups and divided among its members as required. Charles Wise, a part-Fijian son of James Magoun, who had been adopted by his aunt, gave evidence concerning the changed ownership of a piece of land at Vagadace: 'Caroline and James Magoun gave it to my parents, who were always giving presents. It was not a sale—but a gift in a relationship sort of way. My mother and Caroline Magoun were sisters'.[39] Land-holding in Fiji continued along these informal lines until the late 1850s when Europeans with planting ambitions arrived demanding large amounts of land and more formal ownership.

The first requests for Samoan land were made in the late 1830s and early 1840s, by which time the Samoans, who were naturally conservative and wary of foreign ambitions, were fully conversant with the French troubles in Tahiti and the annexation of New Zealand in 1840. To the expatriates, there had appeared to be large stretches of vacant land around Apia harbour, notwithstanding the presence of three Samoan villages in the area. But the chiefs had rights over all the land and were well aware of its value. The missionaries and J. C. Williams, son of the celebrated missionary John Williams, had little difficulty acquiring small sections of land, but later arrivals, men intending to set up trading stations and land speculating whaling captains, found that leasehold was the only form of tenure available. George Pritchard, who was unceremoniously left at Apia as British consul in July 1845, had great difficulty, as he protested to the Foreign Office: 'I have been here more than five months and have not been able either to rent or purchase an inch of ground on which to build a Consulate or Residence'.[40] In 1847, after Pritchard had at last been formally introduced and saluted as the British consul in Samoa by a naval vessel, land was sold to him. During the 1850s

certain small areas around Apia were opened for sale, but large-
scale purchases were impossible until the civil wars of 1869-73,
when the Samoans' desire for guns overcame their scruples about
selling land.

In New Zealand, where land was not at quite such a premium,
the Maori, during this early period, were usually willing to negotiate land sales with foreigners. Deeds of sale of land in the Bay
of Islands area made in the early 1830s contained surprisingly
detailed descriptions of the land to be transferred and emphasised
that the Maori had relinquished all rights to the land. It is impossible to know how much the Maori understood of these transactions, but few of the Kororareka sales were later disputed.
Perhaps twenty years' experience of the missionaries' insistence on
private property had had some effect. The Maori, however, were
still able to manipulate the contracts to their advantage a little.
In August 1833 the merchant Joel Samuel Polack bought a section
of land in Kororareka from the Ngapuhi chief Hone Heke. The
boundaries were carefully delineated and the payment in goods
was accepted. One special clause was included: 'The said J. S.
Polack promises to abstain from building on the Sacred Spots
within his allotments until the persons properly authorized or
Capable shall remove the tapu or prohibition.'[41] Later in 1833 two
Maori groups demanded additional payment from Polack, claiming that the sacred spots contained the bones of their ancestors.
Throughout the 1830s there were few instances when land bought
from the Maori was not subject to this kind of second and even
third payment on account of sacred burial grounds or other land-
related tabus. But once these demands had been met the foreigners
were not further harassed about their ownership. With the growing
number of foreigners moving into Kororareka, the Maori were
quick to appreciate the rising value of land and put up their prices
accordingly. However, they would at no time (not even just after
annexation when prices were sky-high) contemplate selling the
land on which their *pa* was built. The foreign residents were thus
obliged to take up land around the *pa*, which held the most commanding site in the whole town area.[42]

In Papeete the early settlers, who were happy to live under
casual social and land arrangements with the Tahitians, put little
pressure on them for freehold land rights. However, the chiefs

were at no time anxious to sell their lands. When foreign demands increased with the expansion of the Valparaiso and whaling trades, leasehold was the only tenure offered around Papeete, except to a favoured few. The missionaries gained freehold rights to the land they occupied but none of the early foreign residents seems to have to have had enough standing or influence to gain the same for himself. For his services to Pomare II in 1820, S. P. Henry was given land on the island of Moorea. Thirteen years later Pomare IV disputed Henry's rights to this land and the final resolution of the affair found Henry with only half the original area. In the 1840s Joseph Smith, who settled in the Society Islands in 1824, reported that Henry was the only foreigner who owned any sizeable piece of land in the entire group.[43]

Despite the inevitable tensions that resulted from the establishment of alien enclaves in the midst of independent island populations possessing very different political, social and economic interests, the incidence of major crimes was remarkably low. Threats and occasional intimidation were resorted to, but it soon became apparent to both the island authorities and the settlers that each was necessary to the other and that acts which tended to disrupt the *status quo* could destroy the very communities themselves. Foreign residents soon found that the islanders were less likely to steal from them than from visiting vessels. A fine in dollars or goods was the usual punishment for any offence committed either by foreigner or islander, since jails were non-existent and no one in a port town would have had the authority to imprison anybody. No act of intentional homicide among the foreign residents was recorded in any early port town, although there were a few drunken brawls that ended fatally.

In Honolulu it was, as usual, Kamehameha I or his governors who maintained order. Thus on 6 February 1818 Kalanimoku held a public meeting at which he condemned and fined certain foreigners, including Alexander Adams, for drunkenness and for failing to pay the king's taxes.[44] The Levuka residents under Whippy's guidance regulated transactions amongst themselves, exiled warmongers like Pickering, and even held a quasi-trial and hanged the murderers of James Carter. At Kororareka the foreign residents were unable to prevent Maori fighting and raids into the town. A confrontation between Whareumu's people and the

Ngapuhi in Kororareka in December 1827 finally ended without resort to bloodshed, but the Ngapuhi, who were determined on some action before they departed, began pillaging the Europeans' houses and Whareumu was quite unable to prevent it. In 1830 and again in 1837 fighting broke out between rival Maori groups along the Kororareka beach, leaving the foreign residents largely unprotected. Despite this insecurity the foreigners never made any attempt to move their settlement nor arm themselves against the Maori. The convicts who came ashore from the pirated ship *Wellington* early in 1827 found the Maori were as intolerant of them as most Europeans. Within a very short space of time all but six of them had been rounded up by the Maori, and put on board vessels bound for Sydney. The foreign residents at Kororareka were less successful when they tried to impose their beliefs on the Maori. With six companions Augustus Earle, who was in Kororareka for several months in 1827, tried to stop a cannibal feast, but the pieces of human flesh he retrieved from the earth oven and carefully buried were later dug up by the Maori and eaten.[45] Between the Maori and the foreign residents it would appear that two quite different concepts of justice were at work. Most frequently, however, they tolerated each other's idiosyncrasies, interfered as little as possible and the foreigners were, in fact, able to maintain a fairly secure existence. During the early years crimes and disputes between the Europeans in Kororareka were, presumably, settled among themselves.

Foreign numbers in Papeete during the early period were never large and after 1815 the newly constituted missionary laws probably protected them fairly adequately, at least against theft. Captain Kotzebue believed in fact that the laws were too stringent. The Tahitian who stole a sheet from Kotzebue's ship in 1824 was severely punished by the missionaries and the Tahitian magistrate, and called a brute who was not worthy to be treated as a human being. The missionaries, however, did not wield this sort of influence for long and with their fall from all-but-absolute power, particularly after the rise of the heretical *Mamaia* sect in 1826, the foreigners' position also deteriorated. Thomas Elley, acting British vice consul in Tahiti, threatened to quit the island in February 1827, because he felt so insecure in Papeete.[46] The less ambitious foreigners were able to survive this period of instability and do not appear to have been greatly affected by it.

Only in Apia did the maintenance of law and order become a major problem. From the earliest years the consuls and foreign residents proved incapable of settling their differences with the Samoans. The most trivial incidents of cattle or yam stealing were brooded over and stored up until the captain of a man-of-war arrived and was forced to adjudicate. The captains were largely dependent on the consuls and other equally partisan witnesses for explanation of the events, and for interpreters. Further, it was very difficult for naval personnel to act contrary to the consul's wishes without stripping him of the meagre authority he had among the foreign residents and the Samoans. However, George Pritchard so abused the threat of naval power that British captains were forced to criticise his conduct. Captain Maxwell, in Apia in 1848, refused to interfere in a matter that Pritchard himself had done nothing to investigate or settle:

> It might at least have been expected that you [Pritchard] would previously have adopted the usual course of writing to the Chiefs of the District to which the parties belong. . . . At all events until such means have been tried and failed, I must decline any interference in the matter and I [cannot?] for a moment admit the supposition that Mr. Sunderland or any other missionary could possibly desire the intervention of an armed force for the recovery of a few Pigs. Should a demonstration of British Force, ever be required in these Islands, to overawe the Natives I trust the occasion and the object in view will be somewhat more important than the punishment of a few casual instances of Pig Stealing or Cattle Spearing.[47]

The foreign residents' irresponsible dependence on naval justice for the running of everyday life in Apia was exceptional in early beach community development.

Despite the inadequacy of the legal machinery, personal security in Apia was rarely threatened. Although at least two drunken fights in the early 1850s ended in manslaughter, neither should have disturbed the beach community greatly, since those involved were visiting sailors. But in fact the death of a British sailor at the hands of an American, Henry Carleton, occurred at a time of acute consular rivalry and resulted in a refusal on the consuls' part to work together to arrange a trial or deportation of the accused. This lack of co-operation between the American and British representatives in 1854 was closely related to the workings of the Foreign Residents Protection Society, another phenomenon which only appeared in Apia during its formative years. An earlier foreign residents' protection society had been established in Apia in 1848 under the threat of Samoan civil war, but it soon became inactive. The second appeared only six years later, ostensibly for the same reason, although in reality it became a society to protect foreigners from one another's sharp dealings and to free them, or so they hoped, from missionary and chiefly interference. The second society, which was more elaborate than the first, enacted laws to regulate commercial transactions and to maintain order throughout the community. A court was established to try offenders and to allocate the fines imposed to minor public works, but its operations were soon disrupted when the newly appointed American commercial agent, Aaron Van Camp, refused to be associated with the society. It was because of this that the Carleton manslaughter case became such a heated issue: the society and Van Camp clashed over who should handle the proceedings. As Van Camp's schemes developed the foreign residents' court was soon fully employed attempting to protect the Apia residents from his illegal practices. Between 1854 and 1856 barratry, rigged auctions, underhand transfers of property, and embezzlement were among the accusations laid to Van Camp's charge. George Pritchard, with the protection society, led the fight against his colleague and the United States naval officers who tried to uphold him. So far did Pritchard associate himself with the beach element against Van Camp that he sanctioned the fraudulent transfer of American grog shops and dance halls to British citizens so that American officials had no power to close them.[48] Apia, known as the Cairo of the Pacific, had never enjoyed a very savoury reputation and by 1856 it reached its nadir. Naval officers, both British and American, who were sent to establish order from the chaos, were appalled by the situation they found:

There was, moreover, so much exaggeration and so much personal enmity displayed on the part of his [Van Camp's] accusers (none of whom were free from criminality in some shape or other) and on all sides such rude and insulting language and such flat contradictions, that one could not feel otherwise than ashamed and disgusted to be involved in the exposure of so much falsehood and dishonesty; a reproach to the very name of commerce.[49]

Not only those closely involved in the Van Camp intrigues were accused of outrageous behaviour; the population as a whole was seen to be in a degraded condition. Commodore Mervine arrived in Apia in April 1856 and found:

a state of society existing that beggars all description; composed of a heterogeneous mass of the most immoral and dissolute foreigners that ever disgraced humanity; principally composed of Americans and Englishmen, several of whom had been Sidney convicts. Responsible to no laws for their conduct — certainly none that the Natives have the power or disposition to enforce against them — there exist anarchy, riot and debauchery which render life and property insecure.[50]

With Van Camp's departure in May 1856 conditions improved rapidly, but the protection society had proved itself incapable of providing alternative leadership once the two consuls refused to co-operate. Thus after 1856 Apia still lacked any strong social cohesion since it remained dependent on consular rule, and there were no safeguards to protect its inhabitants from similar crises in the future. It should be pointed out, however, that even during the Van Camp affair when most legal procedures were in abeyance, violent incidents occurred very seldom. Economic transactions were greatly restricted between 1854 and 1856 but the foreign residents' lives were not in danger.

While early Honolulu and Levuka could at least boast the presence of accepted leaders and enjoyed a certain degree of internal stability, the residents of both towns were subjected to the threat and even punishment of exile. In 1814 and 1815 word came from Kamehameha I on Hawaii Island that the foreigners in Honolulu without land and skills were to depart: 'that he did not like them'.[51] The continuing influx of deserters was the focus of Kamehameha's anxiety; the well established foreigners were not included. But even they could not always be sure that Hawaiian suspicion or desire to acquire European goods might not extend to themselves. On 23 April 1818 the residents were startled by the arrival of a brig from Hawaii Island: 'With an Indian captain, who informed us that all the white men on the islands were to be put to death at midnight. We were alarmed by a loud cry through the village, when we expected the hour was come; but the natives were contented with the burning of a few houses'.[52] None of the threats was fully acted upon but it kept the foreigners aware of their insecurity and their dependence on Hawaiian goodwill.

Conditions for beachcombing and foreign settlement were more dangerous in Fiji than in Polynesia, since the threat of cannibalism and Fijian intrigue were present for many years after the first European contact. The Levuka settlers considered themselves immune from Fijian wars and attacks, but William Diaper, an itinerant beachcomber with warmongering propensities, who visited Levuka briefly in 1842, had no faith in their supposed security:

> They appeared to be comfortable enough, and I could have remained with them if I had thought proper, but I did not entertain the notion of attempting a civilized life in the midst of cannibals, and thought that they incurred more danger in this kind of semi-civilization and apparent independence than I actually did, who was seeing fresh adventures every day, and trusting to the mercy of savages.[53]

Two years later the 'semi-civilization' was shattered when the Levuka men abused the laws of neutrality tacitly understood between themselves and Cakobau, chief of Bau. Despite their regulations against harbouring partisan foreigners inside Levuka, they rescued Charles Pickering from Lakeba, whence he had escaped after his schooner was wrecked at Cicia Island. Since he was believed to have been carrying information for the chief of Rewa, Cakobau had also been in pursuit of him. Thwarted in his attempt Cakobau vented his anger on the Levuka men, exiling them from Ovalau. Petitions from neither Whippy nor the missionaries weakened his resolve; all the foreigners were forced to depart, leaving a seventy-ton schooner half-finished on the slips. They did not, however, join Cakobau's enemy at Rewa but retired to Solevu, on Vanua Levu, where they took no part in the war. A return to the original town was made early in 1849. The foreigners had had no recourse to any outside power to enforce their reinstatement, nor did they demand compensation, at this stage, for the loss of property they had sustained when the Lovoni men from the interior of Ovalau razed Levuka in 1846.[54] Like the Honolulu settlers their livelihood and security of tenure were dependent on their ability to maintain good relations with their island hosts.

The good relations that were established and maintained in the early beach communities owed a great deal to a number of foreigners who had absorbed so much of the island way of life that they had become sympathetic and tolerant towards the norms of local society, and were equipped to act as mediators between islander and settler. Several of these were beachcombers who, moving into beach communities, brought with them habits of cooperation with the islanders, and used their knowledge to guide the chiefs with newly arrived and more influential foreigners. Whippy's concern for the safety of several bêche-de-mer vessels was probably activated by his loyalty both to the Fijians, who would have suffered severe reprisals had they been successful, and to his fellow countrymen. Later in 1852, at a time when several Americans were intransigently demanding compensation for recent fires and depredations, Whippy went with Captain Home of H.M.S. *Calliope* to Bua as Cakobau's peace messenger, and did much to encourage the combatant parties to make a settlement. During Home's same tour of duty in Fiji, Whippy made it possible for him to capture two 'undesirable' white men on Moala Island. 'Without his most valuable assistance, knowledge of the Natives, and their character', and his 'warm desire to do good', Home stated to his superior officer, nothing would have been accomplished.[55]

John Young and Francisco de Paula Marin were similarly concerned to foster the best interests of their newly adopted homeland, Hawaii. The threat of Russian settlement and perhaps even invasion of the Hawaiian Islands brought Young to Honolulu late in 1815, where he supervised the construction of a fort, and kept Kamehameha I posted concerning the Russians' movements on Kauai. On his advice Alexander Adams and William Sumner were sent to disband the settlement. The attempt was unsuccessful but two months later in May 1817 Schäffer was driven from Kauai and his pipedream of a Russian empire in the Pacific was shattered. When the Russian captain, Kotzebue, who knew nothing of Schäffer or his plans, arrived in Honolulu harbour in November 1816 it was Young who smoothed his way and quietened the Hawaiians' fears that Kotzebue was surveying the harbour as a prelude to annexing the islands. Marin was a trusted interpreter to three successive Kamehamehas and acted as physician to several of the royal household.[56]

The foreigners in Papeete, Kororareka and Apia evinced no comparable sense of responsibility or concern. The Pomare family was renowned for its parsimony in rewarding the services of foreigners in their employ, which may in part have contributed to the lack of loyalty they inspired in foreigners. Even S. P. Henry, who was born and brought up in the islands as the son of one of the missionaries, revealed little vital interest in Pomare II's new economic ventures. Entrusted with certain business transactions for Pomare II in 1820, Henry acted entirely in his own interests without thought of his employer's rights or needs.[57] This lack of consideration towards the Pomare family was symptomatic of the attitudes of the majority of later non-missionary settlers in Papeete. No mediator was concerned to advise or protect the Tahitians' interests, which the foreigners often disregarded in their pursuit of economic gain. Similarly in Apia a quick fortune and return to the civilised world were the goals of the majority of traders, who saw their main avenue to success in the exploitation of the Samoans, not in fostering their concerns. Even Jonas Coe, who arrived in Samoa in the mid 1840s and who rejected several opportunities to return home to the United States of America, did little to protect the Malietoa family with whom he had been closely connected in the early years. The foreign residents at Kororareka had little contact with the Maori chiefs except for their immediate neighbours, the minor chiefs Whareumu and later Pomare and Titore. Presumably they were willing to advise the chiefs if they were consulted but they appear to have been more involved in commercial and social pursuits. Good relations between individual islander and foreigner still existed in the towns of Papeete, Kororareka and Apia but the Tahitians, Maori and Samoans could not rely on any foreigner for disinterested help or advice.

While the settlers were endeavouring to consolidate and, when conditions permitted, to extend their newly-found urban beachheads in the islands, the islanders themselves strove to maintain an uneasy ascendancy over the slowly expanding foreign populations. Exile was threatened and imposed, property was confiscated and business activities were incommoded by tabus, and in Apia in 1855 even by boycott. The Samoan chiefs in the Apia district tried to force the foreign merchants to lower the prices of European goods. When the merchants refused to comply the chiefs posted Samoan 'constables' at their stores. Feeling ran high and could easily have ended in bloodshed, had not a British naval vessel arrived in port and the captain persuaded the chiefs that, while they could control the economic transactions of their own people, they should leave Samoans from elsewhere free to trade in Apia. The chiefs agreed to remove their constables and the boycott soon collapsed, without achieving any of the Samoans' desired aims. Kamehameha I would not tolerate the claim that the English had rights over his islands through his treaty with Vancouver in 1794. The title 'Sandwich Islands' was forbidden and each island had to be called by its Hawaiian name.[58] Other island authorities, however, were not as astute or powerful as he. While the Fijian, Samoan and Maori chiefs were jealously watching the fluctuation of power within their own ranks, the foreign settlers in their territories were slowly usurping political and economic rights which the islanders were never to recover. For a period a few island leaders, notably Kamehameha I and Cakobau, were able to impose some control on foreign activities. But although the early residents, without consular representation, were dependent on their hosts' goodwill, they had much in the way of goods and skills that had become essential to island life. No chief was willing or able to cut himself and his people off from such benefits. Any stand against foreign expansion, therefore, could not be permanently effective. During this early period, however, the islanders were confident of the validity of their own culture and with the exception of the Samoans were not intimidated by threats of naval reprisals. It was only with the arrival of consuls that their precarious power was upset, and their right to control land, trading practices, harbour dues and town development was increasingly denied.

five

Consuls, Missionaries and Company Traders

As the beach communities became established and began to attract more foreign residents they underwent several changes. Old beach community settlers, many of whom had lived or worked quite closely with the islanders, were gradually outnumbered by foreigners who settled at once in the small port areas and had a minimum of contact with their island hosts. The ideas and ambitions of these later arrivals became the common goals of the majority of the foreign residents. Increased numbers and propinquity tended to generate a community of interest among the foreigners *vis-à-vis* the surrounding indigenous population. Similarity of goals, however, did not prevent occasional intergroup friction among the residents, whose economic concerns were often in competition, while their social interests and personalities were also divergent. Tensions were exacerbated by the isolated conditions of expatriate life in the Pacific islands, which had much in common with the restricted lives of Europeans in India and the East. Small enclaves of expatriates living in isolation from their home environment were prone to gossip, rumour and sudden violent upsurges of resentment against their host populations. The diversification of occupation and social status among the enlarged foreign populations in the beach communities was another important factor leading to change, in particular in the patterns of leadership, which resulted in new loyalties and allegiances. The advent and subsequent activities of three immigrant occupational groups — the consuls, missionaries and company traders — were to dominate later development in the beach communities.

In Honolulu between 1820 and 1836 the foreign population grew from about 100 to well over 350 while at the same time the Hawaiians who moved into the Honolulu district increased at a suicidal rate to approximately 6000.[1] J. C. Jones, R. Charlton and

Jules Dudoit settled in Honolulu in 1821, 1825 and 1837 as representatives for America, Great Britain and France respectively. The first missionaries sent out by the American Board of Commissioners for Foreign Missions established a centre in Honolulu in 1820. In an attempt to counterbalance this Protestant thrust a small band of French Roman Catholic priests arrived in Honolulu in 1827 but they were too late to influence the strong bond already cemented between the Hawaiian chiefs and their American mentors, and they suffered for their misplaced zeal. Persecution and exile daunted them until the matter was finally 'solved' in their favour in 1839 by French gunboat diplomacy. Throughout the 1820s and early 1830s the foreign residents were split into a number of hostile factions — the rift between merchants and Protestant missionaries being particularly bitter and disruptive, but not so disruptive as to diminish the merchants' economic activities, which increased over 200 per cent during the period.

Later development in Papeete, between 1827 and the announcement of a French Protectorate over Tahiti in 1842, witnessed a slow growth of foreign population from about twenty-four throughout Tahiti to about seventy foreigners permanently settled in Papeete itself.[2] America, Britain and France were represented in Papeete by J. A. Moerenhout, who took up the office of American agent in 1836 and then changed jobs in 1838 to become the French consular agent, and George Pritchard, who was appointed British consul in 1837. Richard Charlton, British consul for the Sandwich, Society and Friendly Islands, visited Tahiti, once only, in 1826 and appointed Thomas Elley acting vice-consul for the Society Islands. The appointment was never ratified in London and Elley, during the two years he remained in Tahiti, had no influence or control over the other foreign residents in Papeete. S. Blackler arrived as the second American consular agent in 1839, several months after Moerenhout had changed from American to French representative. As in Honolulu, French Roman Catholic priests attempted to establish themselves in Papeete, first in 1836 and again in 1837, and the incidents that occurred during their forceful removal gave French naval officers the means to manipulate the Tahitian government. In the commercial sphere the Valparaiso traders became securely established and throughout the 1830s enjoyed increasing profits.

During its final years as an independent beach community, between 1835 and 1840 when Great Britain annexed New Zealand, Kororareka was inundated by a rush of settlers and speculators who anticipated British intervention. By 1840 there were over 1000 foreigners settled in the Bay of Islands area of whom about 300 lived in Kororareka.[3] In 1838 conditions in the town became so uproarious that the residents formed a protection society to secure their property and persons from other whites. J. R. Clendon took up his appointment as American consular agent in 1839, but he, like J. Busby the British Resident, did not live in the immediate environs of Kororareka. Well equipped shipyards and ship chandlery businesses supplied the large number of whaling vessels entering the harbour, while several agents for Sydney companies organised the trans-Tasman trade. In 1839 the Roman Catholic Bishop Pompallier settled in Kororareka (earlier he had been resident on the Hokianga River) without opposition or much interest from the Maori, the majority of whom had vacated the Kororareka peninsular area by this time.

In Levuka between 1852 and 1865 the foreign population grew from about fifty to over eighty.[4] W. T. Pritchard, the first British consular agent, arrived in the town in 1858, at which time J. B. Williams suddenly found it necessary to move in from the Rewa district. American demands for compensation for every mishap that could possibly be pinned upon the Fijians increased in number and frequency, and when the comprehensive judicial and political powers that W. T. Pritchard had assumed were stripped from him in 1862, the foreign residents were impelled to establish a protection society to bolster up their sudden feeling of insecurity. The church was well represented in Levuka throughout the period, both the French Marists (1851) and the Wesleyans (1852) being in residence. Finally in Apia during this interim period between early development (1840-55) and later large-scale attempts at land ownership and plantation agriculture (1865 onwards), the foreign population increased from 75 to about 150, while commercial activities expanded even more dramatically.[5] The Godeffroy company, established in 1857, was primarily responsible for this growth and the accompanying stability in the economic sphere. The British and American consular agents were joined by the consul for Hamburg (later Germany), August Unshelm, also the manager of the Godeffroy company, and the general tone of society was greatly improved by the arrival of a number of respectable British, American and Scandinavian settlers in the early 1860s. Respectability notwithstanding, the day-to-day management of affairs between the various national groups and the Samoans still remained a fundamental problem.

In all the beach communities the period under discussion was one of instability and increasing disharmony between the islanders and foreigners — each was testing the determination and strength of the other and in almost every minor battle of wills the foreigners emerged with the advantage. Basically the increased foreign population and the close involvement of consuls, missionaries and large company traders in relations between the islanders and the beach community residents were responsible for the new developments. In the following analysis of the changes that did occur the role of the consuls will receive most attention since their influence was unquestionably greatest, while at the same time the effect of the missionaries and company traders was mainly felt within the context of the new situation which consular ascendancy created.

During the early years of foreign activity in the Pacific, neither the British nor the American government was greatly concerned to protect the interests of its nationals or the islanders contacted. But by the second decade of the nineteenth century the British government was forced to recognise that the increasing number of British subjects in the Pacific had to be brought under some sort of control, however minimal. After superficial consideration of the problems of island sovereignty and the effectiveness of gunboat diplomacy, the British government decided on such *ad hoc* arrangements as the occasional visitations of warships and the appointment of Justices of the Peace at Papeete and Kororareka, both of which measures were organised through New South Wales. William Henry, LMS missionary, was appointed Justice of the Peace for Tahiti in 1811, to be followed three years later by Thomas Kendall, CMS missionary, who received the same appointment for the Bay of Islands. Such solutions were only makeshift and by the 1820s both the American and the British governments had been pressured by alarmist reports from naval officials in the Pacific, and by whaling interests and commercial companies working in the area, to provide more efficient protection for their respective nationals and to regulate their activities on shore more closely. Since neither government had any wish to acquire colonial possessions in the area at this time, arrangements for establishing effective control were made on the assumption that the governments were dealing with independent island kingdoms capable of regulating relations with foreign settlers in their territories. Pursuing policies of minimum intervention the British and American governments appointed consular or commercial agents without magisterial powers who, it was expected, would encourage and protect their compatriots' trading enterprises and co-operate with the island authorities to regulate their behaviour. These positions were the lowest grade of appointment available, i.e. part-time agents on a pittance salary (about £200 or its equivalent), or a fee for work basis.

For the first two national representatives in Hawaii the paltry salary was more than offset by their affiliation with successful Pacific business houses. Marshall and Wildes, one of the two major north-west coast and sandalwood trading companies in New England, engineered the appointment of their employee, John Coffin Jones, as the first 'agent of the United States for commerce and seamen', while Richard Charlton, first British representative in Hawaii, was the nominee and employee of Palmer, Wilson and Company.[6] Throughout the century big business interests were to prove a lucrative source of patronage. Jonas Coe slid into the office of American agent in Apia, with the help of his influential brother, the businessman Edward Coe in California. The apparent ease with which commercial companies were able to gain appointment for their nominees was largely due to the dearth of suitable candidates among whom governments could select representatives. Few men of education and responsibility would have been tempted from secure positions at home to be their nation's representative in the Pacific unless they already had some affiliation with commercial interests in the area. Even in the beach communities it was difficult to find hardworking men who wanted to take on a post which entailed much time-consuming and often acrimonious business, rewarded by such a meagre salary. As Thomas Crocker, Jones's temporary appointee in Honolulu explained: 'On my departure from the Islands I did not leave any agent, as there was no resident who would accept of it that was respectable and responsible, owing to the very frequent and troublesome calls upon him, and being a place destitute of all laws as regards the whites'.[7] Under such conditions it is hardly surprising if the actions of the consuls who were willing to fill such positions left much to be desired.

Despite these professional inadequacies, once established in a port town consuls played leading roles simply by virtue of the offices they performed. Only they were able to register deeds and other legal instruments, issue birth and death certificates, provide for the administration of deceased estates and enforce maritime law in respect of European vessels and their cargoes. With and without authority they performed the marriage service and produced the requisite lines. Consuls were not automatically given the right to solemnise marriages: a special licence was required. All the marriages J. C. Williams performed in Apia as British consul between 1858 and 1870 were declared void in England. W. T. Pritchard, as British consul in Fiji, even married himself to a part-Fijian in Levuka in 1861, perhaps hoping to avoid unwanted publicity about his two year old daughter.[8] Although not all consuls sought to enlarge their official duties, none was able to avoid the assumption of more general political powers. Civil and criminal cases and demands for protection and compensation were thrust upon them, as the only foreign residents on the beach who enjoyed any status or authority at all. Thus the arrival of consular agents gave a new focus to beach community life, despite the fact that many were already familiar figures in their respective communities. Once they were recognised as representatives of their home governments, they became the focal point for complaints and the centre of self-conscious, national solidarity.

Not all foreigners in beach communities welcomed the arrival of consuls — some departed unobtrusively as these portents of encroaching civilisation and law and order appeared. One consul in Apia was told, 'We old hands on the beach looked upon the likes of you as we did the police at home — as always trying to run us in'.[9] W. T. Pritchard was welcomed by the British settlers in Levuka and pestered with claims, but he was made to understand that they would brook no interference with their domestic arrangements.

The financial conditions of employment made it imperative for the consuls to participate in general commercial activities, but more important was the fact that the majority of early representatives had been closely involved in beach community life before they accepted consular positions. J. C. Jones, R. Charlton, J. Dudoit, J. A. Moerenhout, J. C. Williams and J. R. Clendon had all traded extensively in the islands, so that when they became consuls they had vested interests to protect and decided views about island authority. Consular entrepreneurs were to be found in almost all major enterprises: J. C. Jones was heavily involved in the Hawaiian sandalwood trade, J. A. Moerenhout was one of the most successful pearl merchants working in the Tuamotus, J. C. Williams initiated the coconut oil trade in Samoa while A. Unshelm was to develop it into a major industry, and a later German consul in Samoa was to introduce the highly successful copra trade. Consular commercial connections extended to the bêche-de-mer trade, purveying, cotton growing and the majority of representatives also had some general trading interests. Consulates were seldom more than warehouses or general mercantile offices, frequently without even a flagpole to distinguish them from the other stores and houses along the beach front.

In Apia G. Pritchard's residence was just one grog shop among many in the town in the early 1850s, while in Tahiti illegally imported spirits were readily available from the United States consulate during the late 1830s. C. Shipley in Apia in 1848 thought the consuls' gun-running activities constituted a serious departure from correct consular behaviour:

> It certainly appeared very odd to see the Captain of a ship whose profession is war, putting himself to great personal inconvenience, and taking a great deal of trouble, to preserve peace between two quarrelsome parties [of Samoans], whilst at the same time the two Consuls, who talked very well, were retailing musquets, powder, and shot to both parties; had they refused to sell the instruments of war, it is very doubtful if any fighting would have taken place.[10]

Other consuls also combined their legitimate trading activities with less acceptable pursuits. J. C. Jones openly confessed to his warmongering activities in Honolulu: 'I am endeavouring to make them [the Hawaiians] believe this will be the case [that a rumoured civil war would in fact break out] in order that we may sell our powder and muskets'.[11] In Fiji both J. B. Williams and W. T. Pritchard speculated heavily in land and attempted to divert settlers and shipping from Levuka to areas in which they had made substantial investments. Neither, however, was successful; nor for that matter was Busby, who tried the same ploy in New Zealand, hoping that with British annexation, the land he had bought would be chosen for the future capital.

These trade and land speculating commitments made it impossible for the majority of consuls to act with impartiality in their official capacities in any case in which their interests were involved. The British and American governments had blithely assumed that the public and private spheres of a consul's life could be and, of course should be, totally and permanently separated. In practice even the most conscientious of representatives found it all but impossible to make the distinction — a number of them were not even concerned to try. On the occasions when the consuls made a real attempt to settle disputes and to maintain law and order, they were handicapped by the minimum of *de jure* power entrusted to them. With the exception of the German consuls and the American representatives after 1870, no representative had magisterial rights; civil cases could only be heard if the persons concerned were prepared to accept a consular court and co-operate with other national representatives if necessary. Even then no fine or punishment was binding.

Murder or kidnapping suspects had to be sent to their place of origin for trial, accompanied by sufficient witnesses and evidence to ensure a conviction, a condition that could rarely be fulfilled in the case of American suspects and only occasionally for British ones. The British-born E. Doyle, summoned to Sydney for trial in December 1837, was found guilty of entering and stealing from a dwelling house in the Bay of Islands in June of that year and for threatening the life of the owner. Henry Williams, head of the CMS mission, was summoned to Sydney as chief witness, on whose evidence and the testimony of Doyle's accomplice, who turned King's evidence, Doyle was hanged.[12] This was an unusually quick passage of justice, made possible largely because of the proximity of the New South Wales courts to Kororareka and the presence of two crucial witnesses at the trial. More frequently persons believed guilty of crimes in the islands were shipped to either America or

New South Wales, only to be discharged because of lack of evidence or relevant laws under which they could be charged.

Most crimes committed in the beach communities, however, were seldom so serious as to defy some sort of settlement. Collection of debts, breach of promise and petty theft could usually be legitimately dealt with by the consular courts in participation with the beach residents and islanders, neither of whom was sparing in the infliction of punishments. In 1866 the American negro, Thomas Tilton, and the German, Henry Nestfall, were brought to trial in Apia by their respective consuls. A jury of eight German and American settlers found them guilty of the theft of fourteen bottles of gin. The punishment awarded, exile. Nestfall was sent to Germany, but suddenly for no apparent reason, the American representative opposed the court decision and Tilton remained in Apia. The settlers' indignant outburst resulted in much consular correspondence, which has preserved the case for posterity; most trials conducted by the court of the Association for the Mutual Protection of Life and Property between 1864 and 1870 were settled without such voluminous records.[13] As in other beach communities, fines and exile were the only punishments that the court had much success in imposing, and even these sentences did not always go unquestioned.

In Levuka before 1860, when W. T. Pritchard established a mercantile court, the British residents had to settle disputes among themselves or leave them until the arrival of the next man-of-war. The American residents could appeal to their agent J. B. Williams for a hearing, but his jurisdiction only covered disputes among the Americans. The mercantile court in which the British and American representatives sat *ex officio* was able to handle a number of land, property and shipping disputes among the foreigners, with a marked degree of success, but its rule was short-lived. In 1862 it was abolished.

In Honolulu until the mid 1830s, accused persons were heard and punished by a joint meeting of chiefs and foreigners. In 1825 when Joseph Navarro shot Captain Sistare twice, neither time causing serious injury, for enticing his Hawaiian woman away from him, the chiefs held a meeting to which all the foreigners were invited, to consider what punishments should be inflicted. Both were sentenced to exile, for stealing another man's 'wife' and making false assertions, and for making an attempt on another man's life. Sistare, a whaling captain, departed for the grounds and Navarro was shipped on the *Eclipse* for Fanning Island on 3 September 1825. For the latter the sentence of exile was not permanent: he was back in Honolulu for a few months in the middle of 1826 and returned to settle in June 1828. In the interim, however, his house and property had been sold. In 1831 Thomas Cooper, a negro, and John Mackey broke into a Honolulu store and stole $2000. The money was later recovered, but Mackey was tied to a cart and given 100 lashes while being dragged through the town, and Cooper received three dozen strokes.[14] Again chiefs and foreigners jointly decided on the punishment.

Justice in respect to the more serious crimes was rough but in a fashion it was seen to be done and the majority of expatriates respected it. A breakdown in consular co-operation and court procedure, as occurred in Apia in 1855-6, could, however, shatter such an *ad hoc* legal system, and a beach community remained without recourse to any form of law until the consuls were prepared to come to terms. For a period in 1839-40 hostility between Blackler, Moerenhout and G. Pritchard in Papeete brought all legal processes to a standstill, since each consul thwarted the other's intentions whenever possible, harboured criminals of their own nationality and refused to bring them to trial or enforce punishments.[15] For a time after the arrival of national representatives the foreign residents were content to use these consular courts but later, led by consular example, they became increasingly eager to place all their affairs beyond island control. Wary of island governments' intentions and of their ability to understand the complexities of commercial and international law, the residents became more self-assertive in demanding what they considered were their rights and privileges as white men. As a result they agitated for extra-territorial judicial procedures, with juries composed only of the nationals of the person accused, whether the case concerned an islander or not. In Honolulu, between 1836 and 1839, the British and the French, and the Americans in an informal way, all made treaties with the Hawaiian government enforcing this requirement.

In Kororareka, Levuka and Apia, where no such treaties were signed between the powers and the island chiefs, protection societies, which earlier had appeared only in Apia, were established.

Their appearance indicated the ambivalence of the foreigners' feelings: on one hand there was the expatriates' self-assurance and sense of superiority, but conflicting with it on the other hand was their insecurity and inability to maintain a dual system of government with the islanders. Direct consular participation in a protection society occurred only in Apia where from the earliest Foreign Residents Society in 1848, consuls had been initiators and leading figures. The Foreign Residents Society established in 1854 subsided into inactivity after the Van Camp affair, although the mixed tribunal created under its auspices functioned until 1860. At this time an attempt, led by J. C. Williams, then British consul, was made to establish a reform government, in which the Samoans exercised an unprecedented amount of control. By 1863 the foreigners, believing that the power had given rise to insupportable arrogance among the Samoan police, withdrew from the experiment and returned to that old stalwart form of government, a Foreign Residents Society — now in the new guise of the Association of Mutual Protection for The Life and Property. Williams, who previously had been so active in the formation of the reform government, willingly assumed the position of judge in the new Association's court, since he agreed with the majority of residents that the former government had been a total failure. The British Government refused to allow Williams to hold the judgeship, but he continued to sit with his American and German colleagues as magistrate in the court, which was able to settle the residents' legal disputes with a large degree of success until the 1870s.[16]

In Levuka the increased population, which had been attracted to Fiji in the late 1850s and early 1860s by the rumour that British annexation was imminent, had their hopes dashed by the announcement of the refusal of the Fijian offer in June 1862. At the same time they were forced to recognise the limitations of consular authority when W. T. Pritchard was relieved of the numerous powers and functions he had illegally assumed. The mercantile court was abolished and all magisterial powers were denied him. The pillaging of an Englishman's house in the centre of Levuka by the Fijians, which coincided with these events, brought home to the residents that their property and interests were virtually unprotected, and led to the sudden appearance of a vigilante committee. There is no evidence to suggest that the committee ever became an alternative form of government, but the instinctive manner in which it was conceived underlines the basic fears and insecurity of the Levuka whites.[17]

In Kororareka the protection society owed its inception to the propertied white minority who feared the hooligan element in their own midst. The settlers who flowed in from Australia and England after 1836 found that the British Resident, Busby, could not guarantee protection or impose justice. 'The man-of-war without guns' — the Maoris' derisive title for Busby — was all too apt. Recognising that the continual disorder which disturbed Kororareka was bad for trade, Busby suggested a protection society to the more respectable residents, but when they approached him with fifteen resolutions inaugurating the Kororareka Association, Busby could do nothing more than approve them unofficially. The major difference between this Association and those of Apia and Levuka was the fact that the Maori were given equal rights in the quasi-government that was established. The Kororareka Association was not an attempt by the foreigners to isolate themselves from Maori depredations or control, but rather dealt largely with crimes against property committed by the rabble elements within the white population. The consuls, Busby and Clendon, and respectable settlers such as Gilbert Mair, held aloof from the Association but the majority of property owners actually resident in Kororareka became members. Punishments (fines, corporal punishment and exile) were imposed and the system achieved an effective, if primitive, degree of law and order, despite moments of blatant partiality. A debt collector from Sydney who tried to settle his account with the leader of the Association was brusquely tarred and feathered, before he could escape.[18] The Kororareka Association was in many aspects similar to the protection societies in Apia and Levuka — in all three towns the foreign residents were obliged to establish some form of government to control and protect their activities but the former did not seek to usurp the power of the Maori who had in fact largely withdrawn from the town area.

Given the isolated environment of the beach communities, the conflicting interests of a multi-racial society and the consuls' position in it, the increased intransigence of foreign attitudes made manifest in the demand for extra-territorial legal rights and the appearance of vigilante committees was all but inevitable. On one hand many residents were eager to believe that the consuls had the power to protect their interests, even in defiance of island law. One's nationality, which in earlier periods had been of little use or significance, was seen as a source of commercial and political privilege. On the other hand the consuls willingly championed their nationals' claims, often regardless of the rights of each case, and encouraged them to believe that with the protection which they could provide, the need to conciliate island governments no longer existed. One outstanding example of consular refusal to acknowledge island authority was revealed by a newly appointed American agent in Apia. When Captain Fremantle attempted to reimpose prohibition on Apia harbour in 1856, he refused to comply, arguing that: 'Any attempt to restrict the Commerce of a Country so long as it in no way conflicted with the laws of Nations in an Island where there is no King, no Government and in many cases no God, would be ridiculous.' Until the Samoans were capable of creating their own unified government and imposing national laws, the American agent was not going to restrict imports of American liquor for Samoan benefit.[19]

Consuls who saw their duty as pursuing their national interests to the detriment of island authority soon found themselves the focus of residents' complaints, and involved in political, economic and religious matters that were beyond the limits of legitimate consular action. Unversed in international law, no island authority understood the bounds of consular rights nor could they afford to ignore the consuls' continual threats of naval intervention, since the occasional visits of men-of-war were the one time when the representatives might have the power to back up their fulminations. If a naval commander could be made to see the situation in the same light as the consul then retribution, punishments and fines followed. Although naval personnel usually made some attempt to view with objectivity the various complaints laid before them, access to non-partisan information or to the other (island) side's story was almost impossible to obtain, unless a captain had his own interpreters. Some captains tackled the disputes brought before them more conscientiously than others, witness the severe criticism G. Pritchard received from a number of British naval officers, but there were more who were happy to lend a little brief authority to their consuls' claims to power and retribution.

One of the most blatant episodes of naval irresponsibility and wilfulness was Captain Boutwell's investigation of the American claims in Fiji in 1855. The history of the origin and growth of the American claims is long and highly involved, but when Boutwell appeared in Levuka the amount agreed upon as owing to the American residents in Fiji, principally to the American agent, J. B. Williams, was $5000. Refusing the assistance of the arbitrators, David Whippy and the Reverend James Calvert, appointed by an American captain in 1851, Boutwell heard evidence for a number of cases, some of which had not previously been brought before an American official, and finally assessed the amount of indemnity at $30,000. This was to be collected from Cakobau, although the chief had insisted that he could not be held responsible for all the Fijians who had allegedly caused the damage. The appearance of Boutwell's superior officer, Captain Bailey, in Levuka with warnings to Boutwell not to overreach his instructions, did nothing to improve the latter's temper. Bailey was obliged to leave, upon which Boutwell reopened the case, increased the amounts of several claims and added three new ones. The final indemnity stood at $43,531, responsibility for which was forced upon Cakobau, who through threat and intimidation was made to sign to that effect. Fourteen years later the American government scrutinised the case and admitted that certain excesses had occurred. All J. B. Williams's claims, amounting to over $18,000, were disallowed — but in the intervening years Cakobau had been saddled with this debt which impinged upon his political powers and threatened the very independence of Fiji.[20] This incident was not typical of the general operation of naval justice in the Pacific, but the powers Boutwell assumed, with J. B. Wiliams's hearty approval, were available to other naval captains had they cared to use them.

The visits of U.S.S. *Dolphin*, Captain Percival, and U.S.S. *Peacock*, Captain T. Catesby Jones, to Honolulu in 1826 were prompted by American sandalwood merchants' demands for the payment of the Hawaiian sandalwood debt which had become impossible for them to collect. (Before this time the merchants had had no cause to ask for a visit from a naval vessel.) The debt was estimated at $200,000, which the Hawaiian government acknowledged to the naval authorities in 1826, and made a great effort to liquidate with the sandalwood resources left to them. In 1829

Captain Finch helped to secure about $50,000 still due to the merchants, principally the United States commercial agent, but the sandalwood account was not finally closed until 1843. These captains apparently performed their duty fairly, at least according to Western lights, and Captain Jones further helped conditions in Honolulu by rounding up thirty American deserters who were not wanted ashore and shipping them off on various vessels. Captain Finch was instrumental in a more positive attempt to bolster the Hawaiian government when he delivered a letter to Kamahameha III, in which it was explicitly stated that all Americans resident in the Hawaiian Islands were subject to Hawaiian laws and were to be held responsible to them.[21] Some naval captains at least were anxious to see that their nationals recognised and respected island authority.

Clearly the practice of naval justice was not precisely set out by either the British or American governments. Without stringent guidelines, each captain was free to judge cases presented to him according to his own preconceived notions of island status and consular authority. Whether their judgment and advice enhanced or ignored island governments, naval officials only remained in the port towns for brief periods of time. Their actions were not likely to have lasting influence unless they favoured the foreign residents, who would then foster them. Finch's attempt to help the Hawaiian government only made the Americans in Honolulu more hostile towards it, as their behaviour made manifestly clear as soon as his ship had sailed from the harbour. Whatever individual captains might do, the very presence of a warship in the islands reinforced the foreigners' feelings of national solidarity and the belief that their interests would be upheld. The more frequent arrival of ships representing one country rather than another caused jealousy and unease in a beach community — fears were rife that one group of nationals would enjoy increased influence over the island government and consequent favours. The American sandalwood traders in Honolulu regarded with suspicion the visit of H.M.S. *Blonde,* Lord Byron, in 1825 and later claimed that his influence had adversely affected their interests. The arrival of two American vessels in 1826 re-established the balance, at least in the Americans' eyes. Disgusted with the pro-islander attitudes of certain British captains, several British subjects in Fiji in the 1850s and

1860s sought American citizenship, hoping to benefit from the more aggressive conduct of United States commanders. From these examples of naval justice, and those that will be discussed in conjunction with the problems of the arrival of French Roman Catholic priests in Hawaii and Tahiti, it seems fair to claim that the most lasting effect of naval intervention in the Pacific was an increasing disregard of the rights of island governments among beach community residents.

Inevitably loyalties and patterns of leadership among the beach residents, both island and foreign, changed during this period. National pride and rivalries, which were stimulated and exacerbated by the consuls, rode rough-shod over any previous feeling of responsibility to island governments or respect for local leaders. Constant demands for the most-favoured-nation treatment and a desire for independence from island control dominated foreigners' attitudes. They took themselves, their livelihoods and their property much more seriously than they had in the early days of beach community life, when they had recognised and accepted the reality of island power. The largely undifferentiated society of pre-1820 Honolulu had looked to Kamehameha I as its source of authority and controller of land, building rights and trading monopolies. With his death in May 1819 and the arrival of a number of new settlers, including the American missionaries and commercial agent, society polarised between two bitter factions: most of the foreigners, led by the national representatives Jones and later Charlton, versus the missionaries, a few more respectable settlers and the Hawaiian chiefs. Intransigence on both sides resulted in a divided community and continual jockeying for control over island affairs in which the Hawaiian chiefs became unwilling pawns. Both Kamehameha II and III were torn between the blandishments offered by the residents — the gay riotous living of the port — and the more substantial and sober benefits offered by the missionaries — literacy and serious counsel about good government. Kamehameha II died in London before he had experienced the degree of pressure that each side was capable of imposing but his brother Kamehameha III was exposed to the full force of both the missionaries' and the merchants' determination to mould the affairs of Hawaii to their own interest. For a time missionary advisers were to gain the upper hand and undoubtedly they sought to protect and enhance island authority, but their intransigence over certain issues and their inability to guard against increasing foreign encroachment made it impossible for the Hawaiian chiefs to develop a truly independent government.

The Tahitian chiefs, who for many years had considered the missionaries as the authorities concerning national and international rights and the correct behaviour towards warships found, after the establishment of consulates in Papeete in the mid 1830s, a rival centre of power in their midst with very different attitudes and demands. It was soon apparent to them that the missionaries had no standing in national affairs and that the consuls were the authorities with whom they had to deal. This realisation helped them little, since the American and French consuls did nothing to strengthen Pomare IV's government: in fact to the contrary they sought almost every opportunity to embarrass it and deny the queen's power. For all his good intentions to protect the Tahitian monarchy, George Pritchard the British consul did as much to undermine its power by his stubbornness and determination to banish the Roman Catholic priests who tried to settle in Papeete in 1836-7, as did his arch enemy the United States, later French, consul, Moerenhout.

Conditions in the Bay of Islands were very different. As British Resident, Busby had even fewer powers than the consular agents in other Pacific port towns. The British settlers in Kororareka, who constituted the majority of the population, soon realised that his presence in no way improved their security. Men like Clendon, who did not become United States consular agent until 1839, and Polack turned, as they had always done, to Henry Williams, head of the CMS Mission, for help and adjudication if they had any difficulty with the Maori over land or property. Busby himself was dependent on Williams to negotiate his early land sales.[22] Kept under a very tight rein by the New South Wales government, Busby was never able to indulge in gunboat diplomacy nor threaten unsubmissive Maori with naval justice. On the other hand the Maori tribes remained highly independent and held aloof from the foreigners' activities in Kororareka. The small number of Maori who remained in the township area refused, as they had done from the beginning of the settlement, to become involved in the expatriates' problems of internal control or in disputes that in other port towns developed into major inter-racial crises. Busby was unable and largely unwilling to assume any decisive role in Kororareka and leadership within the community remained non-existent until 1838 and the creation of the Kororareka Association.

In Fiji the change of leadership occurred gradually. J. B. Williams arrived in 1846, but before the 1850s he had little influence over the white settlers. The foreigners' return to Levuka from exile in Solevu in 1849 was effected without consular or naval intervention. By 1850, however, Williams was demanding naval support to exact compensation from the Fijians for goods stolen when his house was burnt down during Fourth of July celebrations the previous year. Others, including several Levuka residents, who had lost property in wrecks, fires and during their exile, followed his example. While Williams was gathering a following among the foreigners in the early 1850s, Whippy was still able to act as mediator between the Fijian tribes at the Bau-Bua peace settlement in 1852. But he abdicated this role in subsequent years as he too became involved in the American claims and accepted the Levuka residents' more militant attitude towards Fijian authority. By June 1858 Whippy's influence over the Fijians, even his one-time friend Tui Levuka, was so diminished that he had to write to J. B. Williams for help, when he suspected Tui Levuka of hostile intentions: 'I wish you would write him [Tui Levuka] a formal letter and enquire of him what he is about, and allow the Whites to protect their lives and property as far as they are able under your flag'.[23] By the end of 1858 both British and American agents were resident in Levuka and Whippy, with a large following of long-settled whites and part-Fijians, had moved to the island of Wakaya, leaving the chiefs to deal with the consuls alone.

At no time in Apia had a leader been established. The Samoans, divided by their own political rivalries, were unable to capitalise on the foreigners' weaknesses and to put forward their own leader for the multi-cultural community, while from the earliest years of settlement the consuls had struggled to gain some standing. With little support from home governments, the consuls' power to command respect was slight. J. C. Williams, United States commercial agent from 1839 to 1851, was not once visited by an American warship, while George Pritchard was more often humiliated by

British commanders than helped to establish any authority. The economic instability that characterised Apia up to the mid 1850s forced the consular agents to concentrate on guarding their commercial interests and at times brought them into direct conflict with one another. Economic conditions improved with the rise of the Godeffroy company, society became more homogeneous and the competitive spirit between consuls subsided for a while. In co-operation with his British and American counterparts, August Unshelm came, in time, to enjoy a political, economic and social ascendancy over the settlers. Unity among the consuls was by no means absolute, but faced with Samoan opposition they would usually stand firm, which made it increasingly difficult for the Samoan chiefs to safeguard their independence.

Faced with these new leaders, who encouraged foreign development into many fields, the chiefs strove to safeguard their independence and assert their right to impose laws on anyone settled on their islands. In November 1820 Kamehameha II, concerned about the influx of white 'riff-raff' into Honolulu, exiled a number of deserters and beachcombers to barren Fanning Island. Exact numbers were not recorded, but in 1822 it was estimated that there were fifty foreigners and Hawaiians on Fanning, which previously had been uninhabited. J. C. Jones had not arrived in Honolulu with his new commission when the order was promulgated, but it is unlikely that he would have tried to countermand it. Fortunately for the exiles the period of banishment was not long: one of them was back in Honolulu in 1823.[24] In 1829 Kamehameha III and his chiefly advisers refused to be intimidated by the British consul Charlton's demands to be compensated for his cow, which was shot by a Hawaiian for trespassing repeatedly on his cultivated fields. Charlton on his own initiative caught the culprit, tied him behind his horse and dragged him towards Honolulu. In a public proclamation Kamehameha III refused to punish the Hawaiian, who had been cut loose by a friend, or to compensate Charlton, and he rebuked the latter for presuming to take the law into his own hands. But more important he prefaced his edict with a statement of the laws in force in his kingdom and continued: 'If any man shall transgress any of these laws, he is liable to the penalty, the same for every foreigner and for the people of these Islands'.[25] In this proclamation he also upheld Christian marriage,

declaring that every man should live with one woman as a wife —
no polygynous or adulterous associations were to be permitted.
Thus Charlton's blustering attempt to undermine the Hawaiian
government's authority was met with a forceful but judicial statement of the laws and authority of the ruling power.

The indigenous leaders in the other island groups were less
successful in curbing foreign usurpation but no less determined.
From the early 1840s Levuka had been subject to occasional
incendiary raids by the Lovoni hill tribe of Ovalau, whose actions
were frequently determined by Bau or Viwa chiefs. But between
1850 and 1858, the period during which large claims for compensation were being made by the American settlers, the Levuka
residents suffered at least three fires, and possibly more. The 1853
conflagration had been preceded by an incident at Malaki Island
during which the foreigners had taken the law into their own
hands, killed several Fijians and burnt and plundered a town.
Evidence suggests that the chief of Viwa, to whom Malaki was
subject, instigated the Lovoni's subsequent attack on Levuka. Certainly after the Malaki incident the whites expected a raid and did
their utmost to protect their settlement, but to no avail. The
foreigners believed that Tui Levuka was responsible for the firing
in 1858 because of his concern over the white men's growing wealth
and independence.[26]

By 1835 the Tahitians had become similarly disenchanted with
expatriate development and suspicious of their activities: 'The
Chiefs are excessively jealous of Foreigners settling on the Islands
and throw every obstacle in the way of the few that are working
Plantations . . . A law has been recently passed to prevent the
increase of foreign settlers. Rum and all spirits were now prohibited'.[27] Tahitian demands for European goods had if anything
declined between 1829 and 1835; the only luxury item they were
keen to buy being horses. Such conditions did not encourage rapid
economic development or population growth and the majority of
foreign residents could do little more than support their daily
needs.

In Samoa, from the earliest settlement, the chiefs had been wary
of foreign expansion. Their attempts to impose chiefly authority on
the residents had restricted the latter's ability to buy land and
forced them to form protection societies. Pogai and Toetagata,

the chiefs of Apia bay, had unwaveringly insisted upon their exclusive control over the harbour and their right to collect all shipping dues. In 1856 Captain Fremantle persuaded them to provide some services and facilities in the harbour which before neither had been willing to do without extra payment. This agreement did not in any way diminish the chiefs' authority but the arrangement later devised by W. T. Pritchard, British consular agent, whereby the consuls would collect the harbour dues and divide them equally between the chiefs, did constitute a serious diminution of chiefly power, as Pritchard happily acknowledged: 'Having their revenue, small as it is, at our disposal, it will always be in our power to compel their assistance, when required, in matters connected with the Port.'[28]

The Samoan boycott of the foreign merchants in 1855 was another attempt on the part of the Samoan chiefs to control their own people and restrict foreign development. Later, when cotton plantations had been established by the foreigners, the chiefs made another characteristic effort to maintain some control over the situation. At the Vailele *fono* (village assembly) in mid 1866 they passed a local law stating that no Samoan would pick cotton for less than two cents a pound, and that no other island labour would be allowed into the district. Foreign reaction to such a show of Samoan independence and control was immediate and predictable. An American planter wrote to the American agent: 'Now while the man of war is here I should think this kind of thing should be put a stop to. You will see at once that this leaves us at mercy of the Natives'.[29] No action was in fact taken by the naval officer but this total denial of the Samoan chiefs' right to govern their own people was symptomatic of the continual struggle between Samoans and foreigners to control the development of Apia and the growth of foreign commerce.

Both the Hawaiian and Tahitian governments attempted to limit consular interference by addressing petitions to the metropolitan governments concerning the conduct of their representatives and asking for their recall. In the case of Charlton, Hawaiian appeals to the British government in November 1836 that he had continually ridiculed and degraded their people and threatened them with destruction by British naval vessels elicited no response, although British officials had already recognised that their consul had a violent temper.[30] Similar complaints to the United States government concerning J. C. Jones's activities did, however, effect his recall in 1838. Both the Tahitians and an American naval officer protested to the American government that its representative, Samuel Blackler, constantly broke the law and behaved in an undignified and dictatorial manner in the execution of his official duties. Captain J. H. Aulick did not mince words when he reported on the situation to the Navy Department in 1841:

> The result [of the meeting] satisfied my mind that the action and general conduct of our Consul towards these people, have been both injudicious and undignified — that he is in the habit of paying very little respect to either the laws or Authorities of the Island — is dictatorial and overbearing in his Official intercourse and consequently extremely unpopular with them.[31]

Notwithstanding these complaints, Blackler died at his post in Papeete in 1844. In no beach community did foreign development and consular encroachment into the preserves of island authority go unchallenged, but all too frequently island leaders could do little more than voice their opposition and occasionally retard development for a limited period of time.

Among the residents themselves the changes which resulted from the presence of the consuls cannot be assessed in quantitative terms, since in the main their effect was to influence people's attitudes, ambitions and beliefs. Even in Kororareka, where neither British nor American representatives lived in the town, foreign residents' attitudes changed once a consular agent had settled in the area. In 1834 and again in 1837 the residents were most willing to sign petitions to the British government demanding extra powers for the British Resident and strongly advocating British annexation.[32] Their thinking gravitated towards a home government and external solutions, rather than any accommodation with the Maori chiefs. This burgeoning of national and personal ambitions was in part balanced by home governments' reluctance for several years to support their representatives with naval power or magisterial rights. A consul's prestige was therefore strictly dependent on his ability to win the co-operation of other consuls, foreign residents and the islanders. This dependence should have effectively curtailed any consuls' desire to intimidate island governments or to over-estimate their strength, but as long as the representatives nursed the hope of a visit of a naval vessel they were prepared to threaten and fulminate against island governments despite their lack of immediate power and the insecurity they had to put up with from day to day. Given this propensity among the majority of consuls, it is important to realise that only a small stratum of any beach community was directly involved in the consuls' various political stratagems and aspirations. For a large part of the time the majority of small shopkeepers and artisans lived and worked together, and with the islanders, without prejudice or discord. As a class these foreigners had more in common with their island companions than with the larger merchants, consuls and island chiefs who composed the upper levels of beach community society.

Certainly no ordinary sailor or mechanic could expect much help or sympathy from his respective consul. In Honolulu the American blacksmith, John Colcord, was thrown out of a forge establishment by his drunken partner, who refused, with a chief's approval, to return all his property. Colcord accepted the situation philosophically: 'I knew it was of no use for me to fight against the whole Sandwich Isles. I also knew it was of less use to apply to the Consul as I had never known him to do anything for a poor sailor'.[33] Such minor injustices were settled in an out-of-court manner or just let pass, which helped to maintain a certain harmony on the beach. Even in Apia, where jealousies and rivalries were most intense, a reasonable degree of co-operation was maintained on all but one occasion: the Van Camp affair. Thus the bulk of beach residents, the traders, grog sellers, shopkeepers and mechanics, had a minimal interest in the political setup as long as it guaranteed good working conditions. Their attitudes to law and order and to the consuls themselves were well analysed by the American commercial agent for Samoa, James Dirickson, in 1859:

I have always found them [the foreign residents] ready and willing to assist all the Foreign Consuls in their Official Capacity as long as there was no gross assumption of power, and firm supporters of law and order . . . I fully believe if Consuls appointed here would only attend to their official business as Consul, or if they engaged in business as merchants would carefully refrain from allowing their private and public business to come in contact, they would have no cause to complain of the Foreign Residents who are shrewd business men and as quick of perception as they are honorable.[34]

While honour among the foreign residents may not always have been at a premium, it seems fair to accept the remainder of Dirickson's remarks. Unless the residents' security or economic livelihood were at stake, they were not likely to become involved in consular controversies.

In times of peace, therefore, the effect of the consuls' presence in beach communities should not be over-emphasised, but in a crisis, and the consuls were adept at manufacturing crises out of the smallest incidents, the foreign residents led by the consuls became aggressively self-assertive for the honour of their respective countries and for their own pockets. Ready to increase their power and influence, and that of their fellow countrymen, at any opportunity, the consuls were always a discordant element in society; a rallying point for national solidarity and a potential threat to island independence.

The early missionaries stationed in or near the beach communities were not, initially, held responsible by their boards of directors for the spiritual well-being of the foreign residents. They were, however, seriously concerned about the influence non-missionary Europeans exercised over the islanders, and consequently made their presence felt in the port towns in a number of economic and political matters. Their attempts to regulate foreigners' trading practices with the islanders and to influence law-making aroused hostile opposition from the residents and resulted in dissension within the community on which the consuls battened. The traders and merchants were justified in their belief that the missionaries spoiled their opportunities for making large profits by teaching the islanders the value of European goods in the Western world. J. C. Jones complained to his employers in November 1821 that little would be received for the frame houses then being built, since the Hawaiian boys belonging to the mission had told the chiefs that such houses sold for only $300 in the United States.[35] The consuls were just as capable of undermining missionary efforts, as the Reverend J. Orsmond complained in Tahiti: 'Wicked, Letsherous, Debauched Mr. Elly [acting British vice-consul] has his bottom marked all over with the native tatoo, did all he possibly could in company with Mr. Charlton [British consul to the Sandwich, Society and Friendly Islands] to injure & displace Missionaries'.[36]

In all beach communities, however, except Honolulu, missionaries and other foreigners lived side by side, remonstrated occasionally against one another's practices but rarely had any significant or sustained contact. The Protestant and Roman Catholic missionaries in Levuka, from the early 1850s onwards, seldom had any serious disagreement with the foreign settlers. The Protestant missionaries frequently berated them for their addiction to alcohol but little notice was taken of such remarks. The only major source of conflict was the rival land claims of the Wesleyan mission teacher, John Binner, and David Whippy which were quickly settled, and reveal if anything a certain affinity of goals between the missionary and the foreign residents. Similarly in Kororareka and Papeete the foreign settlers and missionaries had hardly a respectful word for the opposite party, but neither interfered directly in the other's affairs. In Apia the missionaries became part of the intricate, changing loyalties and rivalries between Samoan and expatriate and thus sometimes found themselves opposed to the foreign residents and sometimes in collusion with them.

Only in Honolulu did serious friction occur. For more than twenty years the foreigners had traded and lived in the Hawaiian Islands without any interference or competition. When the missionaries first arrived in Honolulu in 1820, they were warmly welcomed by a large number of foreigners, who offered shelter, food and other useful gifts. But the initial friendship was severely strained by the puritanical standards of morality on which the missionaries insisted — standards not to be found in similar communities in the United States. Furthermore the foreigners soon realised that their influence and powers of intimidation over the Hawaiians diminished in direct ratio with the missionaries' ascendancy.

The flashpoint that severed good relations occurred in May 1821 — fifteen months after the missionaries' arrival. An expedition to Tahiti in one of the Hawaiian chief's newly acquired schooners was planned by the missionaries, who wished to visit their fellow evangelicals and to introduce the accompanying Hawaiian chiefs to a converted island people. The foreigners strongly opposed the plan, giving a number of spurious reasons, behind which lay the hard economic fact that the Hawaiian chiefs were deeply indebted to them. The vessel scheduled to sail to Tahiti was required in Hawaii to collect sandalwood and the chiefs were needed to organise their people to gather it. The missionaries were accused of encouraging the Hawaiians to repudiate their debts, and while the incident itself was minor (the missionaries capitulated), the feelings and frustrations underlying it were not assuaged for over a decade.[37] A struggle for influence over Kamehameha II and III ensued, each faction endeavouring to safeguard and extend its own interests. As the missionaries gained the upper hand with some of the chiefs, 'blue laws' were promulgated forbidding, among many things, the sale and consumption of spirits, gambling, adultery and the long-established custom of girls swimming off to the ships at anchor. At this, sailors, beach residents and even a few ships' officers combined in anger against the missionaries whom they rightly believed to be the initiators of the legislation. The first attempt by the Hawaiian chiefs to impose a 'Ten Commandments' code of law in December 1825, under the indirect auspices of the missionaries, was thwarted by the foreign settlers, the sailors then in port and Boki, a chief unsympathetic to missionary interference. Again in 1826 and 1827 similar attempts to prohibit prostitution gave rise to disturbances in Honolulu and Lahaina and the chiefs were obliged to relax strict enforcement of the new laws.[38] But missionary persuasion continued to attract Hawaiian converts so that by 1829, in his public proclamation after the cow incident, Kamehameha III was able to introduce a number of moral laws.

At no time in the ensuing decade were these laws consistently or steadfastly enforced. After the death of the queen regent, Kaahumanu, a devout Christian, in June 1832, Kamehameha III rebelled against the strict discipline imposed upon him by the missionaries, and sought to consolidate his position as king over and above both the clergy and the other Hawaiian chiefs, several of whom were strongly influenced by the missionaries. Between 1833 and 1836 the 'blue laws' frequently went into abeyance, but they were re-enacted in 1836, notwithstanding strong foreign protest, when Kamehameha III was once more drawn into the missionary fold. For the numerous owners of taverns and gambling houses, and for the small traders who relied heavily on the sale of goods to women who visited the ships, it was a period of great financial uncertainty for which the missionaries were largely blamed. At the same time the large-scale merchants were also antagonised because their leisure hour entertainments — billiards, drinking, gambling, and riding on Sundays — were greatly curtailed or subject to interruption by Hawaiian constables.

The reaction of the islanders to Christianity in its various forms lies beyond the scope of this book, but certain political effects arising from island conversion to Protestantism and the later arrival of Roman Catholic missionaries had substantial repercussions in the beach communities, particularly Honolulu and Papeete. In both Hawaii and Tahiti the Protestant faith became closely identified with the ruling chiefs, who felt dangerously threatened by the subsequent appearance of Roman Catholicism and reacted accordingly. In New Zealand, Fiji and Samoa, where the Protestant missionaries were unable to establish themselves behind a recognised king, the introduction of Roman Catholicism did not have such a profound effect. Generally the advent of Catholicism offered islanders and foreigners alike the opportunity to voice their opposition to the *status quo* and to organise under a rival political and religious banner. In Kororareka the arrival of the Roman Catholic bishop Pompallier in June 1839 occasioned little political interest or activity. No immediate threat to Maori independence was discernible at this time, but once annexation was mooted in January 1840, and it became apparent that the CMS missionaries were strongly in favour of it, the bitterest Maori opponents to the treaty of Waitangi were found among the Roman Catholic converts and also the heathens. Incidents such as Tui Levuka's defiant conversion to Catholicism in 1868 in a bid to throw off Cakobau's control, or J. B. Williams's invitation to the French Catholic priests at Lau to settle in Levuka in opposition to the Wesleyans whom he disliked, were the outcome of personal pique and usually not of lasting importance.[39] In Honolulu and Papeete, however, the consequences of the introduction of Roman Catholicism were to undermine island authority and give foreign residents an unprecedented chance to enhance their power to the islanders' detriment.

Both the Hawaiian and Tahitian governments recognised the threat an alternative Christian organisation posed to their authority, which was so firmly based on Protestant doctrines and guidance. As they feared, the Roman Catholic priests became a rallying centre for all islanders and foreigners dissatisfied with quasi-Protestant rule. In both island groups the Protestant missionaries had stressed the idolatry of Rome, the moral bankruptcy of the Roman Catholic faith, and had conjured up the spectre of the Antichrist. It is impossible to gauge how much of this propaganda was understood or taken to heart by the ruling chiefs but there can be little doubt that they moved against the Roman Catholic missionaries for political rather than religious reasons. (The actual tenets of Catholicism were never a crucial issue.) With at least tacit missionary approval, the Hawaiian and Tahitian chiefs exiled the priests from their islands. Armed with appropriate instructions from Paris, both Captains Laplace and du Petit Thouars interpreted this treatment of France's holy representatives as a national insult requiring immediate compensation and rectification. In both Honolulu and Papeete these naval officers found consuls who, recognising the advent of the Roman Catholic missionaries as an opportunity to embarrass the island governments and increase their own power, had from the beginning championed their right to remain, to preach their doctrines and to enjoy the privileges and protection granted all residents, particularly the Protestant missionaries. These representatives upheld the French naval officers in their efforts to have the priests reinstated and the island governments suitably reprimanded.[40] Other foreigners involved themselves in the ensuing incidents as it suited their interests. In neither town was any desire to protect the rights or comply with the orders of the island governments manifested.

The first Roman Catholic mission arived in Honolulu in July 1827 much to the embarrassment of the American missionaries who were enjoying their first major successes. Through government default the small colony was able to establish itself unobtrusively, but their opportunities to gain converts were greatly restricted. By 1830 opposition within the Hawaiian government to Catholicism had grown and the disappearance of the priests' protector, the Hawaiian chief Boki, exposed them and their handful of Hawaiian converts to increasing persecution. In December 1831 the priests were forcibly deported. This did not prove a permanent solution to the problem, which was to harass the Hawaiian government until 1839. Although this later date is beyond the period of Honolulu development discussed in this chapter, it will be analysed here for the sake of coherence, and because the attitudes and actions of the consuls and foreign residents are strictly in keeping with those under review. After an unsuccessful attempt to rein-state the Roman Catholic missionaries in 1837, the matter was finally settled in July 1839 when Captain Laplace sailed into Honolulu harbour and, under the threat of immediate hostilities, demanded that Roman Catholicism should be tolerated through-out Hawaii and enjoy all the privileges granted to Protestantism, and that a bond of $20,000 be deposited with him to guarantee the government's future good faith. The Hawaiians were forced to sub-mit even before Kamehameha III had time to arrive from Lahaina. The bond money was raised from the resident merchants, who would have lost most if Honolulu had been bombarded, and a treaty was finally signed which included a further two clauses: one permitting the importation of French wine and brandies, which effectively nullified the prohibition laws of 1838; and the second allowing a jury to consist entirely of foreigners, summoned by the French consul, for any Frenchman accused of crime. According to Com-modore Wilkes the number of Frenchmen present on Oahu in 1839 to benefit from this law was not more than four. To the foreigners in Honolulu, regardless of nationality, Laplace was a hero. A letter of respect and gratitude was sent to him and a grand dinner given. The American, Stephen Reynolds, resident in Hono-lulu since 1823, wrote in his journal for the 17 July 1839: 'Glorious Day King signed the Treaty with the French!!'. One foreigner, the American publisher James Jackson Jarves, later sided with the Hawaiian government, and accused Laplace of extorting a treaty from Kamehameha III under threat of force, but a jury of his fellow countrymen unanimously agreed that he had failed to prove his case. Not even the missionaries were prepared to support Jarves wholeheartedly and the virulent controversy his stand had aroused among the residents forced him to retire to Hawaii Island until tempers had cooled. Meanwhile the merchants reclaimed the $20,000 bond money they had put up, through taxes on the Hawaiians, and Ladd and Company extended their premises in expectation of a greatly increased liquor trade.[41]

In Tahiti the struggle between Pomare IV and the French

consul, Moerenhout, over the introduction of Roman Catholicism led to the later establishment of a French protectorate. Divided within itself the Tahitian government was unable to control or resist Moerenhout, who used the deportation of the French priests and later breaches in the 1838 French treaty to encourage French interest in the group and to create the conditions under which a protectorate could be promulgated. The first attempt by French Roman Catholic priests to settle on Tahiti was made in November 1836, when two priests landed discreetly on the south coast of Tahiti and travelled overland to Papeete. Moerenhout, then American consular agent, sheltered them, although he was fully aware that they had come ashore without Pomare IV's permission and in defiance of the port regulations. Certain Tahitian chiefs who sought to embarrass Pomare IV's government welcomed the priests at this time, but they were unable to protect them. Acting under George Pritchard's orders (at the time he was officially only a missionary) the Tahitians broke into Moerenhout's house in December 1836 and forcibly deported them. On 31 January 1837 the priests again attempted to come ashore at Papeete but were sent back to the vessel which had brought them, since the Tahitian authorities refused to allow them to land.

In August 1838 Captain du Petit Thouars arrived to defend the honour of France, which he did through the time-honoured practice of collecting an indemnity (this time 2000 piastres) and forcing the Tahitian government, under the threat of bombardment, to sign a treaty allowing the French priests to settle, build a church and practise their faith. Pritchard paid part of the 2000 piastres demanded and collected the remainder from two or three other English settlers. At the same time du Petit Thouars insisted that Moerenhout be recognised as French consul. After August 1838 any complaint of governmental injustice from a French resident (who numbered not more than ten in all) or any failure to observe the conditions of the French treaty added grist to Moerenhout's mill. Faced with Moerenhout's determined intriguing the Tahitians loyal to Pomare IV could not depend on the majority of non-French, foreign settlers to advise them or help protect their interests. Heartily dissatisfied with Pomare IV's regime and particularly with its chief adviser, that Pooh-Bah, Pritchard, the foreigners, by the early 1840s, looked to annexation by any power as the only means of establishing order and good working conditions.

Pritchard's departure for England in early 1841 presented Moerenhout and the Tahitian chiefs who were openly in favour of foreign intervention from which they were to benefit with the opportunity to undermine Pomare. Thus the stage was set for French action, which was not long in coming. In September 1842 du Petit Thouars returned to Tahiti to check up on the government's performance under the 1838 treaty. Presented with a long list of French grievances du Petit Thouars demanded a 10,000 piastres indemnity. No foreigner was prepared to furnish any part of the sum or even advise the government, which in the persons of four chiefs signed a document asking for French protection. Pomare IV later reluctantly added her signature and du Petit Thouars complied immediately. On 11 September 1842 the French Protectorate over Tahiti was declared.[42] Thus in both Honolulu and Papeete the crisis over the introduction of Catholicism, combined with the French government's determination to establish its power in the Pacific, gave the consuls and foreigners several opportunities of enhancing their influence and economic standing to the detriment of the island governments, which were exposed to intimidation and abolition.

The third major group to join the consuls and missionaries in the beach communities were the company traders. Like the consuls many of them were directed by decision-makers in their home countries and were concerned with company and national prestige. Once the Godeffroy company had established its trading empire in the central Pacific, it could bring economic and political pressures to bear upon the Samoan authorities in any matter concerning its interests. Guided by instructions from Germany, the consul-cum-manager of the company was well placed to manipulate events to the company's advantage. The Valparaiso merchants who set up trading establishments in Papeete after 1827, and those involved in the supply trade to whalers, did not have the backing to wield any great influence over the Tahitian government, but they did everything in their power to keep their persons, premises and activities beyond the reach of local laws and to bring the government into disrepute. Similarly in Fiji the merchants who settled in Levuka in the early 1860s were dependent on the newly established cotton planters for a livelihood. They took little interest in the Fijians unless expatriate development was threatened by island opposition when they became actively concerned to protect it. In New Zealand the owners of shipyards, the ship chandlers and the Sydney merchants established a highly profitable economic base in Kororareka and the Bay of Islands area between 1830 and 1840. By the late 1830s a number of these merchants had begun to accumulate surplus capital, only to find that investment opportunities were limited, since sufficient grog shops, stores and servicing facilities for the whaling trade had been established. Land, however, was available, and in March 1839 the wealthy settlers set up the Korarareka Land Company, which concentrated on sales in the township area.[43] These activities posed little threat to the autonomy of the Maori, who had left the Kororareka settlers very much to their own devices. But at the same time there was a rush from Australia and Britain of land speculating companies and would-be settlers, who bought up large acreages throughout New Zealand. The presence and exploits of the latter were to have profound repercussions on the Maoris' independence.

In Honolulu commercial activity was extensive and although it was concentrated almost exclusively on the supply trade to whalers, by the mid 1830s it sustained eight large commercial houses, one shipwrights' establishment, fifteen grog shops and hotels, and over eighty artisans—ships' carpenters, ordinary carpenters, blacksmiths, masons and coopers.[44] Close consular participation and interest in business frequently gave the merchants and consuls together decisive powers over the Hawaiian government. During the Laplace affair, they collected the $20,000 bond money and strongly urged the Hawaiian government to capitulate to French demands. Most merchants attempted to keep their businesses beyond island interference and control. Determinedly extra-territorial in attitude, they wanted freehold rights to their land and their own law courts. They questioned the government's authority to impose any law, especially import restrictions and duties, and always expected their interests to be paramount in any government decision.

The arrival of consuls, missionaries and company traders gave the growing foreign populations in beach communities greater stability and self-awareness. Casual friendships between islanders and residents were succeeded in many cases by more formal relationships in which a settler's place of origin and his status as a white man were 'properly' emphasised. Consuls, backed by occasional naval power and sometimes the force of a home government, became the foci of the residents' complaints and ambitions. Island authorities found it increasingly difficult to enforce their laws among the foreigners, who ignored or reversed them if it suited their purposes. The missionaries were genuinely interested in the rights and welfare of the island people, their converts, but their close identification with island authority, especially in Tahiti and Hawaii, and their rigidly puritanical outlook, frequently made it impossible for them to advise island governments effectively or to mediate between the islanders and the foreigners. More seriously their intransigent stand against Catholicism in Honolulu and Papeete gave the already antagonistic foreign residents the opportunity to intrigue against the governments, which was to lead to the abrogation of several Hawaiian laws and the establishment of a French protectorate in Tahiti.

Company traders brought with them the complex trading procedures and large establishments of Western commerce, in which few islanders could find employment. Beyond the port towns island labour was still used for pearl diving and to some extent in the coconut oil and copra industries, but increasingly on large company plantations non-indigenous labour was used. In spite of experience in inter-island trade the islanders seldom succeeded as traders or shipowners when they entred the European commercial system. Difficulties in book-keeping and organisation were partly responsible but basically it was the islanders' inability to resist their relations' demands for credit. Stripped of their sandalwood and bêche-de-mer resources they had no product except coconuts attractive or profitable on the world market, while their land was either sold in small portions, rented for minimal prices, or retained and in most cases worked in traditional non-profit-making methods. The Maori were the only islanders during these early years to make radical changes in their agricultural production to grow crops for sale. Throughout the Pacific the major economic enterprises gradually devolved into foreign hands. Sometimes the islanders put up a struggle, as did the Fijians against the European-imported coconut oil extracting machines. They refused to supply an adequate quantity of nuts since coconut oil was their only means of purchasing European goods. Their opposition, however, was not long-lasting.[45] Ultimately in both political and economic spheres the consuls and merchants assumed the initiative, which the island governments, through lack of power and experience in world affairs, could no longer exercise. Thus each incident or crisis between the foreigners and their hosts was manipulated by the new leaders of the beach communities to strengthen their control over island governments and commerce.

six

The Pattern of Daily Life

The majority of English and American residents in Fiji live in a state of unblushing polygamy: the number of their wives and women is unlimited, and it is not uncommon for two or three of them to be confined at the same time. In this particular, as well as in other sensual indulgences, they are ready to conform greedily to the customs of their adopted country, and their domestic life is grossly immoral. There are amongst them some very degraded characters, and it would be no easy matter to discover from whence they have congregated. In Levuka they number between fifty and sixty, with some two or three hundred half caste children. They mostly hail as shipwrecked mariners; and there is not one in the whole Society in what may be called a respectable position, nor is there a dwelling except the Missionary's house better than a common barn. The village where the houses are concentrated is filthily dirty, and better deserves the appellation of pigsty than of a town. . . . The White people I must say are comparatively industrious and live on good terms with each other; their principal occupation is boat-building.[1]

Such a reaction was typical of an educated visitor, conditioned to the *mores* of civilised life, to one of the beach communities. From a port town anchorage the vegetation looked lush, the sea and shore sparkling, and the scattering of island and European style houses through the trees most romantic, but once ashore the lack of sanitation, roads and bridges, the jumble of jerry-built houses and the unconventional social and familial arrangements among the Europeans and islanders shattered the first illusion and often prejudiced all subsequent judgment of the community. Captain Fremantle, the author of the above quotation, was finally forced to admit that the Levuka men were peaceable and 'comparatively industrious' but he found nothing further could be said in their favour, although he had just left Apia about which he had written: 'a more unruly, disreputable community cannot be conceived'. To Fremantle, as to many men of his social standing, the lack of regular hard work and the sexual laxity of the beach communities could not be condoned whatever other virtues the inhabitants might possess.

While economic and political factors impinging upon port town life changed with the availability of resources or the arrival of official representatives of the metropolitan powers, the social complexion of beach communities remained relatively stable. Neither the basic population composition nor locally sanctioned domestic and marital arrangements was affected by changes in economic pursuits or in patterns of leadership. In these frontier towns men of sailor and mechanic origins were the foundation of society. Some were content to loaf their days away on the beach with the islanders, drinking gin by the keg full and only taking on odd sailing jobs when it was necessary. Others became sailor-traders plying their craft within the island group, collecting coconut oil, tortoise-shell and any other marketable products, in exchange for European goods. Opportunities for skilled artisans, carpenters, coopers and blacksmiths were always available and high standards of workmanship or perseverance were not insisted upon. Other residents who took it upon themselves to supply the alcoholic needs of their fellow Europeans, and sometimes the islanders, seldom lacked customers. Harry Zupplien, one of many grog sellers in Honolulu, accumulated a fortune in the trade. This predominant working class was supplemented by a number of more substantial shopkeepers and merchants, most of whom had arrived after the port towns were firmly established, but who still thought it prudent to come without wives. The totality of white society was completed by the missionaries and consuls, a number of whom brought wives with them.

As on other frontiers of European expansion the scarcity of white women was compensated for by the incorporation of indigenous and part-indigenous women into the foreign communities. In the Pacific there were no island customs inimical to liaisons between foreign men and island women and the practice was accepted without stigma in the port towns for several decades.

Many such arrangements were based on great affection and were considered as marriages. Stephen Reynolds's grief, when the part-Hawaiian girl he had lived with for over three years died, is revealed in his journal:

> Her Native Simplicity and Kindness had drawn from all with whom she was acquainted their friendship & esteem. How much more then from me who had every opportunity of Knowing and experiencing her attentions and disposition. Her Behaviour since my acquaintance has gained my esteem which will ever be Remembered with feelings of tenderness & Respect.[2]

His language may now appear rather stilted but there can be little doubt that he was completely genuine in his grief. He noted the anniversary of her death for several years after in his journal. Inevitably not all liaisons were so harmonious. Reynolds's second marriage, aged 45, to the seventeen year old part-Hawaiian Susan Jackson, was not without frequent argumentative incidents. Only a month after the marriage Reynolds discovered that she had spent part of every day since that date with the young king, Kamehameha III. Infidelity was only one problem. He also had to keep a very sharp eye on Susan's friends and relatives, several of whom demanded presents from Reynolds's store, to which Susan had access. Many men with island wives faced this difficulty. The demands of one's wife's relations for credit or straight-out gifts, which an island woman found very difficult to refuse, could threaten a man's livelihood and often was the cause of separation. Dominic Ferrau, a Genoese carpenter living in Kororareka in the mid 1830s, married a high-born Maori woman only to discover that his union with her necessitated a continual flow of goods to her brother to ensure his keeping her.[3] Richard Hinds in Honolulu in 1837 claimed that a number of foreigners with Hawaiian wives had to keep the extent of their property and money a secret from the latter because a chief could easily ask the women for as much as half and they would feel compelled to give it. Hinds reported that: 'Mr Mitchener, a respectable man, now compelled to keep a billiard table through misfortunes, is in this awkward situation'.[4] To overcome this difficulty many traders acquired wives from islands distant from their permanent trading establishments. Women from the Gilberts and from Manihiki Island were greatly sought after.

Wives were usually not included at dinner parties or other social entertainments in the community and several were poorly treated, beaten and thrown out. In many ways the foreigners considered their marital relationship with an island woman in a master-servant light. The woman was acquired, often by purchase (through presents) from a chief or relatives and could be discharged like any other domestic servant in the event of not giving satisfaction. Some masters at least relented later. The Reverend R. B. Lyth recorded in his journal in June 1848: 'Joseph Rees sailed for Rakiraki in search of his wife whom he had dismissed 2 or 3 weeks ago, on some slight offence'.[5] An island wife was afforded little of the respect which a European wife would have expected, but her lack of equality was also suffered by her white counterpart, if perhaps to a lesser extent. The island and part-island women did, however, have means of redress — they were free to leave their *soi-disant* husbands whenever they wished and they frequently did, some taking with them the lands they had brought into the liaison. Thus a certain balance did operate and there is much evidence to suggest that many separations were not permanent. Certainly for many foreigners the bonds were lasting and their regard for the island people high. On his deathbed John Sullivan, a settler in Fiji, made sure that all his wives and children were taken care of: 'I give all my property to John, Matthew, James, Hannah and Mary, my illegitimate children, to be divided equally among them — annually to the amount of fifty or sixty dollars . . . I give my women, eight in number, their liberty and permission to return to their own towns'.[6] His offspring also received certain pieces of land. Matthew Hunkin, a permanent resident on Tutuila, was glad that his eldest daughter was marrying a Samoan, whom he believed was: 'much superior in every respect to the generality of Europeans in these parts', and he stated further: 'if a girl is to marry in Samoa, she is likely to be happier with a native'.[7] Both wives and part-island children were treated with a degree of casualness, but there was much genuine affection as well; a relationship perhaps typical of the Polynesians themselves, among whom marriage was essentially a contractual arrangement to be dissolved at will.

Island and European style houses were mingled together in the beach communities without distinction, many foreigners preferring to live in the cheaply built island variety which were better suited to the climate and to the families under their protection. Apia as late as 1874 was typical of all the port towns for many years: 'The middle ground along the beach is filled up with small white houses and native cottages, savage and civilized life strangely blended together'.[8] Except in Honolulu, little money was spent on ostentatious architecture, and even in that town the mixture of houses was characteristic until later in the nineteenth century. In February 1842 Sir George Simpson wrote: 'The town of Honolulu presented a strange admixture of the savage and the civilized, stacks of warehouses rising amid straw-huts'. Papeete in 1839 was perhaps more unpretentious that the others: 'Among all its dwellings, the royal residence, and the house of Mr. Pritchard, are the only ones which possess the luxury of glazed windows'.[9] But in Levuka and Apia island houses out-numbered European types until the 1870s. Kororareka was dominated by a Maori *pa* around which the familiar jumble of island and European dwellings were scattered.

Superficially the simplicity of island life seemed most attractive: 'Several Mechanics and Seamen have left their Vessels here [Papeete, 1828] and have taken Native Wives and appear to live extremely Happy. Living here in a manner costs nothing and they get employment from the Vessells who put in here to refresh'.[10] But some travellers recognised the squalor to which foreigners without property or skills were often reduced:

> The working class, are sadly addicted to drinking, and lead a miserable and degraded life; indeed the humbler classes of white men in all the islands, with their careworn faces and haggard looks, exhibit a wretched appearance. Allied as a general rule to native women, they live as the natives do, have no social comfort, and make no effort to get it, making up for their poor bill of fare and discomfort by seeking for its deficiency in the stimulus and excitement of the glass.[11]

Without a good deal of determination and a certain element of luck it was not at all easy for the less influential foreigners to make a comfortable living in the beach communities. E. R. Butler, who settled in the small community of Lahaina, Maui, early in the nineteenth century, spent the greater part of his life on voyages to the north-west coast or around the Hawaiian Islands, acting as mate, pilot and sometimes as master. Despite a lifetime of hard

work he was destitute in 1838 and compelled to call upon Kamehameha III, for whom he had performed many services, to look
after his wife and child while he set off on yet another voyage.
Similarly even the educated bachelor A. H. Fayerweather struggled
for four years as a book-keeper and accountant in Honolulu before
he gained regular employment.[12] Many lower class whites failed to
establish themselves in the small, highly competitive Western
economic sphere and those who, nonetheless, remained in the
islands became closely identified with island living patterns, frequently from necessity.

Much in the living conditions and behaviour of the foreigners
in beach communities must have disenchanted the new arrival; the
latent attractions of these port towns were revealed only on further
acquaintance. During one of his early visits to Papeete in 1833-4,
the doctor John Coulter found: 'The white residents there were all
a sordid, speculative set, with few exceptions'. Two years effected
a marked change in his attitude:

> I felt so completely at home and in security at Tahiti, that when
> I left it for the last time, I felt much regret. I was charmed with
> the island, I liked the natives, and received unlimited kindness
> from the missionaries, and several English residents. In fact, we
> all felt as if leaving a home port, more than a distant island in
> the Pacific.[13]

Little of the glamour associated with island life was to be found in
the beach communities, but the tradition of island hospitality, combined with the foreigners' desire to hear the latest news from
Europe and America, opened society to the visitor, who, in time,
was better equipped to judge its essential quality.

The long-established settlers achieved a status and standard of
living in the early port towns that would have been quite beyond
their reach in their natal societies. With limited aspirations, and
content to live the rest of their lives in the islands, these beach
patriarchs were renowned for their open-house style of hospitality,
their island wives and numerous part-island children. In the island-
style houses of Jonas M. Coe, past Samoan wives visited and lived
with present ones, and from three of his six quasi-formal unions
Coe recognised eighteen children whose names were recorded in the
family Bible. According to R. W. Robson in *Queen Emma* many

others were brought up within the same household but Coe never revealed the same strictness or sense of responsibility towards them. Recognised Coe children were obliged to observe European table manners, to sit at table with their father and use cutlery. They were also made to wear shoes. Robson gives no documentary evidence for these intimate statements of Coe family life, nor have any been found in recent research.[14] The price and scarcity of shoes in Apia, as in all early beach communities, makes that regulation seem unlikely. Few of the old residents themselves sported such articles. But that Coe was a disciplinarian was confirmed by his daughter Phoebe Park, née Coe, who described her father as a strict man. Except for two frail daughters who were educated at the local convent, all the recognised children were sent away from the contaminating influences of the beach to school in New South Wales or California. Phoebe Park further explained that Coe's daughters were only allowed to marry white men, but any suggestion of latent racialism is modified by her later remark: 'I was one of the girls chosen to chew the kava for King Malietoa and my father'.[15]

In Levuka David Whippy lived in a large Fijian *bure* which accommodated his own wife and children and the orphans, and sometime companions, of deceased or departed foreigners. A shipwrecked sailor who was billeted in the Whippy household in 1855, until he could arrange a passage from the group, found the Whippy children entertaining bilingual companions. While he was there Whippy's first wife came to visit after an absence of almost twenty years. At the time Whippy was living with his second wife Dorcas, to whom he had been married by the missionary, James Calvert. From appearances his marital relations seemed unexpectedly conventional, but the sailor talks of further Whippy offspring born of Dorcas's women attendants; these, however, were not recognised in their father's will.[16] The favourable image that Whippy projected among missionaries, naval personnel and casual visitors to Levuka owed much to the social role he played within the township. He held himself responsible for several part-Fijian children, safeguarded the land left to them, and cultivated it on their behalf. In 1835, hearing of the plight of James Magoun, stranded among a Fijian tribe which was keeping him captive, Whippy wrote to him outlining his plans and later was able to organise his escape.

On beach community standards he justly earned his title of 'Old gentleman'.

In Honolulu the older residents had greater scope and opportunity to live in style. Oliver Holmes, for many years governor of Oahu, owned extensive plantations on Oahu and Molokai, with about 180 Hawaiians to work them. As a visitor in 1812 Ross Cox was lavishly entertained by him and waited upon at table by Hawaiian servants with napkins. Holmes's part-Hawaiian daughters were bilingual and greatly sought after by Honolulu society. As the missionary Elisha Loomis succinctly stated, the Holmes girls were all prostituted to respectable foreigners. Hannah Holmes was mistress to no less a person than J. C. Jones, the American commercial agent, with whom she lived for many years, until after one trip to California in 1838 he unwisely returned with a Spanish wife. The Hawaiian government accused him of bigamy, refused to recognise him as United States representative any longer and offered Hannah Holmes the right to a divorce on account of Jones's outrageous conduct.[17] The energetic, eclectic Spaniard, Don Francisco de Paula Marin, physician, tailor, horticulturist, builder, interpreter, adviser and vigneron to the Hawaiian chiefs, lived in good style in the stone house Kamehameha I had allowed him to build for himself in 1810. His Roman Catholic affinities were obvious in the drawingroom, which was decorated with Chinese pictures and crucifixes: 'but on removing a sliding pannel from the opposite side, subjects of a far different nature were represented!'[18] After 1812 his house and large compound were the rendezvous and information centre for the incoming American sandalwood traders. The captains, supercargoes and agents came and went as they pleased, stayed with Marin or just ate meals there, set up Hawaiian houses and installed their entourages. Nathan Winship, captain of a sandalwood vessel, frequently stayed in Marin's compound and readily fitted into this society with his seven 'wives'.[19]

Later in life Marin's Roman Catholicism, which he adhered to despite many inconsistencies, caused him considerable difficulty, particularly after the arrival of the first Roman Catholic priests in 1827. Although he gave them no assistance, the ardent Protestant convert, Kaahumanu, the regent of the islands, grew suspicious of Marin's activities and in 1829 ordered him to stop celebrating mass and baptising his children and the Hawaiians in his employ, something he had practised for many years. Father Short, one of the first Roman Catholic priests to arrive in Honolulu, praised Marin's faith and behaviour:

> Withal he sticks firmly to the old religion. He baptizes all his children and teaches them their prayers in Spanish and does not allow them to communicate with the pseudo-missionaries. Morning and night he makes them say their prayers and the beads; on Sundays he reads the greater part of the mass, his family gathering around him, and he gives them an exhortation in Spanish. . . . If polygamy were allowed, he could pass for a patriarch.[20]

Notwithstanding prayers and exhortations, Marin's children had inherited their father's promiscuous proclivities. Two years after Kaahumanu's prohibition on Marin's religious activities, she told him he must stop his daughters committing adultery. Lahilahi Marin, another accepted member of J. C. Jones's menage, bore him several children. Previously she had consorted with Kamehameha III. The permissive atmosphere that prevailed in beach communities and the minimum of labour required to enjoy many of the comforts of life did not encourage European moral standards among the young part-islanders or the older white settlers.

Relations between foreigners in port towns were subject to a number of different influences among which the isolation of each beach community was of basic importance. These small enclaves of expatriates in alien territory naturally clung together and stood united in the face of island hostility. Negroes and men of different religious convictions, including Jews, became accepted members of beach society, which often comprised representatives from all the European nations, plus a handful of Chinese, Malays and Africans, who would act in concert whenever the need was recognised. In the absence of any obvious threat, petty rivalries and jealousies tended to disrupt this unity and in beach communities with larger populations, cliques appeared. The divisive strength of these groups should not, however, be over-estimated — they were characteristic of aliens huddled together, among whom gossip and rumour were always active. Such associations never became immutable or insensitive to fundamental community needs.

In Honolulu John Colcord faced the united opposition of the four established blacksmiths when he tried to set up a forge in

1826. They provoked him into fights with them and did their best to injure his trade, but Colcord, refusing to join their drunken carouses, persevered and in time built up a lucrative position for himself. In 1838 Dumont d'Urville believed the Levuka men were dangerously disunited. Perhaps they perceived and admitted the correctness of his concern, since two years later the community had a recognised leader and enjoyed a large degree of internal cohesion. A. H. Fayerweather in Honolulu in the early 1830s found it extraordinarily difficult to find gainful employment as a book-keeper and accountant. Competition for positions left him without friends or advisers until he finally secured a place with Peirce and Brewer and was accepted into the firm's social milieu.[21] Fragmentation was more obvious among the large population of Honolulu, but it occurred in all beach communities to varying degrees. The prosperous and respectable in the Bay of Islands had no truck with the rabble in Kororareka, while in Apia the Germans employed by the Godeffroy company were housed together and formed an independent social group apart from the rest of the foreign community. Despite tensions, in no beach community did these divisions threaten the existence of the towns. Further, the division did not affect the reception of a visitor, who would be received with great hospitality by all groups in a port town. In small beach communities survivors from shipwrecks were generously taken care of and billeted among the residents until arrangements could be made for them, while in Honolulu the consuls were responsible for housing or hospitalising their sailors until they could be reshipped home. A craving for news from the outside world and for novelty, which is symptomatic of any isolated community, was at the bottom of this hospitality but it was nonetheless genuine. Any visitor or shipwrecked sailor who decided to become a permanent resident inevitably became associated with one or other group and assumed its outlook.

The observance of national days reflects the complexity of beach community loyalties and interests. For the majority of foreign residents identification with one's place of birth was or became fundamental. Residence in a beach community, even if permanent, was not considered to modify in any way one's national status as British, American or whatever. In fact for many, beach community conditions led to increased patriotic zeal. One national group would accuse another of spoiling their trading opportunities or of putting undue pressure on the island government during the visit of a naval vessel. In Honolulu, once the sandalwood debts became difficult to collect, Jones accused Charlton of telling the Hawaiians that the American government would outlaw the debts.[22] It frequently occurred that members of a particular interest group were of the same nationality and the usual beach squabbles often assumed a nationalistic flavour. In keeping with this, the celebration of national days provided an opportunity to display nationalistic pride. The Americans in Honolulu provided sumptuous luncheons or dinners on the Fourth of July, to which a large number of the foreign residents were invited. Thus the honour of the United States was vaunted, but at the same time community solidarity was also enhanced. On 4 July 1812 three American ships then in Honolulu harbour received permission from Kamehameha I to celebrate. The national salute was fired three times during the day and evening, and in the afternoon a large banquet was prepared to which all the foreigners on the vessels and ashore were invited, including the Englishman Young and the Spaniard Marin. Kamehameha I, his chiefs and priests were also present.[23] An even earlier Fourth of July celebration was recorded in Honolulu in 1807 — this time the Hawaiian chiefs seem to have been the major participants: 'The grand anniversary of American Independence was ushered in with a salute, and the ship dressed in all colors, while the king with royal family etc., celebrated the day in streams of gin.'[24] After the arrival of the United States representative in 1821 the celebration became an annual event to which the leading residents irrespective of nationality, the chiefs and the missionaries were invited. The Fourth of July 1829 was heralded with many gun salutes. A splendid dinner was held at the Oahu Hotel. The company of about fifty included the American and Catholic missionaries, the English consul and residents, the Dutch and Spanish and many Hawaiians, as well as the American settlers. On this day the whole community stood united — the hostility between merchants and Protestant missionaries, the Roman Catholic/Protestant split and any other minor disturbances in the town, were transcended. During the following decade Fourth of July celebrations became even more elaborate. No less than $360 were subscribed for the dinner in 1834.[25] Throughout the Pacific the

Americans gave the most lavish parties and in Honolulu, where the foreign population was large and the wealthiest predominantly American, their national days were regularly celebrated with much display. In Apia and Levuka, where the more respectable portions of the population were British, Queen Victoria's birthday was occasion for picnics, sports days and a few more drinks in the bar. In 1872 even Guy Fawkes was remembered in Levuka.[26] But on the whole the British were less flamboyant than the Americans.

Everyday entertainments in beach communities were characteristic of those found in any frontier society: alcohol, gambling, billiards, bowling alleys and cards were the only pastimes that enjoyed regular patrons. Whatever the prevailing laws, alcohol of some variety was always available to foreigners, and to islanders and part-islanders, if they wanted it. The Pomares, Kamehameha II and III and Tui Levuka were encouraged to indulge their partiality for liquor by the foreign residents, who found it greatly to their advantage to have the chiefs under the influence. Before the Temperance Movement engaged the loyalties of the missionaries in the Pacific, they too were glad to accept gifts of wines and porter from visiting captains. The grog shops and taverns attracted men from all levels of beach society. On 24 June 1828 Reynolds recorded that the chief Boki and Kamehameha III had been gambling until three o'clock that morning with several of the mechanics in Honolulu. Boat and horse racing, cards, billiards and bowling, which was most popular in Honolulu and Apia, where there were significant American populations, could all be gambled upon. In Honolulu Messrs Mitchener and Boyd lost over $100 in one evening playing billiards at $3 to $5 a game.[27]

A high rate of alcohol consumption was an enduring feature in all beach communities, except Levuka for a limited time. John Colcord, temporarily a teetotaller, found he had more work than he could handle in Honolulu in 1826 because: 'My Brother Blacksmiths continued to carouse, some times 2 or 3 weeks together and would not work at all'. If weaned from their addiction they 'began to look and act like men', but few remained teetotal long.[28] Reprimands for excessive drunkenness chequered Alexander Adams's long piloting career in Honolulu, but do not appear to have ever blighted his material or marital success. In September 1828 the Reverend Hiram Bingham refused to marry Adams to a Hawaiian woman because he was 'crazy with rum', but Governor Boki was prepared to officiate instead. When Adams presented himself for marriage to another Hawaiian girl three years later Bingham again refused to perform the ceremony for the same reason as previously. Boki was dead by this time and it is not recorded whether anyone else was prepared to act.[29] Similarly in the other port towns alcohol played a major role. At Levuka in 1860: 'Intemperance still prevails among the whites here. We hoped to have had a little respite after the burning down of the grog shop, which occurred a few weeks ago, but the "Jennie Dove" has brought an additional supply and started the people off again'.[30] Before prohibition laws were introduced into Papeete in May 1834, the town was over-supplied with grog sellers and accompanying dance halls:

> The abundance and indiscriminate sale of ardent spirits, as well as the laxity of the laws which permitted the sensuality of a sea-port to be carried to a boundless extent, caused scenes of riot and debauchery to be nightly exhibited at Pápeéte that would have disgraced the most profligate purlieus of London.[31]

The immediate effect of prohibition was a general quietening of tone in the community. Lucrative raids were made on a number of stores round Papeete, some white residents were brought to trial and others departed. Total prohibition was, however, impossible to enforce. Grog shops continued to operate in secret, while occasional confiscation became an established form of licence, and seizure from ships a form of port revenue.

Conditions were little better in Kororareka, which in 1837 was described as 'a filthy looking miserable place the residence also of several white people, whose principle occupation is to furnish Rum and Tobacco to the crews of the Whalers'.[32] Grog sellers did not limit their activities to supplying alcohol: some unwary sailors (or willing participators) found themselves kidnapped and later ransomed off to other vessels, which, victims of the same practice, found themselves short of hands. Such a deception led to a riot in Kororareka in August 1839 when an irate captain tried to recapture his men. One of the more notorious saloons was partially dismantled, curses were exchanged between the crewmen and the drunkards ashore, but the captain was unsuccessful.[33] In drinking as in gambling the lack of moderation exercised suggests the tedium endemic in beach communities and the craving for excitement among the anti-intellectual foreigners. There was little attempt to diversify the leisure-time activities of the beach residents, most of whom were well satisfied with the pleasures of the taverns. W. T. Pritchard's failure to establish a reading room in Levuka in 1860 underlines the residents' continuing lack of interest in the cultural aspects of the societies they had left.

In keeping with this general indifference to anything except immediate gratification was the irresponsible attitude many fathers had towards the education of their part-island offspring. Unless outside pressure was brought to bear, most children who were not brought up within their mothers' culture were left to roam the beach without restraint. The more affluent and conscientious settlers sent their children to school in the United States, New Zealand or Australia, but the majority were not in a position to afford such expense or to appreciate its desirability. Men like Whippy, Cummins, Coe and Colcord, however, who started life in the islands with nothing, did earn the money and have the inclination to send at least one of their children to school outside the islands.

Soon after their arrival in Honolulu the missionaries opened a school for the numerous part-Hawaiian children in the town. The foreigners responded enthusiastically to the plan, offering gifts and money, and by September 1820 thirty pupils attended the school regularly. Most of the children had so little English that lessons had to be interpreted into Hawaiian for them by Sally Jackson, the Hawaiian wife of one of the foreign residents. In 1822, after the school was well established, the missionaries decided that all their efforts should be concentrated on the redemption of the Hawaiians. By this time the early co-operation between merchant and missionary had disintegrated and no foreigner had the time or interest to prevent the school's closure. Part-Hawaiian education was then neglected for another decade, until the establishment of the Oahu Charity School in 1833. The formal opening of the new school was attended by the foreign merchants, seven of whom constituted the school committee, several Hawaiian dignitaries and a number of American missionaries. Latent hostility to the mission was, however, evident in the school laws which limited religious instruction to the reading of the Bible without any explanation.[34] Despite these tensions the new school won approval throughout Honolulu and became a permanent institution for the education of foreign and part-island children.

In Apia the missionaries first attempted to establish a school for the children of foreign residents in 1846, but it was not until June 1856 that they finally pressured the foreigners into action. A school house was built and a teacher provided under the guidance, but not the patronage, of the missionaries. The school's subsequent history of closure due to lack of funds to employ a teacher emphasises the foreigners' lethargy. In Tahiti, where the children of mixed liaisons were less numerous, the missionaries took some of them in and brought them up with their own families. But as late as 1840 education for the remaining part-Tahitians was still most uncertain. The school that had been established for them and the Tahitians by the missionaries was far from successful. The CMS missionaries in the Bay of Islands refused to be in any way responsible for the education of the children of foreigners. Captain Hansen, who had been allied with the mission since its inception in 1814, was angered, justifiably perhaps, that his children were left without any means of education. J. R. Clendon, one of the wealthiest settlers, engaged a tutor for his children.[35]

Similar apathy characterised the foreign residents' attitudes towards religion; in most communities the mission activities were considered relevant to the islanders only. In Honolulu the situation did become much more volatile — a bitter, anti-missionary prejudice developed, preventing any interest or co-operation in religious or educational matters for over a decade. This hostility between merchants and missionaries was not constantly at fever pitch in the town but both parties eyed with suspicion the behaviour of the other and almost invariably imputed the worst motives to them. The first minister sent to the Pacific from the American Seamen's Friend Society appeared in 1833 at Honolulu, where a seamen's chapel was opened. The Reverend John Diell, who considered both visiting seamen and the local foreign residents as his especial charge, was warmly welcomed by the foreigners, in particular by such men as J. C. Jones, R. C. Charlton, William French and Eliab Grimes, all of whom had been stalwart opponents of the mission. This suggests that these men were not basically irreligious but rather strongly averse to the missionaries for political and economic reasons. They had no cause to fear Diell, who was grateful for their attention: 'The gentlemen of the village took an early opportunity of introducing me to the king and principal chiefs, and in every way have manifested a spirit of kindness, for which I feel myself under many obligations'.[36] But as had happened in the previous decade, early goodwill dissipated in the face of Diell's denunciations of theatricals, dancing and card-playing, which were becoming fashionable in Honolulu at the time. Neither Diell nor the missionaries before him were able to moderate the rigorous moral standards that evangelical Protestantism demanded; not even in an attempt to gain the loyalties of the foreign community. Church members in New England were not excommunicated for dancing, but this was threatened and imposed in Honolulu in 1836.[37] Amid fast waning enthusiasm Diell established the Oahu Bethel Church — the first church for foreigners in the Hawaiian Islands — in May 1837. The number of communicants remained small throughout his tenure.

Later on the idea of the seamen's Bethel Church spread to Papeete and Apia, where the established LMS missionaries started services for the foreign settlers and sailors in their churches, but they met with the same lack of success as was experienced in Honolulu. Few residents were prepared to join a movement dedicated to the principles of abstinence and quiet Christian living. The small congregations in port town chapels usually consisted of whaling captains and sailors on temporary visits. In Apia in 1845-6 a flash of interest was shown in a temperance society, to which the leading expatriates belonged. Three years later a subscription was raised to buy and bring out from London a corrugated-iron chapel, twenty feet by forty feet, part of which was to be screened off as a reading room. The foreigners assembled the chapel and attended its opening in January 1849, but by November of the same year they handed over all responsibilities to the mission and were seldom to be found there themselves. Interest in the temperance society had been even more short-lived, not lasting out the year of 1846. A very small chapel for English services was built in Papeete under G. Pritchard's guidance in 1834, but even in his most optimistic moments Pritchard could never say more than the attendance was 'pretty good'. In fact it fluctuated greatly and, as in Apia, frequently only visiting captains and captive crews made up the congregation.[38]

In Kororareka a church for the foreign residents was built in 1834, but previously English services had been offered in the town when a CMS missionary was available. Earle claimed in 1827 that it was the custom of the Kororareka settlers to shave and put on their best clothes every Sunday and to hear Divine Service if the missionary arrived. Extracts from the journal of Henry Williams, the missionary who usually performed this duty, reveal that Earle's sanctimonious picture of the Kororareka settlers was not quite the whole truth. Frequently Sunday attendance was small, due to widespread intoxication among the settlers and once in 1828 Williams received a note requesting him not to come because all but one or two were drunk. The service was discontinued during the same year. However, the missionary printer, William Colenso, who was made responsible for the English services in 1834, found the Kororareka settlers sympathetic towards the idea of a temperance society, which they founded in August 1835. Fifty people attended the second meeting in May 1836 and the first book to be published in English in New Zealand was the *Report of the New Zealand Temperance Society* (May 1836).[39] Notwithstanding the new church and temperance society, drunkenness and uproarious living were in the ascendancy again throughout Kororareka before the end of 1836. The urge towards material betterment and the leisure-time entertainments which attracted men to beach communities were so incompatible with the aims and standards of the Bethel movement, temperance ideas or general Christian philosophy that their failure among most foreign residents was hardly surprising.

For about a decade between 1840 and 1850, the settlers at Levuka appear to have acted quite out of character with residents in the other beach communities. From Lieutenant Wilkes to Captain Erskine, naval officers expressed their surprised approval of the Levuka foreigners' concern for law and order, cleanliness, education and Christianity; the last not only for their part-Fijian offspring but for their Fijian wives and even themselves. While Wilkes was in Levuka in 1840, one of his officers encouraged the settlers' attempts to establish a mission school for their children. He bought a suitable piece of ground from Tui Levuka and presented it to the missionaries for such a purpose. For three years, 1840 to 1843, the whites repeatedly asked the Wesleyan missionaries stationed at Viwa for a teacher and missionary. In 1842 a deputation went in person to the mission, but they only succeeded in procuring a teacher. An itinerant missionary did, however, include Levuka in his circuit and in June 1843 he was well pleased with his labours:

> *Levuka, Vuna, Lovoni.* At these three places on the island of Ovalau we have 147 professing Christians. Twenty-one of these are white people, chiefly English, and the greater part of the rest are their wives, servants and children. Four of the white people have been married to native women during the year. They attend the means of grace at every opportunity when I visit them and some of them attend the native services on the Sabbath . . . They are all anxious that their children should be well instructed, and do all they can to induce them to attend to school and the ordinances of God's house.[40]

In 1844 this godly community was exiled to Solevu but relations between them and the missionaries remained most cordial. After the destruction of Levuka in 1846, the missionary John Hunt rescued material from two whale boats that were destroyed, and returned it to the men at Solevu. In gratitude for this and many other acts of kindness they built him a comfortable wooden house at Viwa. On a visit to Solevu Hunt was welcomed 'with great cordiality'. But the foreigners' amiability and exceptional interest in religious and educational matters still left them open to missionary reproof. Hunt found some Fijian women were hindered in their religious instruction by a handful of foreigners and he felt compelled to warn 'the white men against reading certain books and pamphlets which I had seen among them containing Socinianism, and universalism in its most insinuating forms'.[41] A year later Hunt still held the Solevu settlers in high esteem and urged the British consulate in Tahiti to afford them greater protection.

> I have had many opportunities of knowing them [the Solevu men] during the last seven years, and my opinion is, that it would be difficult to find fifty such men, circumstanced as they are, with a character more unexceptionable. They have improved in many respects during the last few years, and show much good feeling towards Missionaries and Mission work.[42]

This unusual situation did not survive the foreigners' return to Levuka in 1849. When Captain Erskine visited the settlement later that year he praised the tone of society and the industry of the residents, but there was no school or church. In July 1851 the Levuka men were urged by an American naval officer to stop drinking and turn to religion — the first of many similar sermons. Levuka's population increase from about thirty to fifty between 1848 and 1852, the decline of Whippy's position, and the residents' changed allegiance to the United States commercial agent, J. B. Williams, all had some part in Levuka's fall from moral rectitude. With the arrival of the trained schoolmaster John Binner in 1852, a school for part-Fijians was re-established, but neither religion nor education had much relevance in a community with such changed motivations and outlook.

With time and the increase of settlers coming to the islands with European wives and set economic aims, a modicum of respectability and staidness was imposed upon the beach communities. Slowly the more uproarious beachcomber activities disappeared — groups of foreigners and islanders no longer sat on the beach for days on end drinking a cask dry. Then the stigma fell on the long-established habits of gambling and tavern drinking and the taking of island 'wives'. The influence of the slowly increasing number of white women can be seen in several of these changes, but not all women were bastions of Victorian morality. Busby was scandalised by Mrs Guard, who lived with a chief's son on the payment of six cannisters of powder to her European husband. Mrs Cooper at her third or fourth trial in Papeete became most abusive and refused to pay her fines for having been in possession of seventy crates of gin.[43] Despite such lapses, civilisation and respectability were seeping into the beach communities. From the diary of Levi Chamberlain, who was the secular agent for the American mission for over twenty years, the change and growing complexity of society in Honolulu is clearly revealed; the transition from grog shops to hotels and well-appointed private dinner parties, from frenetic mission baiting to a tolerant acceptance, and from Hawaiian grass *hale* to stone or wooden mansions. Over a period of twenty years, and within a population that had grown to about 600 foreigners, the process was not unusual. It occurred in the other beach communities, as in most frontier societies, but nowhere in the Pacific did it have a significant effect on the sailor-mechanic class.

In Honolulu the arrival of the missionaries and of permanent merchant settlers marked the beginning of a new era. But the example of the missionaries, the godly merchant Hunnewell and several pious captains, was counterbalanced by the pleasure-seeking, distinctly secular activities of the majority of merchants and sandalwood traders, led by the consular agents J. C. Jones and R. C. Charlton. The funeral in 1825 of ex-governor Holmes, for whom the missionaries had held great hopes, underlines the limitations of merchant respectability:

> The mourners followed the coffin the females being supported by foreigners. The most decent of the foreigners, those who pride themselves on being above the vulgar, walked in procession arm in arm with their paramours . . . To add to the scene the keepers of grog shops displayed flags, which are hoisted as signals of their traffic, at half mast.[44]

For six years between 1826 and 1832, the blacksmith, John Colcord, struggled to give up drinking. When he finally succeeded and took the pledge in October 1832, taunts and tricks were played upon him, and many people refused to employ him. With industry, however, he rapidly built up new custom and expanded his forge to include a store, three salesmen, three shoemakers and a tailor. He considered the Oahu Charity School not good enough for his part-Hawaiian daughter whom he sent to Boston for her education in 1837. By 1839 Colcord's second Hawaiian wife had died and he decided to visit the States with his four sons. Before he left, his property was valued at between $7000 and $10,000. In May 1841 he returned to Honolulu with an American wife and his daughter, having left the four boys at school. From beginnings as a destitute artisan he was accepted as a member of the merchant class and became a frequent visitor at the mission.[45] Opportunities were not lacking in Honolulu for those who could break themselves from the taverns and gambling houses, and money, a white wife and children at school in New England guaranteed one a place among the élite of Honolulu society.

In other beach societies a similar quasi-respectability was to be found among sections of the merchant class. A frequent visitor and resident in the islands from 1857 contended that:

Levuka, Ovalau, at that time [1860], was about on a par with Apia as regards the quality of the denizens of both. All the original residents had either died off, killed one another, or been killed by the natives, and a new class of men had come into the groups, some of very superior education and antecedents.[46]

He was not without bias. Writing in 1912 he was obviously trying to establish that beach community society was quite as respectable as anything to be found in Australia at the same time. A number of the new arrivals in Apia in the late 1850s had, however, proved more amenable to the missionaries than earlier settlers. Among the old residents, furthermore, the diehard beach leaders Pritchard, Yandall and Hamilton had all turned to the church for spiritual comfort. Pritchard had become bankrupt, Yandall had lost almost all his property by fire and Hamilton, in a drunken moment, had nearly killed somebody. New interest was shown in the little iron chapel, erected in 1849. One hundred and twenty pounds collected from the residents and visiting captains made it possible in 1860 to move the building to a more suitable site and improve its facilities.[47]

By 1860 Levuka was no longer the residence of David Whippy, who, accompanied by William Simpson, Isaac Hathaway and several part-Fijians, had left the town after a devastating fire late in 1858, for the island of Wakaya. All David Whippy's property was destroyed in the blaze, and since Levuka and his standing in it had altered so much in the previous eight years, the time was advantageous to leave with what remained of his following. But the superiority of those who succeeded him, either in education or antecedents, would be difficult to establish. W. T. Pritchard arrived in November 1858 as British consul and in his wake came a medley of people from Samoa and the colonies, attracted to Fiji by his reports of its great potential. The missionaries at Levuka certainly found no reason to welcome their arrival:

We are getting an accession of Foreigners to these Islands. And I am sorry to say that too many of them are fearfully addicted to intemperance. Since Mr Pritchard came, I suppose not fewer than 20 whites have come from Samoa . . . This is by far the worst station in the group. Here most of the whites reside. Here grog is drunk to the greatest excess.[48]

Similarly in Apia the new élite showed no aversion to alcohol, associations with island women or appearing for work in pyjamas, which were in fact the day-time uniform of many foreigners on the beach.

Even in Kororareka, some pressures to conform to outside standards of respectability began to be felt. The big ship-chandlers and shipyard operators, Clendon, Mair, Stephenson and Wright, had always held aloof from the riff-raff population of Kororareka, but after 1835 a division between respectable merchants and a handful of professional men and the rest of the residents was discernible within the town itself. Ben Turner, a shipwrecked sailor, began his career in New Zealand as a trader in dried tattooed heads. Prohibition of the trade forced him to set up as a grog seller in Kororareka in the early 1830s. Business prospered to such an extent that he soon became a substantial owner of lands and property in and around the port town. Despite slight wounds after a gunbattle on the beach with J. S. Polack, a well established merchant, Turner continued to succeed, and in 1839, as the only professed Roman Catholic in the town, he welcomed and entertained Bishop Pompallier as his house guest, before Pompallier settled in his own establishment. (Later Turner became the Bay of Islands representative in the Auckland Provincial Council.)[49]

Beach community life encouraged and indulged eccentric behaviour, and illusions of grandeur among its foreign settlers. Many of the 'captains' and 'colonels' in port towns owed their titles to personal acts of promotion since their arrival as destitute shipwrecked sailors, deserters or ordinary soldiers. The number of *soi-disant,* disinherited or remittance men of European aristocratic families to find their way to the Pacific was also prodigious. In Apia John King Bruce, a Negro born in Liverpool, insisted on calling himself the first white man on the beach: 'I am British born and bred, thank God! and at that time no people in the islands but British were called "white" '. He refused to countenance the claim of two British convicts who were in Samoa when he arrived, since they were covered in tattooing and more savage than their hosts. The rights of a Portuguese to the title were similarly brushed aside.[50] To Charles Pickering the marriage of a part-Fijian girl to a chief was totally against his principles. Rather than let the daughter of a white man marry a Fijian he added her to his already extensive household. The eccentricity of Stephen Reynolds, revealed in many aspects of his behaviour and daily dress, was most obvious in his pyrotechnic displays of temper which periodically led him to refuse to do business, even of a consular nature, with persons he did not like or approve of. These outbursts were mitigated in many peoples' eyes by his genuine interest in the welfare of part-Hawaiians and the time he spent playing his fiddle while teaching the girls to dance. The boisterous activities of the pirate Bully Hayes would be classed by most people as criminal rather than eccentric, but his exuberance and flair for deceiving persons in authority made him a much admired figure during his intermittent visits to Apia.[51]

The conventions of Western society had little relevance in beach communities, where no one questioned the background or upbringing of his neighbours too closely unless he was prepared to face ostracism. For many years after the arrival of the missionaries and the few godly merchants, hard drinking, marriage and living with island women, together with a marked reluctance for sustained work, were predominant features of port town life, despite admonitions to reform. But such society was not without some affectation. In 1868 twenty-four British residents in Apia sent a letter of loyalty to Prince Albert, who had recently been attacked in New South Wales:

> We regard with the greatest indignation the murderous assault made on your Royal person . . . We assure your Royal Highness that although far from our beloved country, we still have the deepest devotion of loyalty towards your Royal Mother, Her Majesty Queen Victoria, the Prince of Wales, and all the members of the Royal family. We can confidently assure your Royal Highness that though living in these so called uncivilized islands, we should have heartily welcomed your Royal Highness had it been your good pleasure to extend your visit to us.[52]

Such sentiments were not everyday phenomena in beach communities but the smallness of society and its whimsical, momentary interests and loyalties often made it possible for one man to initiate a pet project or petition and carry many of his immediate colleagues or fellow nationals with him. Sudden effusions of intense group loyalty, combined with the intrigue endemic in most beach communities, left little room for respectability as the Western world understood it.

All port towns suffered from primitive public facilities and some lacked particular amenities completely. As late as 1840 Kororareka was still without a public jetty. The foreigners' strong extra-territorial attitudes, and their feelings of impermanence, plus the fact that few of them owned the land on which they lived, made the development of a sense of community almost impossible. Beach towns grew at the whim of island and foreign settlers without reference to any housing or street plans. Any project for community development thus fell victim to the total lack of concern evinced by the large majority of foreign residents. Burials were casually performed in close proximity to permanent settlement, roads were inadequate, bridges non-existent or precariously temporary and any system of sewerage completely unknown. There can have been little to attract either eye or nose along the beach fronts littered with rotting animal and vegetable matter. The death rate in the beach communities was high but despite the unhygienic conditions, alcohol rather than contagious diseases such as dysentery or typhoid was the killer:

> In the Navigator Islands, as in Fiji, disease of any kind . . . is to be attributed, not to the effects of climate, but to those of intoxicating drink. When one considers the astonishing quantity of alcoholic drink, chiefly 'square gin', consumed during any one month in either Apia or Levuka by so disproportionate a number of white settlers, one need not be surprised at hearing an outcry about disease.[53]

Yaws and elephantiasis were two tropical diseases to which Europeans were particularly prone but neither was likely to prove fatal. Except in Honolulu the beach communities were often without the benefit of any medical practitioner, another profession which, by default, often fell upon the consuls. While epidemic diseases were not a serious hazard for the European populations in the port towns, any increase in population was a potential threat to public health, and the islanders, if not the foreigners, were ready victims to a number of minor infections which could have been controlled if the foreigners had had any interest in public sanitation.

For many years beach community populations were a casual

combination of foreigners and islanders, the latter mostly women. The men came from a wide section of European society but with a preponderance from the working class. Among the island women there were some of high rank, and in Fiji at least it was possible for a minor chief (Tui Levuka) to marry a part-Fijian girl (Elizabeth Grundy, widow of an expatriate).[54] Social gatherings between the chiefs and leading foreigners were frequent and easy — island feasts and foreign celebrations were well attended by both races. The visits of mercantile and naval vessels provided further opportunities for mixed entertainment. The Hawaiians, who proved most adept at many European games, revealed their expertise on board the *Tonquin* in Honolulu harbour in 1812: 'In the course of the evening the queens [of Kamehameha I] played draughts with some of our most scientific amateurs, whom they beat hollow; and such was the skill evinced by them in the game, that not one of our best players succeeded in making a king.'[55] Repeatedly visitors to the islands remarked on the ease with which Polynesians and Fijians acquired Western table manners. Hugh Cuming in Papeete harbour, early in January 1828, invited Pomare IV and her retinue to dine on board. They drank sparingly in the missionaries' presence but after the clerics' departure, a large quantity of wine disappeared and the women quarrelled over a length of scarlet ribbon. However: 'At Dinner the Ladies behaved with the greatest propriety used the Knife and Fork in an admirable manner'.[56] The islanders' adaptive and imitative skills were combined with polite but dignified bearing, which made mixed social intercourse easy for both races.

Social differentiation within a tribe was commonly practised among the Fijians and Polynesians, who were quick to recognise the personal worth and standing of most immigrants, and to respect them accordingly. Once beach communities began to grow, society divided quite naturally into two or more classes. By 1824 in Honolulu there were numerous shanty grog shops kept by runaway sailors, but there were others: 'fitted up in a superior style, for the exclusive accommodation of Yeris [chiefs] and ships' officers, admission being refused to Kanackas and sailors'.[57] Christmas dinner 1827 was celebrated in Honolulu at the governor Boki's house, at the American agent's and among the mechanics and other Hawaiians.[58] In the other port towns social status was of little significance in ordinary daily life, but the visit of a man-of-war or large merchant vessel revealed a sharp distinction between those who entertained, and were entertained by, the officers and captain, and those who met only the common sailors — island chiefs and leading foreigners belonging strictly to the former group.

Early beach communities provided a meeting place where both races could participate in economic and social activities. Any inequality of opportunity arose from the division of society, which had a class rather than a racial basis. Later when the number of foreigners in port towns increased the islanders and part-islanders found that preference in employment was always given to the expatriates and that they had no place in the newly emerging Western-dominated society. But before this development race relations in beach communities, although subject to moments of suspicion and tension, were predominantly easy and flexible. Captain Fremantle considered beach community life in Levuka to be immoral, the inhabitants the scum of the Western world, and the conditions sordid and squalid in the extreme. His terms of condemnation may have been exaggerated but a description of the other beach communities has shown that basically Levuka in 1855 was not an exception. The exigencies of frontier society made the foreigners insensitive to the moral standards of the West, while their pursuit of wealth and, for many, their desire not to remain permanently in the islands made them indifferent to the conditions in which they lived. The mitigating aspects, such as the generous hospitality and good race relations found in beach communities, were ignored by their more hostile critics.

Primarily, however, these towns came into being to serve Western commerce, and Fremantle, like so many others, had to admit that the foreigners were at least periodically industrious. Frederick Bennett condemned Papeete in 1834 for the depths of iniquity to which it had sunk, but despite its depravity the town had an 'air of commercial importance'. Similarly Apia, soon after the Van Camp crisis, appeared to be a prosperous settlement: 'Although of a most mixed character, and built without any regularity, yet with its European stores, native houses, chapels and public houses, [it] constitutes a considerable township, and has quite a business look with it'.[59] Whatever social conditions prevailed, the port towns were capable of serving the mercantile ventures undertaken in the Pacific, and they were always ready to offer shelter and entertainment to any newcomer willing to accept the standards and modes of life he found around him.

seven

The Later Years

Although several aspects of beach community life were slow to change, increased contact with the outer world and the continued growth of foreign populations, which occurred during the later stages of development in the port towns, did introduce new economic and political interests, which brought in their wake new social patterns. Levuka experienced the largest population increase with a rise from about 60 residents in 1858 to over 500 late in 1870, but both Honolulu and Apia grew in size, if not so dramatically, during their later years. British annexation of New Zealand in 1840 and the declaration of a French protectorate over Tahiti in 1842 brought to an end independent beach community life in Kororareka and Papeete. In the last few years before the British intervened in New Zealand, Kororareka and the Bay of Islands area had experienced a rapid increase in foreign population but there had been little comparable growth in economic enterprise, since the majority of the new arrivals were land speculators gambling on the expectation of annexation. No such influx preceded Tahiti's sudden change in political status. Papeete's foreign population, which had grown slowly throughout the 1830s, numbered about seventy in 1842, the majority of whom were employed in the supply trade to whalers, or the export of island products among which pearl-shell was still important. Development in Kororareka and Papeete after 1840 and 1842 respectively was controlled indirectly from the capitals of Britain and France and directly by colonial officials sent out by those European governments. The affairs of both beach communities were henceforth the concern of foreign powers, in place of nominally independent island authorities, and therefore cease to fall within the limits of this book.

Between the mid 1830s and the early 1840s Honolulu's population rose steadily from about 350 to between 500 and 600 in 1843, while the Hawaiian population in the area grew to approximately 8000. The supply trade to whalers, including peripheral activities, was still the economic mainstay for the foreign residents, but interest was developing in Hawaii's agricultural potential. The company run by Brinsmade, Ladd and Hooper pioneered a sugar plantation on Kauai late in 1835 and in subsequent years a number of foreigners followed their example on other islands. On Hawaii Island silk manufacture (started in 1837) and cattle ranching (started in the late 1830s) were also experimented with. Despite much seeming activity these new enterprises were beset with many problems, especially the vagaries of the Hawaiian climate, and the non-availability of capital, labour and necessary machinery. During this period none was to become a major export industry.[1]

Apia's population, estimated at about 120 in 1860, declined to 50 in 1865, but increased again to reach about 150 in 1877. The sudden decrease in 1865-8 was due to a minor cotton boom. High cotton prices on the world market, during and immediately after the American civil war, enticed many Apia residents to take up cotton production on the small areas of Upolu land which the Samoans, seriously affected by drought, made available at this time in exchange for trade foods. In 1866 and 1867 cotton was Samoa's leading export. The following year, however, the overseas market eased for kidney cotton, on which the foreigners in Samoa had concentrated, and conditions in the group made the islanders most reluctant to engage as wage labour. Without Samoans to pick the cotton, the small traders and artisans were forced to leave much of the 1868 crop to rot on the bushes while they returned to their safer occupations in Apia. In addition to these former residents, Apia's population was augmented during the 1870s by a number of settlers, who were employed by the Godeffroy company, two or three men with capital who established mercantile and trading houses of their own, and other less reputable foreigners who were predominantly interested in land speculation and intrigue. During the early 1870s a handful of Chinese traders and restaurateurs also settled in the town.[2]

Levuka's first marked increase in population occurred in 1859-60, when over 100 foreigners, some from Samoa and many more from the colonies of Australia and New Zealand, arrived in Fiji in response to W. T. Pritchard's private and public statements (many of the latter were published in the colonial papers) about the islands' economic potential and the likelihood of early annexation by Great Britain. Disappointed in their expectations, many left the group, while the majority of those who remained took refuge in Levuka. Throughout the 1860s there was a steady inflow of foreigners, many of whom sought in Fiji the quick fortunes that had evaded them on the Australian and New Zealand gold fields, whose production during the decade greatly declined. A general economic depression in Australia and the Maori wars in New Zealand encouraged further colonials to try their luck in the islands. The high prices for cotton in the late 1860s provided the incentive to go to Fiji, not only to would-be planters, but also to merchants, some with substantial capital backing, surveyors, land and real estate agents, lawyers, auctioneers and professional gamblers, who all anticipated a share in the cotton boom profits. The rapid increase and diversification of advertisements in the *Fiji Times* between September 1869 and December 1870 are proof of the numerous new services and goods available in Levuka — cases of preserved ginger, Hobart Town jams and sausage machines were among an extraordinary collection of goods offered for auction in October 1869. By December a steam hair brushing and shaving machine was expected daily from the colonies. A year later at the end of 1870, pianofortes could be tuned and regulated, a mender of watches, chronometers and musical boxes offered his services to the residents and the latest tucked skirts and muslin dresses were available.[3]

This continued growth of foreign populations in the port towns resulted in a distinct modification of settlement patterns — the foreigners no longer occupied dwellings interspersed among those of the islanders, but moved together into what became sizeable nuclei of predominantly white settlers. Islanders still lived in close proximity to the foreigners, but certain areas became recognised white preserves in which the former were visitors or employees (usually domestic) rather than neighbours. The new expatriate arrivals, few of whom considered themselves permanent island dwellers, increased the beach communities' contacts with the outside world. Letters, newspapers and journals kept them relatively up to date with colonial, American and European events. Steamship communications across the Pacific made mail and passenger services more frequent and reliable. At the same time international interest in the islands was heightened; naval vessels from England, the United States, France and Germany became expected visitors in the port towns. New commercial interests also made it imperative to keep in constant contact with the outside world. The profitable production of sugar and cotton, and to a lesser extent copra, was closely linked to the prices current on the world markets. Boom cotton prices lasted only as long as the cotton fields of southern America were out of production. None of the island plantations, which were already hampered by adverse climatic conditions, could compete against the enormous exports of Negro-grown cotton from America.

Many new settlers established themselves on plantations distant from the port town of their island group, but this spread of foreign population and interest to the hinterlands did not weaken the beach communities' importance. Unlike the expatriate village shopkeepers and the bêche-de-mer or copra traders who were scattered round the islands and remained as self-reliant as possible, the planters depended on the foreign centres for equipment, supplies, credit facilities, news, hospitality and often to gin and export their crop. These new commercial and agricultural enterprises greatly influenced foreign attitudes towards island authority and even to the whole structure of island society. The predominantly trader-artisan populations of early port towns had had minimal political interests as long as good trading conditions prevailed. This did not, however, prevent them from provoking incidents of a political nature, but these were nearly always a mask for trading rivalries. With the advent of a planter community and the growth of interest in the development of agriculture, many foreigners became vitally concerned in island policies. The planters' prerequisites — security of land tenure, the continued availability of land for sale, and an adequate supply of cheap labour — often brought them, and other foreigners with property interests, into direct conflict with island governments and their rights. Once beach community establishments became involved in exporting commodities for the world markets there was an increasing demand for political stability and governmental efficiency, without which it was impossible to attract capital for investment or to arrange monetary and credit systems. No island government, however, had mastered the complicated and advanced Western political and administrative methods required to meet the foreigners' needs. The attempts made by island authorities to deal with the changed conditions strictly belong to the history of island political development, but since beach communities were major initiators in most reform movements and vitally affected by them, some analysis of them must be made.

By the late 1830s in Honolulu the bitter hostility between merchant and missionary, which had been rife in the port for over a decade, was gradually losing its intensity: 'A warfare was, however, kept up between the individuals belonging to the rival nations of England and the United States, which afforded ample room for the tongue of scandal to indulge itself'.[4] Thus the town still lacked harmony among its foreign residents and between them and the Hawaiian government. Jealous of American business and investment, which dominated the economic scene in Hawaii, the English accused them of bringing unjust influence to bear on the Hawaiian government through the agency of the American missionaries, and especially the ex-missionary advisers to the King and his chiefs. William Richards, appointed in July 1838, was the first of a series of these advisers. Conversely, the sudden expansion of British trade through Honolulu at the end of the 1830s alarmed American merchants — one British resident claimed that the annual value of British trade through the port rose in the three years 1839-42 from $20,000 to $150,000. The increase was largely due to the activities of the Hudson Bay Company, which established a permanent agent in Honolulu in August 1834. Anglo-American rivalries became so intense that probably for the first time in Honolulu in 1840 the British were not invited to join the Americans for their Fourth of July celebration.[5]

Convinced that their extravagant agricultural and mercantile ambitions would succeed if only the authorities would co-operate, the foreign residents put increasing pressure on the Hawaiian government through their consuls and naval officers visiting the port, demanding commercial and extra-territorial rights and freehold land tenure. Lord Russell in 1836 and Captain Laplace in 1839 both proved willing to act on their nationals' behalf. The treaties they imposed against the Hawaiians' will negated laws previously promulgated and undermined land policies of long standing. No foreign resident, however, would counsel or uphold the Hawaiian government in its struggles against the militant demands of these men, since every concession granted increased their ascendancy and advantages. In daily life the residents kept the pressure on the government with a stream of claims which could be blown into 'international incidents' on the arrival of the next man-of-war, if the foreigners and the incoming captain agreed on it. In 1840 Charlton laid claim to a large block of land in the heart of commercial Honolulu. The government agreed to his right to part of it but denied his claim to the most valuable section. This suit was to harass the Hawaiians for many years but in 1840 the English residents were prepared to see it as further evidence of the chiefs' hostile attitude towards all the British. In October 1841 a dispute over the interpretation of a contract between an Englishman, Skinner, and a naturalised American, Dominis, was brought before an all-foreign jury for trial. When Skinner withdrew from the court on the pretext that the jury was predominantly American, Governor Kekuanaoa dismissed the case without further hearing.[6] This added more heat to the national rivalries and these two cases plus other claims, several of which involved many thousands of dollars, hung over the government and were obviously to become matters of contention when next a naval vessel arrived.

Although the Hawaiian chiefs, with missionary guidance, had begun to modernise their processes of government — a bill of rights had been promulgated and land reforms mooted — the foreigners remained clamorous for more reforms and concessions. The likelihood that an alien might precipitate an incident which could lead to naval intervention and to the possible loss of independence was very real. In an attempt to forestall such an event the Hawaiian government sought to have their independence formally recognised by the great powers. An ill-organised and unsuccessful bid was made in 1840, followed by a second, equally unproductive, in November 1841. The agent of the latter attempt was P. A. Brinsmade, United States commercial agent, who was working on behalf of Ladd and Co. The government had given the company permission to lease all the unoccupied lands in the entire group, but the lease was conditional on the recognition of Hawaii's independence by the great powers. Clearly the government was prepared to pay a high price for Ladd and Co.'s assistance in their bid to bolster Hawaiian sovereignty. The third envoy, William Richards, the ex-missionary adviser to the government, and the chief Timothy Haalilio, was finally successful in 1844.[7] The Hawaiian monarchy survived for another fifty years, although not without several threats to its independence. Behind the façade of full sovereignty, however, a largely Westernised government dominated by foreign-born ministers and representatives passed legislation to ensure expatriate development.

The Fiji cotton boom of 1868-71 attracted hundreds of settlers to the group, and more significantly to Levuka. Of a total foreign population increase of 716 in 1870 about 400 remained in the town.[8] A large majority of these were intent on establishing any kind of business that did not involve capital or hard work. Arbitrators, commission agents, notaries, brokers, land and real estate agents all hoped to make a fortune from other peoples' labour. By 1871 jerry-built, weatherboard houses with corrugated zinc or iron roofs, stores, warehouses, two gins and many hotels and boarding houses straggled south in a double row along the beach front, from Levuka Vakaviti over Totoga creek and down to the point towards Nasova.

In the beginning of May this year [1871] the town had one European and one native Wesleyan church, supported by missionary funds; one Episcopalian, supported by voluntary subscription; and one Roman Catholic Church, divided between Europeans and natives. There were between 100 and 120 houses and warehouses of European construction, and about twenty-five of native architecture, inhabited by settlers; of these thirty were private residences at the back of the business part of the town. Sixteen new houses were in course of erection. There were thirteen public houses, but I don't think that more than one third of the number could have been doing a profitable business, although there is no license fee, nor any import duties. Fourteen retail stores competed for the favours of a population, which, though fluctuating, cannot be set down at more than 350. But it is not the permanent residents who sustain the commercial credit of Levuka as much as the visitors, particularly those who come for 'recreation'.[9]

Enclosed by rugged hills, Levuka had a minimum of land for expansion; overcrowding and a deterioration of living conditions were inevitable. As late as 1875 there was no permanent building in Levuka. Accommodation in the town was always at a premium; planters on business or holidaying competed with new arrivals and travellers for a bed. The boom, however, was short-lived; prices for Sea Island cotton eased late in 1870 and by April 1871, after a severe hurricane which ruined more than a quarter of the total crop, cotton was obviously not able to provide the basis for a new Anglo-Saxon empire in Fiji. On 22 June 1872 fifty foreigners in Levuka agreed to form a company and to subscribe £1500 to emigrate to New Guinea. Within two or three days one-third of the amount had been contributed.[10]

Earlier, while the boom was still at its height, a tide of optimism had helped to disguise the many difficulties, particularly financial, besetting the commercial community. Without a properly functioning government or any recognised security, no banking or formal credit facilities could be established. Furthermore, the British residents, who constituted a large proportion of the foreign population, had no recourse to legal procedures since their consul was not granted magisterial powers. Commercial transactions, land sales and transfers, in fact all contracts, depended upon a man's word, which was not sufficient in the densely populated and highly competitive Levuka society. Two attempts had been made in the 1860s to establish Western-style governments for Fiji but neither proved capable of withstanding the disruptive influences of island political rivalries and foreign demands. The united confederation of 1865 collapsed when the presidency was to have been transferred from Cakobau to the Tongan chief, Ma'afu, who was trusted by even fewer Fijian chiefs than the former. Two separate confederations were subsequently established in 1867, one in the eastern islands headed by Ma'afu and the other in the west with Cakobau in charge. Ma'afu, an astute politician, advised by responsible foreigners, governed well and offered planters the security of land tenure they required. Cakobau's kingdom, burdened with a greater number of clamorous foreigners, many of them concentrated in

Levuka, and a heavy debt to the United States, was doomed from its inception.[11]

By June 1871 the collapse of the cotton industry combined with chaotic commercial conditions in Levuka induced a handful of newcomers to establish yet another government. It was planned and set up in such secrecy that the crowning of Cakobau in Levuka in June 1871, which was the government's first official action, took the majority of Levuka residents completely by surprise. However, despite some grumbling among the old hands about the lack of consultation, the merchants and planters welcomed the Cakobau government as, they hoped, a genuine attempt to improve the highly unstable position of the expatriates in Fiji. But at no time during its three years in office was the Cakobau government able to realise these hopes, partly because it was highly unrealistic of the foreigners to believe that the cotton industry could be revived. (Only the introduction of a new export crop and new investment and credit facilities could provide a secure base for expatriate development, and such were not forthcoming at this time.) The other major factor contributing to the government's failure was the refusal by the majority of foreigners to admit that the Fijians had equal rights and powers in it. Without the support of both the Fijians and the foreigners the government could not obtain official recognition from the British government and thus its powers were further weakened. Opposition among the more rebellious Levuka residents crystallised in the formation of a Ku Klux Klan which was later transformed into a British Subjects' Mutual Protection Society. Many merchants in Levuka defied the government at every opportunity and the murders of two isolated planter groups at Ba by hostile Fijian mountain tribes underlined the insecurity of the planters and led in one instance to armed confrontation between the planters and the government troops who, the former believed, were totally inadequate as a punitive force against the mountaineers. The Cakobau government proved quite unable to restore commercial and financial confidence in Levuka or to guarantee security to the planters. Not only was it faced with insurrection, the foreigners' refusal to pay taxes and widespread obstruction, but it also over-spent its own much-extended credit.[12]

By late 1872 the actions of some ministers led many foreigners to believe that Cakobau's cabinet was not interested in promoting regular government or general, that is, foreign, prosperity:

> The government of Fiji was constructed on such an extensive
> scale, as to at once suggest the idea, that its projectors were not
> in earnest; but had simply got up a very elaborate speculation,
> a sort of bubble company, by means of which they hoped to gull
> the public, and having filled their own pockets, make good their
> retreat, when the affair should collapse.[13]

Philp, the author of this quotation, had been refused the Attorney-
Generalship, the offer of which had brought him to Levuka early
in 1872. Embittered by this experience he had nothing commendable to say about the government or its officers. John Bates Thurston, who had been responsible for Philp's rejection, had been
appointed to Cakobau's ministry in April 1872 and had done
everything in his power to limit government spending, but despite
this effort, which should have won him the foreigners' approval,
his concern to protect and enhance Fijian interests guaranteed the
opposition of most residents.

While the total foreign population in Fiji declined after 1871,
in Levuka numbers fluctuated between four and five hundred until
after annexation; thus a continued strain was put on the town's
resources. When the commissioners Goodenough and Layard in-
vestigated the state of Fiji in 1874, their final recommendation of
annexation to the British government was strongly influenced by
their knowledge that the government had survived previous crises
only by the intervention of H.M. naval vessels, that it was heavily
indebted, and still spending beyond its income, and that many
foreigners faced ruin if the British did not intervene. The political
and financial anarchy generated by the foreigners during the cotton
boom forced the Fijians to accept annexation in 1874 as the only
way to safeguard their land and interests, and transfer the intri-
cacies of government into more experienced hands.

In Apia the growth of the foreign population after 1868 was
not as great as in Honolulu or Levuka at similar stages of their
development, but among the new settlers there were a handful
who were determined to acquire substantial land rights throughout
the group. The conflicting claims and ill-feeling generated by these
land speculators were to dominate political manoeuvres in Samoa
until the 1890s. For the first time during the civil war of 1869-73

Samoan land was readily available to foreigners in return for guns and ammunition. Several Apia residents, particularly T. Weber for the Godeffroy company and J. C. Williams, and a few speculators from America and the colonies, took advantage of the situation, but the major investors were agents of the Central Polynesian Land and Commercial Company (CPLCC), a west coast American firm of somewhat disreputable origins and intentions. Tracts of unsurveyed land were made over to CPLCC agents, who included Jonas Coe, the American consular agent, and J. C. Williams, the British consular agent, in 'sales' that were not always authorised by the proper Samoan owners or sufficiently documented — the boundaries and total acreage were often left blank. Further the CPLCC agents paid only nominal deposits for the land they alienated, avowedly while they were awaiting the results of survey.[14] By 1873 it was apparent to both Samoan and foreigner that a halt and some rationalisation of the situation were essential. Had all the sales been validated the Samoans would have been perilously short of land, but the haste with which most transactions had been concluded resulted in several lots of land being sold more than once and even more being sold by Samoans who had no right to them. This very irregularity gave the Samoans grounds to dispute the foreigners' claims while the expatriates were similarly aware that no island tribunal was likely to give their cases a very sympathetic hearing.

Into this atmosphere of confusion, hostility and frustration stepped Albert B. Steinberger, an American political adventurer about whose antecedents little is known, apart from his informal connection with the CPLCC, which had been declared bankrupt in 1873, and a vague friendship with President Grant. The reactions of the Apia residents to the course of Steinberger's filibuster in Samoa between 1873 and 1876 fluctuated from enthusiastic support to unrelenting opposition and determination to depose him. Among the Samoans his status remained high long after 1876, despite foreign disclosures of his duplicity and self-interest. From the moment of his arrival Steinberger was happy to advise the chiefs about the making of a new constitution, and later in 1875 he willingly assumed a position of far-reaching power in their new government. During his first visit (August-October 1873) he promised all things to all people and on the most vexed question of land alienation he diplomatically called a moratorium of a year before any commission should be set up. The prospect of American annexation before the completion of the year was widely anticipated by the foreign residents, among whom the assiduously spread rumour had been welcomed. In two months Steinberger succeeded in gaining the approval of the Samoans, the foreign residents, the Godeffroy company and the missionaries, both Roman Catholic and LMS, to his cause. But on his return to Apia in April 1875, without any documents for American annexation, everyone looked to him to execute his contradictory promises. The foreign residents soon became disillusioned, questioned his status with the United States government and finally with missionary approval (the missionaries had also been disappointed in their expectations), they combined to effect his downfall. With the aid of the meddlesome British Captain Stevens this was achieved in January 1876 amid determined Samoan opposition, and the town reverted to the inadequacies of consular rule.[15]

In 1876 and 1877 several of the fortune seekers and agitators who had lived in Levuka before annexation found the formalities of colonial rule most uncongenial. The confusion and lack of organised government, under which they had previously thrived in Fiji, now attracted them to Apia, where they continued to prosper.

The whites [in Apia] are mostly riff-raff of a very low order; and in short, the Samoa of today is simply a reproduction of what Fiji was before annexation. Many of the scamps who are now working its strings are the identical men who, finding Fiji no longer a happy land of misrule, have just moved on to the next group, there to repeat the intrigues of their previous life.[16]

The ensuing political and economic unrest in which the consuls inevitably became involved led Arthur Hamilton Gordon, the first governor of Fiji, and also responsible for British subjects in the neighbouring island groups, to intervene and expedite the establishment of a municipal government for Apia in September 1879. Within the municipality, which included the township of Apia and several adjacent Samoan villages but excluded the Mulinuu peninsula, the three consuls of America, Britain and Germany gained unprecedented power. The foreign settlement became in fact a self-governing enclave in which the Samoan government had no effective role. In addition to this deprivation of power, international treaties between Samoa and Great Britain, the United States and Germany gave the foreign residents complete control of Apia harbour and exempted them from paying any import or export taxes. Understandably the Samoans were hostile towards the municipal act and the new treaties which stripped them of a substantial portion of their revenue and virtually annulled their sovereignty over an important part of Samoa.[17]

By the 1870s the Imperialist impulse in Europe, the colonies and even in America was undoubtedly stronger than it had been in the 1840s, the period of the Hawaiian development discussed above. Thus events in Fiji and Samoa during the 1870s were greatly influenced by international rivalries and ambitions which consuls and foreign residents manipulated as well as typified. But despite the difference in foreign attitudes between the 1840s and the 1870s, the effect of the increase in foreign population and of the proliferation of their commercial and political interests on the Hawaiian, Fijian and Samoan governments was very similar. In all three groups foreign expansion resulted in the diminution of island sovereignty either in fact or in practice. Political movements and pressure groups originated and had their greatest influence in the beach communities, where the concentration of expatriate population and financial investment led the foreigners to assert their rights and demand reforms in government. Isolated on plantations in the outer islands, foreigners soon realised the necessity of conforming, at least superficially, to island standards, but this did not prevent them from being compensatingly vocal and antagonistic towards island authority once they returned to their protective port town. Honolulu's foreign residents welcomed French intervention in support of Roman Catholicism in 1839, precipitated the judicial crises of 1840-1, and throughout the late 1830s and early 1840s were clamorous for freehold title to their land. International recognition of Hawaiian independence did not solve the Hawaiians' difficulties, but rather left the foreigners undisturbed to manipulate the newly formed, Western-style government in their own interests. Attempts to establish quasi-democratic style governments in Fiji in the 1860s and 1870s benefited neither Cakobau nor the foreigners. In 1871 the Levuka residents accepted a king and government, but later opposed it when it overspent its budget, and sought to annul it when its ministers pursued policies inimical to their interests. The resultant chaos, plus great financial difficulties, was only resolved by annexation. In Apia the removal of Steinberger who, whatever his faults, had done much to create a workable system of Samoan authority, multiplied difficulties and left the community open to renewed agitation from the CPLCC agents and the recalcitrants from Levuka. The municipal government treaty of 1879 virtually denied the Samoans any powers or control over the Apia area, while it left the foreign residents free to foment factionalism among the Samoan chiefs and to interfere disruptively in Samoan affairs.

Political unrest among the islanders and foreigners made it increasingly difficult for island and consular authorities to impose law and order in the port towns. In Honolulu until the mid 1830s, juries for the trial of foreign defendants were composed of an equal number of foreign residents and Hawaiians, but these were gradually superseded by consular courts with all foreign jurors, who were usually selected from a government list of respectable residents. After Laplace's visit in 1839 even this shred of control was stripped from the Hawaiian government, and consuls became solely responsible for the entire proceedings of foreign trials, including the selection of jurors. In these new courts the passage of justice was sometimes obstructed by national hostilities and refusal to co-operate, but most cases were settled, to foreign satisfaction at least. Minor crimes were still handled by Hawaiian authorities, often without recourse to the jury system. Visiting sailors guilty of disturbing the peace found Governor Kekuanaoa rigorous in inflicting punishments. Lieutenant Wilkes, while upholding the governor's authority, complained in Honolulu in 1840 that one of his sailors had been punished for his part in a brawl in an arbitrary and most informal way, a fine and twenty-eight lashes having been inflicted. Kekuanaoa refused to admit Wilkes's complaint, maintaining that the meeting to impose the punishment had been honestly conducted. The differences of cultural background influenced the two men's attitude to justice: in the American's eyes no punishment could be considered legal without a properly constituted trial with sworn witnesses.[18] Kekuanaoa's extrajudicial methods of dispensing justice similarly concerned Honolulu's foreign residents, who were intransigent in their efforts to remove all judicial procedures involving foreigners out of Hawaiian control.

The process of justice in Levuka was greatly impeded by the British consul's lack of magisterial powers, and that in a population which was of predominantly British origins. I. M. Brower, J. B. Williams's successor to the American post, had been granted full magisterial rights, which meant that at least transactions between American subjects in Levuka could be made binding. Lacking such power the British consul, Edward March (in office 1869-73), obstructed the Fijian government attempts to establish law courts, warned British subjects that allegiance to the Cakobau government would deprive them of their rights as British citizens and did nothing to discipline a coterie of British agitators who advocated lynch law and at times practised it in a mild form. The diehard British malcontents refused to recognise the legality of the Levuka police court, constituted by the Cakobau government in October 1871, and when thwarted in an attempt to undermine it, they stormed the jail and released a British prisoner. After a series of meetings and an improvised trial the man, who had confessed, was found guilty and taken to March at the British Consulate where it was hoped he could be held until the next H.M. naval vessel arrived — thus by-passing the Levuka court entirely. But March, who had done nothing to restrain the British subjects involved in these proceedings, was not prepared for this development. He refused to meet the deputation with the prisoner, who was finally returned to the government jail — the only prison establishment in town. Despite this anti-climax the residents maintained they had acted constitutionally and had proved the Levuka court illegal and unnecessary.[19]

Despite the lawless activities of this group of recalcitrants, who were loudly condemned by the majority of residents, Levuka did not succumb to rowdyism for any length of time. The unprecedented expansion of the port in 1870 and the failure of the cotton crop in 1871 combined to make the latter year crucial for the maintenance of justice in the group. The romantically inclined Earl of Pembroke found Levuka society in 1871 as pleasant, orderly and often as clever as any he had ever met, but he was convinced that the continued rush of fortune-seeking foreigners would inevitably end in disorder.[20] Litton Forbes, also in Levuka in 1871, emphasised the difficulties which faced the town: 'In 1871 the numbers of this semi-criminal class in the islands had increased to such an extent that the very name of Fiji was looked on in Sydney and Melbourne with loathing and contempt. "Gone to Fiji" bore the same significance in Australia as "Gone to Texas" did in America a few years ago'.[21]

Disputes among the British subjects over accounts, breaches of promise or faulty land transactions were settled all too frequently by club law. Debts, which were notoriously hard to collect, were customarily squared away by debtor and creditor fighting it out in the rotunda behind Manton's hotel. A swaggering, arrogant attitude was adopted by many foreigners in Levuka. Public protest meetings, held in the local hotels to condemn the government or the disgraceful state of the main street, became weekly events — to the undoubted benefit of the publicans who were accused by more than one cynical observer of promoting the meetings in the first place. The planters moved along the beach in gangs known as the 'Taveuni Lords, Nandi Swells and the Rewa Roughs', followed by their labour boys, but single-handed duels or combat were the extent of their belligerence and courage. In fact despite the disreputable nature of many of Levuka's new residents Forbes was forced to admit that the community was essentially English and intent on making money. Even the Ku Klux Klan and the members of the British Subjects' Mutual Protection Society, who were sworn to overthrow the government, never were a party to, or encouraged any major crime.[22] By 1874 the town was as peaceful as it had been in the years before 1871: 'I had heard so much of the rowdyism and ruffianism at Levuka that I was surprised to find it during the whole of my stay as quiet and orderly as a town in England'.[23] Between 1870 and 1874 there were sporadic incidents of rowdyism but serious crimes were exceptional. Probably the most disturbing crime committed in Levuka was the assault with vitriol on an amateur actress, Mrs Vernon, who was severely burned.

Until 1877 the mixed and consular courts of Apia were able to dispense such justice as the community required, except in 1875 when they were temporarily superseded by the Steinberger government courts. In 1877, however, amid intense political intrigue between the residents and the Samoans, renewed attempts were made by the successors to the CPLCC claims to realise their investment. The resultant struggle attracted a number of free-booters from Fiji, including a one-time leading member of Cako-bau's last government. The British and American consuls, who were again in hostile opposition, broke open warehouses sealed off by the other and generally encouraged and participated in a wave of illegal activities that brought much of Apia's business to a stand-still. Only the German residents, whose land claims, concentrated in the hands of the Godeffroy manager, were less controversial, remained aloof and largely unaffected by the lawlessness and com-mercial chaos that convulsed the rest of the population: in many ways this outbreak was reminiscent of the Van Camp fracas in 1855-6. Alarmed by the vandalism and impending anarchy, the old established residents of Apia petitioned Edward Liardet, British consul, in June 1877 to deport the worst offenders in an effort to stop the prevalent 'spirit of ruffianism and utter lawlessness' from spreading.[24] But violence and commercial skulduggery continued until intervention from Governor Gordon became essential, after the lynching of an American, Cochrane, in November 1877.

Cochrane pleaded guilty to the unintentional murder of a sailor, James Cox, when drunk. The fatal brawl had occurred at William Henry's notorious shanty saloon, between two men who had never seen each other before. (It is highly probable that both were visit-ing sailors in no way connected with the other disturbances on the beach.) Having been found guilty by an American consular court, Cochrane was put on board a vessel without guards, to be trans-ported to the United States. At a meeting of more than 80 per cent of Apia's foreign residents straight after the trial, it was decided that the immediate punishment of Cochrane on shore would have a salutory effect on the riotous beach elements, who had become increasingly violent and uncontrollable during this period of widespread disorder. Cochrane was hanged that night in the presence of many foreign residents, including the medical missionary, Dr G. A. Turner.[25] Later reports of the incident by par-ticipants and others stressed their awareness of the enormity of the act in normal circumstances, but claimed that in a town riven by dissension, without law courts or police, the measure was essential to maintain law and order. Even Consul Liardet argued:

I believe, my Lord, it would be injudicious to visit any punish-

ment on Mr Pritchard [chairman of the lynch meeting]*, who
has acted under force of circumstances, and which action has
indirectly produced a quieter feeling among the community, who
had been previously so disturbed by the lawless acts committed
by the agitators who came here from Fiji.[26]
With the deaths of the British consul, Liardet, and the principal
CPLCC agitator, J. M. Stewart, early in 1878 and the arrival of
Governor Gordon in Apia a modicum of commercial and social
order was re-established. The sources of potential discord in Apia,
however, had not decreased; no final judgment about land rights
had been given and the scope for political intrigue was not lessened
by the Municipal Act, introduced the following year.

Against this background of political upheaval and legal uncertainty, the tempo of social life in beach communities fluctuated
from unrestrained enthusiasm to utter despair as each pet project
followed its mercurial course. Even in Honolulu, which was not as
disturbed as Levuka and Apia in later years, residents became
closely identified with one rival clique or another and their suspicious competitiveness kept society in a perpetual state of tension.
Revisiting Honolulu in 1839, R. B. Hinds found that:

> There is a want of conciliation which give rise to numerous
> differences when we arrived the families were much divided,
> and presented numerous shades of hostility, sometimes they did
> not visit but spoke when meeting at a third person; sometimes,
> a coolness existed at all times, and here and there they were in
> the most decided hostility. Even we as strangers found a little
> tact necessary in stearing among these social breakers.[27]

Even residents who attempted to ignore these divisions found
themselves affected by the febrile atmosphere.

> The old fashioned quietude of domestic life, here, seems much
> interrupted by continual excitement. You cannot imagine what a
> bustle an arrival produces — or any trifling affairs — I do feel
> it injurious to anyone, who lives upon excitement. It is an
> artificial stimulus, giving vivacity, and cheerfulness to the de-
> pressed, and lonely; however, it is the order of the day, and I
> do not consider myself free from its influence.[28]

* Mr George Pritchard was son of the former British consul, George
Pritchard and a brother of W. T. Pritchard.

Late in November 1872 the mayor of Levuka and the British consul brawled publicly on the beach over a matter which could easily have been settled more peaceably and privately.[29] Isolated, vulnerable and subject to boredom, many of the foreign residents placed undue importance on the minutiae of daily life and over-reacted to any chance remark or new development.

While port town society was periodically convulsed by the latest scandal or rumour, much of the rough frontier atmosphere familiar in the early beach communities was giving way to more conventional standards of living. The arrival of a number of expatriate women was the most influential single factor in this process, but white women *per se* were no guarantee of respectability. In Levuka Mrs Craig of the Balmain Hotel, situated in the Fijian town of Levuka Vakaviti, was fined for repeatedly selling liquor to the Fijians, in defiance of the law. The majority of women, however, brought with them the attitudes and many of the movable attributes of Western civilisation. Upright pianos, silver salvers, visiting cards and elegant clothing, all became part of the social ritual in Levuka and Honolulu. In the presence of the newly arrived women some of the older residents in Levuka became aware of their lack of polish and lapses from Western standards. They admitted that: 'obscene language [was] used in the hearing of the gentle-nutured females', but they argued: 'We are yet too new to have worn out altogether the influences on men of weak minds, created by habits of self indulgence, savage communion, and long severance from the restraints and usages of society'. In April 1872 twenty-four Levuka gentlemen expressed their appreciation to Mrs Perrin for her admirable conduct when she slapped a man's face on his refusal to give up his seat to a lady: 'We . . . present you with this brooch as a token of our admiration of your pluck in doing what was the duty of every gentleman present to do'.[30] Men in Honolulu re-entered mixed society without such an effort:

We have now quite a different state of society lately — so many ladies that the parties are really interesting, on every Wednesday eve' we have what are called free easy's or converzaciones [sic] given by the ladies alternately and everyone to call during the evening and go when they please without ceremony — they are really very pleasant.[31]

Few women would countenance an island-built house, however cool or suited to the climate. In Honolulu the pleasant New England style mission houses were copied by many of the wealthy Americans who followed later. Others built in wood or stone according to their means. In Levuka and Apia the predominantly colonial populations had no comparable tradition of attractive domestic architecture to draw upon and also little experience of tropical conditions: 'The people who have gone to Fiji have no idea of the construction of houses suited for a warm climate. They build these shantys as they would build them on some Australian gold field; and they furnish them as if they were in England'.[32] In 1874 Miss Gordon Cumming, accustomed to expatriate British life in India, was more outspoken about the discomfort of Levuka houses:

As to the houses, they are all alike hideous, being built of wood (weatherboard is the word), and roofed with corrugated iron or zinc, on which the mad tropical rains pour with deafening noise; or else the burning sun beats so fiercely as well-nigh to stifle the inmates, to whom the luxuries of punkahs and ice are unknown.[33]

Hotels and stores were built with a similar lack of amenities and comfort.

Individual weatherboard houses, which tended to symbolise both social and racial differences in beach communities, were only one index of the greater exclusiveness among foreign residents. Within several such houses complete expatriate families could be found divorced from the indigenous and part-islander populations by wealth, property and ideology. Mixed racial marriages and liaisons became increasingly unacceptable in the merchant class. Ambitious young merchants in Honolulu returned to the States to choose wives, since: 'having a regular wife perhaps may look a little better in the eyes of respectable strangers'.[34] For those unable to afford the time or money for the voyage home to New England, there was a chance to catch one of the single American girls who demurely ventured out to the islands, frequently under the wing of a missionary family. Their investment in a one way passage was usually quickly rewarded by marriage. 'By the Helles-

pont [July 1833] is a contingent of 2 young ladies which are to be
disposed of to those who bid highest for wives. A few good looking girls might sell well'.[35] In Levuka, hoteliers with an eye for
business brought in attractive barmaids from the colonies. A girl
with any looks at all could be guaranteed five or six offers of
marriage in her first six months.[36] Planters who had Fijian or
part-Fijian wives were careful to keep them discreetly in the
background when they were visited by other Europeans.

With the advent of white women, a number of new entertainments appeared. Balls and informal dancing, picnics and mixed
concerts became part of the daily round. These did not necessarily
increase white exclusiveness, but few islanders were at home at such
gatherings and the tendency was towards segregation. As soon as
sufficient women were present dancing was taken up with
enthusiasm. The arrival of a naval vessel — the Americans often
with their own band — led to a whirl of parties and dinners given
by and for the visiting personnel. Officers and men fresh from the
civilised world found the communities unskilled in the latest dancing fashions, even in Honolulu, the most advanced port town:
'There was some dancing, but little waltzing as there is few or
none of the residents (men) who can, and the officers waltzed so
very fast the ladies found great difficulty in keeping time with
them'.[37] Jigs, reels and highland flings were still being danced in
Apia in 1872.

Among the Pacific islanders, the Hawaiian chiefs had adapted
themselves more fully to Western life than any others. Between
1836, when dancing became a permanent social feature in Honolulu, and 1843, Kamehameha III and his court were among
invited guests at balls and dinner parties, particularly on board
naval vessels. But the foreigners taxed them with 'great listlessness,
and want of conversation' and they were sometimes excluded from
residents' functions ashore.[38] By the 1870s, when dancing became
an established pastime in Levuka, white attitudes towards coloured
people had taken on a distinctly racist tone, which was evident in
Fiji as it was elsewhere in the colonial world at that time. The
Tongan chief, Ma'afu, and the Fijian chief, Judge Marika, were
both invited to different Levuka balls and accepted, but their
presence was exceptional in a society more exclusive than Honolulu
had ever been. At a Levuka fancy dress ball in early January

1872: 'Every preparation for the comfort of the guests had been made, by a fence to make the premises private and so to exclude the natives from window views'.[39] Picnics also became a strictly expatriate entertainment in Levuka, while in Honolulu and Apia they were more frequently mixed affairs. On 25 November 1842 Kamehameha III gave a picnic (*luau*) at his house in the Nuuanu Valley. Forty to fifty foreign residents, missionaries and Hawaiians attended the Hawaiian style meal, eaten on the ground.[40]

Amateur theatricals came into fashion in Honolulu about the same time as dancing, both much to the disapproval of the missionaries, Diell and the pious trader, Brinsmade. The members of the Oahu Dramatic Club, which was established in 1834, favoured the last scenes from famous plays interspersed with songs and comic sketches rather than full-length, serious dramas. Talent was drawn from among the young clerks and a few of the merchants in the town, but all the ladies and a large number of Hawaiians were present at their performances. Despite good attendances the club accumulated $300 worth of debts in its first six months and collapsed completely in 1836. By the 1870s ladies were more willing to appear on stage, so the Levuka theatrical company, established in 1871, could offer diversified programs to their mixed audiences. Dramatic entertainment was predominantly of the Grand Concert style with excerpts from operas and plays, full-length works seldom being performed. But again as in Honolulu enthusiasm within the club fluctuated greatly, debts mounted and it did not become permanent.[41]

Self-improving clubs of different kinds appeared during this stage of development in Honolulu, Apia and Levuka. The Sandwich Island Institute, founded in Honolulu in 1837, was designed along the same lines as the Mercantile Library Association in New York. It boasted a library and a cabinet of curiosities, but its major activity was fortnightly lectures, given by leading foreign residents to other foreign males. At Levuka the Mutual Improvement Club, started in August 1872, was transformed into the Levuka Mechanics Institute a year later, in keeping with educational fashions in the colonies. Lectures and debates on educational and moral subjects were the basic activities, but a reading room, chess club, painting and choral lessons, and even classes in Fijian, were organised. Apart from its' self-improvement institute, Apia had no formally established societies until the 1880s.[42] Political intrigue dominated the foreigners' activities throughout the 1870s, while the small population with relatively few females limited the scope of dramatic or choral entertainment, and the incentive to arrange it.

The pinnacle of social development was the inauguration of Masonic Lodges. The first lodge in the Pacific, Lodge le Progrés de L'Océanie, was established in Honolulu in 1843 by French and American merchants. In Apia the brethren were called to a preliminary meeting in December 1877 but nothing further eventuated.[43] The first attempt to establish a lodge in Levuka early in 1871 also failed owing to personal differences, but by the end of the year the Free and Accepted Masons of Polynesia were ready for initiation: 'The Regalia and requisite paraphernalia having arrived from Sydney, the above Lodge will be opened in due form and according to ancient custom and pristine usage, on Wednesday, 27th December (St John's Day) at high twelve'.[44] Despite proscription early in 1872, owing to a confusion with the Ku Klux Klan, and a difficulty over a charter, the lodge, unlike the other clubs and societies, kept the interest of its members, held regular meetings and is still functioning today.

The pioneer island newspapers, which appeared with the increase in foreign population and the expansion of economic interests, played an important role in reinforcing residents' group identity and exclusiveness, and fostering a sense of community among them. In all three ports the first attempts at publication were hindered by the lack of skilled printers, the irregular supply of suitable paper and inks, and the failure to gain sufficient financial support from the relatively small commercial interests the newspapers served. Despite these problems pioneer island newspapers were published in the following years:

Honolulu *Sandwich Island Gazette* 1836-9
Sandwich Island Mirror 1839-40
Polynesian 1840-1
The Friend 1843- (this was a Bethel publication)
Levuka *Fiji Weekly News and Planters' Journal* 1868
Fiji Times 1869-
Fiji Gazette and Central Polynesian 1871-4
Fiji Argus 1874-6

Apia   *Samoan Reporter* 1845-70   (this   was   published
       quarterly by the missionaries)
       Samoa Times 1877-81

Only the *Fiji Times,* which succeeded the *Fiji Weekly News and Planters' Journal* in 1869, became a permanent publication and is still published today in Suva.

Despite their short lives and intermittent appearance the newspapers covered local economic conditions and reported movements on the world markets as they were received. In their pages public entertainments and dates for club and lodge meetings were widely advertised. Editorials and leader articles brought to the residents' attention the dangerous and unsanitary state of the community. Through newpaper advocacy fire brigades were established, bridges were made more secure, committees to improve the state of cemeteries were set up and some effort was made to ensure efficient sewage disposal and rubbish collection. The predominant characteristic of the pioneer island newspapers was their prompting and encouragement of all efforts to replace the raw squalor of beach community life with the amenities, and even some of the niceties, of the civilised world.

Like the clubs and societies, however, attempts by editors to improve community conditions were met with momentary enthusiasm followed by inertia and unconcern. Most foreigners agreed with editorial condemnations, but effective action was difficult to organise and almost impossible to sustain. In Honolulu several attempts were made to tidy up the major business and residential area, but in 1840 the streets were still ankle deep in dust, or mud depending on the season, and offal: 'In some places, offensive sink-holes strike the senses, in which are seen wallowing some old and corpulent pigs'.[45] Despite repeated warnings in the *Fiji Times* that rotting matter would increase the likelihood of dysentery and other infections, Levuka's health officer Dr Ryley reported in January 1873 that cesspools were everywhere in use and offensive piggeries and fowl yards were built very close to houses: 'From the inequalities of the ground stagnant water is sometimes found in back yards, and slop water in a putrid state . . . and to complete the picture, we sometimes find mole hills of rubbish, offal, and filth indescribable, reeking and seething after rain in a broiling sun'.[46] In time basic safety and sanitary precautions were taken but the tendency to revert to former conditions was always present. Little was done to install more general public facilities. A scattering of kerosene lights was put up in much frequented places and in Honolulu in 1843 the maze of pot-holed, dust or mud lanes was transformed into a modern grid of wide streets crossing at right angles. But the editors' dreams of well built jetties, gardens and squares in Levuka and Apia had to await annexation and were realised in Honolulu only after the problems of land, labour and other aspects of expatriate development had been dealt with.

The diminished rapport between foreigners and islanders that had survived the arrival of the consuls was further undermined by the greater political, economic and social complexity which overtook the port towns in later years. Political control, which had devolved first upon foreign consuls, was subsequently transferred to filibusters or foreign-born ministers and parliamentary representatives in island governments. Some of the latter were anxious to safeguard island rights, but their attempts were nearly always compromised to a greater or lesser extent by their desire to maintain their own positions, or by the activities of other self-seeking Europeans. Major economic enterprises were controlled by foreign personnel, capital and knowledge. While the early sandalwood, bêche-de-mer and coconut oil traders had worked in close contact with the islanders upon whose co-operation and labour they were dependent, the later cotton growers, land speculators and company merchants avoided island contact and control as much as possible. Similarly in society the foreigners became more exclusive. Balls, picnics and sports days frequently barred the islanders and sometimes the part-islanders, while in most of the clubs, including the Levuka Lodge, and even in some churches, segregation was an established fact. Efforts to improve living standards and bring an aura of civilisation to the ports reinforced these exclusive tendencies. Fear of fire led to the prohibition of island-built houses in the heart of beach communities, and in an attempt to improve the facilities of the natural, fresh water bathing pools in Levuka one was set aside for white use only.[47] Visions of wide plantations, wealth and power divorced the majority of Europeans from the islanders, whose land was required, and basic rights and freedoms denied. The beach communities were transformed into small scale Western port towns which became the organising centres for foreign political and economic aggrandisement. No longer was there any identity of interest between islander and foreigner — the latter demanded, and increasingly enjoyed, supremacy in all spheres, political, economic and social.

eight

Race Relations in the Beach Communities

The growth and development of the beach communities, due largely to the rise in foreign and island populations and the expansion of expatriate economic and political interests, inevitably led to increased tension between the multi-racial settlers.[1] In an attempt to analyse the patterns of island/foreign relations in the port towns during the early years, it is necessary to go back and discuss the different expatriate groups that arrived, their aims, ambitions and the particular prejudices or predispositions they brought with them. But firstly, on a very general level, it is important to realise that inherent in any inter-cultural situation is the possibility of conflict over rival economic and social interests or over concepts of leadership and legal rights. Further Western penetration of the islands of Polynesia and Fiji, as in any non-industrialised area, was characterised by a number of developments which had a profound effect on race relations despite the fact that the processes themselves were largely impersonal. The introduction of a number of manufactured goods, superior to corresponding items of island design, led to the acceptance and use of many. Traditional skills were gradually lost and the islanders found themselves dependent on foreign goods, and obliged to furnish supplies or services in exchange for them.[2] Thus from the earliest beginnings of the beach communities the islanders were continually adapting to new circumstances, while their dependence on goods of Western manufacture undermined their political authority. Opposition to any foreign development was always compromised to a certain extent by this dependence.

With the arrival of European explorers in the Pacific the islanders recognised, perforce, the existence of peoples with completely different racial and cultural backgrounds and with certain highly attractive material goods. The subsequent development of relations between the two groups was directly affected by the goals of the European immigrants who settled in the islands. The slow but perceptible increase in tension in the beach communities during the pre-colonial years can be analysed in terms of the pressures of competition between island and foreign interests. Mutual feelings of intolerance, misunderstanding and straightforward opposition multiplied in the port towns in proportion to the various demands made upon the islanders' land, labour and ways of life by incoming groups of Europeans. Given this premise it is not surprising to discover that relations between the islanders and beachcombers were noted for their ease and harmony. The beachcombers, the first representatives of the Western world to settle for any time in the islands, were insignificant in terms of numbers and had no grandiose ambitions to change island life. Most were happy to be accepted into an island society and to be offered a wife or consort. Dependent on an island chief and his people for food, shelter and a livelihood, the onus was most definitely on the beachcomber to do everything in his power to integrate his ways into those of the dominant population. Even at this stage, however, the islanders found it necessary to modify their behaviour a little in deference to the whites, who had the knowledge to use and mend much of the new equipment introduced, and to tolerate the beachcombers' lack of knowledge of correct behaviour, since they were a source of European goods. The islanders quickly learnt that acts of cannibalism, even upon other islanders, did not ingratiate them with foreigners, and sometimes frightened trading vessels away.

In Fiji in the late 1840s a beachcomber, Saunders, abused all the rules of hospitality, insulted the chief, who was his host, lowered him in the eyes of his people, spoke in his disfavour to visiting shipmasters and ill-treated a woman. A letter was thereupon written for the chief concerned, Cakanauto, to J. B. Williams, newly appointed American commercial agent: 'I do not choose [that] he should remain any longer on the Island of Nukulau but for your sake who have prevailed with me to let him have his woman again, and for me not to treat him harshly, I am willing not only to help him move all his goods but my people shall build him a house on some other land round the Harbour'.[3]

Cakanauto refused to tolerate Saunders's presence any longer, but he was still concerned to remain on good terms with J. B. Williams, who had close dealings with the Salem bêche-de-mer traders — an important source of Cakanauto's wealth and power. For this reason, perhaps, Cakanauto was prepared to help Saunders to move away from Nukulau. In Samoa a European who deliberately ignored island custom was not punished by the chiefs, but regarded as someone of no breeding who could not be expected to do or know better.

The traders' designs on the islanders were more extensive than the beachcombers', but while in theory they hoped that a wide range of Western goods would be rapidly incorporated into island economies, in practice the traders found the islanders extremely selective in the items they would accept, and fully capable of keeping the prices of their own produce high. Only during the earliest stages of contact was it possible for the traders to indulge in fraudulent or highly exploitative practices to sell their goods, and frequently even at that time their tricks rebounded upon themselves. Once the traders were permanent members of a beach community shady dealing from either side occurred less and less frequently. Increasingly Western goods formed an essential part of indigenous society, while on the other hand traders became closely associated with island life through their newly acquired wives: a relationship mutually beneficial to both islander and trader emerged. Like the beachcomber, the trader still had to ingratiate himself with the leaders of his host society and had to keep abreast of the islanders' fast-changing wants. The American agent J. B. Williams never seemed satisfied with the trade goods sent to him by his brother in New England. Inevitably the time lapse between Williams's requests for new goods and their arrival was more than sufficient for the Fijians to have changed their desires.[4] Similarly in Honolulu, J. C. Jones found himself over-supplied with goods no longer attractive to the Hawaiians: 'I wish our gunpowder, guns, pots and kettles would assume the form of blue cloth, and I think we should be able to turn it into Sandallwood'.[5] The goods and knowledge introduced by the traders and beachcombers were to have profound repercussions on island societies but in the early years this influence was partially balanced by the islanders' numerical predominance, their control over most food production and their selectivity when bartering.

It was the missionaries, the third component in early beach communities, whose attitudes and plans seemed to pose a real threat to good community relations. Theologically they were bound to give doctrinal support to the equality of all races, but their assumptions concerning the superiority of Western civilisation as well as Christianity made them very intolerant of island culture. Years after their arrival there were still some missionaries (from all denominations and parts of the world) who could discuss the islanders of their close acquaintance in terms of 'darkness', 'lust', 'stupidity' and 'total lack of gratitude'. Unadulterated, this intolerance and abysmal lack of understanding could have created very unpleasant relations, but their effect was counterbalanced by the missionaries' dependence on the islanders for protection and sustenance, and their desire to attract island souls to Christianity. Neither coercion nor discrimination was suitable in such a context. The islanders' gradual acceptance of Christianity, which appeared to offer access to a more powerful god in material, military and medical terms than traditional gods, further neutralised the intolerant aspects of the missionaries' beliefs, and relations between the two became predominantly easy.

The reactions and the balance of interests between island authorities, foreign traders and evangelising missionaries during the early stages of development is well illustrated in R. A. Cruise's description of relations between the Maori and the foreigners in the Bay of Islands area in 1820. The British vessel, *Dromedary,* which had transported convicts to New South Wales, anchored in the Bay of Islands in February 1820 to take on a cargo of kauri spars for its return voyage to England. For ten long months the captain, who refused to trade muskets, had to negotiate with the Maori chiefs of the Bay of Islands and Hokianga over the availability of trees, and Maori labour to fell them. The presence in the Bay throughout most of the period of at least one or two whalers, who had no such trading scruples, often left the *Dromedary* without provisions or an incoming cargo. The CMS missionaries, who had been settled in the area for six years, had had minimal success in interesting the Maori in the benefits of Christianity or Western civilising arts. Like the crew of the *Dromedary* the mission was dependent on the Maori for food, and also for protection, which left them open to continual petty depredations and insults. Clearly the Maori were in control of the situation and manipulated the traders and missionaries alike. Symptomatic of their confidence in their own civilisation and power at this time was the anger of one chief whose daughter was living with a young deserter from the *Dromedary*. When the captain captured the youth and forced him back on board, the chief threatened to kill any *Dromedary* crew member he found in his territory. 'He continued to express his astonishment that the white men should prevent the union of one of their body with his daughter, whom he considered far superior in rank to any individual holding a subordinate situation in the Dromedary [that is anyone below the captain]'.[6]

The Maori believed themselves to be in complete control of the situation and except on the level of internal ship's discipline, they certainly were. But Cruise stresses towards the end of his narrative that throughout their stay individual Maori proved most hospitable and generous, Maori women lived on board the ship during the ten months, single sailors on shore were never molested and ultimately a complete cargo was collected without recourse to a trade in muskets. While patience amongst the British was essential, the trade was finally adjusted to the satisfaction of both partners. The balance of power lay with the Maori, about that there was no question, but the allure of Western goods was sufficient to make them participate, admittedly somewhat grudgingly, in the timber trade, especially when other trading opportunities were not open to them.

Power, such as the Maori enjoyed in the Bay of Islands in 1820, and other islanders had during the early stages of contact, was not permanent. The continual growth and diversification of island demands combined with increased foreign settlement and trade, undermined the islanders' former position. In 1844 Cakobau exiled the foreigners at Levuka, apparently without second thought, but when he realised that he had severed his most reliable connection with Western goods, especially firearms, and that the very fighting strength which had enabled him to intimidate the foreigners was endangered, he quickly reversed his decision. Unconcerned with Cakobau's dilemma, the foreigners refused to return to Levuka immediately, but when, five years later, they finally agreed, they found the chief very willing to accommodate them. By the mid 1840s in Fiji power was more delicately balanced between islander and foreigner than it had been in New Zealand twenty years earlier. In the early beach communities influence and interest fluctuated between the foreign residents and the islanders. Without external support or protection the foreigners were usually in no position to question chiefly decisions concerning rates of exchange, the availability of island wives or land ownership, but on the other hand their hosts, eager for manufactured goods, encouraged foreign settlement and were prepared to protect them. This identity of interest and the need for security to maintain stable trading relations helped to establish a basic harmony in the beach communities. Tensions were never eradicated, but while foreign numbers remained small and both sides realised that a breakdown in relations might destroy the settlements completely, the compromise was workable.

With the arrival of consular agents the foreigners believed they had gained considerable influence, and imperceptibly the sources of authority moved out of island control. This did not occur overnight, but once consular agents were established in the beach communities, merchants and traders tended to seek their support over any subsequent difficulty with island authority. In fact the consuls awakened the expectation of Western governmental support and intervention among the foreign residents and offered them an alternative source of security. In succeeding years the chiefs and consuls found themselves competing for the loyalties of the beach residents and the right to control their trading and social activities. Inevitably areas of potential discord expanded between islander and foreigner, as well as within the foreign community, which divided into different national groups with rival interests. However, despite the fact that there were times when national factionalism or the foreigners' refusal to respect island authority threatened to undermine the easy relations established by early settlers, incidents of overt hostility were not long lasting. While the port towns remained basically trading communities a modicum of stability and co-operation was essential; after most outbursts of hostility a semblance of harmony was restored. But new attitudes had infiltrated into the towns and precedents had been set that were to expand into an established expatriate philosophy and outlook when the planters entered the community.

While consular agents were testing the political strength and viability of the chiefs, large company traders were creating a monopoly over the major economic activities in the Pacific. In most mercantile fields, including the bêche-de-mer, pearling and ship-chandlery trades, the islanders lacked the capital and expertise to establish rival trading complexes, while in the provision and coconut oil trades, although they did become major suppliers, the foreigners continued to control the lucrative export markets. From the earliest beginnings of the beach communities island products, especially sandalwood, bêche-de-mer and pearl-shell, were heavily exploited, but their eventual diminution did not seriously affect the islanders. Sources of European goods were diminished but the islanders' land and food supplies were still virtually intact. This situation was to change dramatically with the arrival of planters and land speculators—the very bases of island life were threatened and the islanders found themselves in direct competition with the foreigners who were demanding their land and labour. Although planters and land speculators worked outside the beach communities, the deterioration of race relations consequent upon their activities had serious repercussions on those port towns affected by them. In Hawaii, large-scale plantation agriculture was not successfully established until the 1850s and 1860s, well after the period discussed in this book. Similarly in Tahiti plantation agriculture was insignificant before annexation, while in New Zealand very few settlers had taken up farming before Britain took possession of it. The activities of the large number of land speculators who plagued New Zealand after 1836 did little to affect race relations either in Kororareka or beyond at this time, since few buyers actually settled on their land or started to develop it. Fiji suffered from an influx of prospective cotton planters between 1865 and 1871, while Samoa was troubled by land speculators in 1872-3 and in the following two decades by their attempts to have their land claims officially verified.

The majority of cotton planters in Fiji between 1865 and 1871 looked upon Levuka as the centre of commerce and social life, the stronghold of the foreign population and the forum of foreign dissatisfaction and vocal dissent. During the boom years, however, Levuka was essentially the centre of entertainment and hospitality. Little thought was given at this time to Fijian opposition over land sales and refusal to work as plantation labour. But with the failure of the cotton industry in Fiji in 1871 the patronising self-assurance of former years gave way to bitter frustration. Many bankrupt planters were forced to leave their land and take refuge in Levuka. There, with other foreign malcontents who had suffered in the financial collapse, they intrigued against the Cakobau government and sought to undermine it. Other planters clung to the hope that the cotton industry could be revived, but they still used the columns of the *Fiji Times* to denounce the government, and refused to submit to it: 'We [planters], who are making Fiji at the risk of life and health; daring all, and enduring all, are to pay for the flummery of Royalty in our midst, while those of the savage monarchs own despicable race who are land owners, as we are, shall be allowed to hold lands free of tax?'[7] These reactions to financial embarrassment and failure were not peculiar to Levuka. In all beach communities any commercial difficulty or embarrassment suffered by the Europeans caused discord. It brought into the open latent attitudes and expressions of white superiority. Rather than analyse their failure in terms of the relevant commercial and climatic factors, many Europeans preferred to blame everything on the laziness, stupidity and obstinacy of the islanders.

In Levuka, where the cotton collapse was perhaps the most severely felt economic failure in the pre-colonial port towns, the most aggressive and racist organisations appeared: at first the Ku Klux Klan established in 1872, followed by the British Subjects' Mutual Protection Society. Despite its name the former was not responsible for any lynchings. In fact both societies limited their activities in Levuka to voluminous newspaper correspondence and unarmed scuffles with other foreigners. There were several incidents between 1871 and 1874 which threatened to divide the town into warring factions, but a compromise was always accepted or forced upon the insurgents before serious hostilities eventuated. In May 1872 the Ku Klux Klan fomented a crisis in Levuka which could have sparked off serious hostilities but for the intervention of Captain Douglas. Again, the riot at Nasova on 5 September 1873, when an unruly mob of British subjects broke through the first picket of Fijians and Tongans guarding Cakobau's house and fired on a second group of island soldiers, could have ended in a racist war, if Captain Simpson had not been able to pacify both sides.[8] Despite this reoccurring ground swell of frustrated, often racist activity, which was largely directed against the Cakobau government — the only visible source of authority — there were still a number of people in Levuka who persisted in pointing out the weakness of the Europeans' position and the inadvisability of exacerbating the Fijians further. Their arguments were usually weighted in terms of expediency, particularly to facilitate British annexation, rather than in any belief in racial equality or fairness: 'It is always to our interest to conciliate the natives, and more especially so at the present time, when we want their co-operation in the interests of annexation'.[9] But at least there was an element in the population who advocated non-aggressive, if not equal, relations with the Fijians.

In Apia the cessation of land speculating activities in 1873 did not generate the degree of discord and hostility that was caused by the cotton collapse in Fiji. Fewer foreigners were involved in the former enterprise and not more than ten lived for any length of time in the town. Samoan reaction, when they realised the extent of the land that had nominally been sold to foreigners, was horror, and new bitterness towards the residents, a number of whom, including J. C. Williams, had previously assisted them. Between 1873 and 1879 speculators' attempts to make good their land claims caused increasing resentment and political unrest within the town, while their deliberate attempts to foment Samoan factionalism made it impossible for the Samoan chiefs to unite against the foreign community. By 1879 the American consul had no illusions concerning the effect of this foreign intermeddling, but equally clearly he had little sympathy for the Samoans:'I believe the Samoans are utterly incapable of establishing or maintaining any form of Government in the presence of the large foreign interests here, and the determination of the foreign population not to respect or observe the authority of those so far beneath them in culture and intelligence.'[10] Although aware of the foreigners' tactics, the Samoan chiefs were still unable to combat or control them and were thus finally forced in 1879 to relinquish their nominal authority over the multi-racial community in Apia to a municipal government headed by the consuls. By 1874 the Fijian chiefs were similarly incapacitated and forced to accept British protection. Thus in both Apia and Levuka the discord and financial chaos caused by the failure of over-ambitious Europeans were largely responsible for subsequent foreign intervention and the diminution of island power. All semblance of racial equality was lost. Relations between a number of individual islanders and foreigners remained fairly easy, but in Apia and Levuka the Samoans and Fijians became second-class citizens stripped of the influence and position they once enjoyed.

While the activities of company traders, planters and land speculators increased economic and political tensions in the beach communities, the arrival of a significant number of white women, at about the same time, put a further strain on race relations. The hypothesis that the permanent residence of expatriate women in multi-cultural frontier settlements is not conducive to the maintenance of harmonious community relations gains weight from the experience of Fiji and to a lesser extent from that of Samoa, and of Hawaii up to the early 1840s.[11] In these three areas white women, the large majority of whom came as wives, or at the invitation of residents, arrived at a time of rising European economic interests and ambitions. The living styles and liaisons with islanders which had been accepted in earlier years were no longer considered appropriate by men who had visions of substantial mercantile and planting enterprises. Not surprisingly in these new circumstances the expatriates expected their womenfolk to cultivate the civilising arts and domestic comforts which previously they had ignored. Well-defined and rather restricted roles thus awaited the incoming white women, who had little opportunity or reason to make close contacts with island people. On one level they became symbols of the male expatriates' rising status and success, which were so frequently achieved at the expense of the islanders. However, the role that expatriates expected of their women was one to which they were accustomed and probably most women assumed it willingly, feeling little desire to fraternise with the islanders. These women were not imposing unwanted standards on the men nor should they be considered more racially prejudiced than them. Together white couples established living patterns similar to those of their home societies and inevitably community relations suffered in the process.

Competition between island and foreign women accounted for some of the new problems. On their arrival white women immediately felt threatened by the position island girls had made for themselves in the port towns and this encouraged the expatriate females to set up boundaries between themselves and the islanders, and to cling to familiar social standards. They sought to safe-guard their vulnerable positions by denouncing mixed marriages and island style houses, in this way reinforcing their husbands' attitudes. These fears and prejudices isolated white women from islanders of both sexes, and their lack of knowledge and feeling of insecurity led them to criticise their hosts in typically racist generalisations: 'It is certain Samoans hardly know what gratitude means' or 'The natives [the Fijians] are utterly devoid of gratitude, and their character for lying, stealing, and trickery is well known all over the Group'.[12] The conception of the 'other' group in such stereotypic terms, which is characteristic of racial prejudice, was one few white women seemed capable of avoiding.

In Fiji a number of European women arrived during the height of the cotton boom, at a time when the planters believed that fortunes were guaranteed. Congregated together in Levuka these women, many of whom came from Australia and New Zealand, had little knowledge of the Fijians and even less interest in their welfare. Many newly arrived men revealed similar attitudes. The women built up around themselves a replica of colonial society, but they were not alone in insisting on the standards and customs of home. The men were also eager to civilise their ways and offer their women the comforts of a former life; most frequently it was they who demanded improvements on the women's behalf. By mid 1870, when female numbers were rapidly increasing, a jetty for Levuka harbour, which 'old hands' had done without for decades, was suddenly deemed essential, at least by the male editor of the *Fiji Times*. 'Ladies accustomed to the decencies of European life prefer almost any way of getting ashore to being hugged in the arms of a half-naked savage.'[13] Church attendance, in which few Europeans in former days had indulged, was considered an essential Sunday activity for those seeking status and respectability. Of necessity, services were held in both Fijian and English, a language division which was used to enforce racial segregation. At the same time picnics and sports days became exclusively European entertainments. This insidious segregation of social life in Levuka was widespread by late 1870 and had greatly undermined the easy inter-racial contacts of earlier years.

With the hurricane and the fall of cotton prices in 1871 white exclusiveness hardened among many settlers into unrelenting racist hostility. What responsibility lay exclusively with European women for this erosion of understanding cannot be ascertained. But it is clear that the demands and aspirations of the planters put a strain on Fijian-European relations, and the whole tenor of white society, even before the arrival of a significant number of white women, had grown more insistent on expansion and success. By the beginning of 1870 it was widely accepted that the triumph of the planter over the indolent Fijian was only a matter of time:

> There is no help, it appears to me, for the savage; the laws that ordain his disappearance before the civilized man are as certain as those that govern the heavens: too far inferior to us in mind to keep pace with our rapid advance, too far behind ever to hope to overtake us; so long as the two races keep apart all goes well, in a fashion with him, but as soon as civilization encroaches upon savagedom the conditions which seem necessary to his existence change, and the savage, if left to himself, inevitably perishes; bind him to our chariot wheels, and drag him along, in spite of his outcries, and he would live.[14]

The appearance of European women, very few of whom were independent of white men, strengthened and encouraged these visions and stimulated the growth of many colonial institutions and entertainments. Later, when the economic conditions underlying this efflorescence of civilisation and domesticity collapsed, the expatriates of both sexes, faced with defeat, found solace and a sense of superiority in the comprehensive reconstruction of colonial society they had created.

Earlier in the century the steady arrival of American women in Honolulu did not presage a dramatic change in the existing patterns of community life. Notions of empire were not an article of faith at this time but most women migrated to Hawaii to join expatriate traders and shipowners who believed their economic prospects were improving and that domestic patterns similar to those at home should be established. Class and, in time, racial prejudice among the foreigners in Honolulu became more apparent. On several occasions Stephen Reynolds mentioned with displeasure the cliquishness which was developing in Honolulu. In mid July 1840 all the foreign women in the town were invited on board the British man-of-war in the harbour. Not a single English woman attended and a number of Americans who could have gone refused. The reason given later was that some of the American women asked were mechanics' wives.[15] The raising of class barriers in Honolulu at this time was an inevitable development given the new commercial enterprises and aspirations of certain expatriate families. Tensions between foreigners increased, but also on the racial level relations deteriorated. The opportunities and status being denied the lower class foreigners were also denied the islanders and, as has been maintained for other societies, there are strict parallels between the way people speak and feel about those of a different class and the way they speak and feel about those of a different race.[16]

R. B. Hinds visited Honolulu in July 1837 and again in May and June 1839. On both occasions he found a great want of conciliation among the foreigners and a marked disinclination among all foreign cliques to include the Hawaiians in their social activities. Similarly, letters written by the wives of merchants in Honolulu reveal not only their pretensions in white society, but also their total lack of interest in, and latent hostility towards, the Hawaiians. Frequently the only mention of the Hawaiians in such letters was derogatory and very similar in tone to the racist generalisations quoted above: 'Mrs Wood like everyone else, is troubled with her natives — oh dear I will never attempt to keep house with nothing but natives — 'tis dreadful beyond endurance'.[17] Snobbery among foreigners and prejudice towards the Hawaiians made it increasingly difficult to maintain any corporate community spirit in Honolulu, the total population of which was well over 8000 in the early 1840s.

During the 1870s race relations in Apia were severely strained by the activities of land speculators, but the town did not experience a contemporaneous increase in the number of white women residents. The handful of expatriate women in the town who were the wives of missionaries and traders revealed attitudes and aspirations very similar to those voiced in Honolulu in the 1840s. Mrs Williams, the wife of the British consul and one-time acting American commercial agent, J. C. Williams, believed that the Samoans were ungrateful. She felt that the man who had been appointed to take over the American agency from her husband 'will do very well for the Office, but he has a Native Wife & one of the worst specimens, so that it is very unfortunate'.[18]

With new social and economic conditions, including the advent of expatriate women, the organisation of society followed the path already taken by commerce, which had become increasingly complex and Western oriented. Positions in mercantile companies and the newly evolving beach societies were more and more difficult for islanders to find. As many island elements as possible were removed from the port towns. The kind and scope of entertainment and the locally held canons of good behaviour were altered to conform to Western standards. The leisurely atmosphere which pervaded the early port towns was no longer tolerated. Public clocks or the firing of cannon at noon were instituted, public holidays respected and fixed business hours observed. This piecemeal process of Westernisation gained concentrated support and direction from the island newspapers, which consistently encouraged improvement in the beach communities. Their continual appeal to community spirit gave rise to a strong sense of group identity among the Europeans, who were led to see themselves as an élite in an unreliable and often unstable island culture. Any advance, from a newly built jetty to a neatly walled-in cemetery with tidy individual plots, was considered proof of the superiority of Western civilisation over the indolence and lack of interest that characterised island life. Inevitably the islanders were made to feel out of place in communities which posited such emphasis on Western *mores*.

The loss of status and influence experienced by the non-white inhabitants of the port towns as a result of the continued expansion of foreign population and enterprises is clearly illustrated by the history of the part-islanders in the beach communities. Only calculated guesses can be made concerning the number of people of mixed origin in any island community. Many part-island children were assimilated into their mothers' culture without record, while information about those associated with the Europeans is slight. However, during the early development of the island trades, the handful of Europeans in the beach communities had to rely largely on the part-islanders for many of their trading activities, especially in collecting native products and transporting them to the central depots. Many part-islanders in Hawaii, Samoa and Fiji became adept boat builders, sailors and pilots and enjoyed a major share of all shipping within the island groups. Part-islanders who were fortunate enough to gain some education were employed as clerks and salesmen in the trading companies, and as interpreters. At the Oahu Charity School in the mid 1830s nearly twice as many girls as boys were enrolled, since the latter had all been taken into business.[19]

But only a few foreigners took a vital interest in the development of those part-islanders who were European-oriented. Some benefited from missionary education and care, but the majority had few skills and little, if any, social standing among the Europeans. Island attitudes towards the part-islanders varied widely. In Hawaii it was possible for the granddaughter of the English beachcomber, John Young, to marry a Hawaiian prince and later to become Queen. The Fijians showed a similar tolerance for persons of mixed descent. In Samoa, however, during the 1870s, the leading chiefly families became increasingly unwilling to pass their high-ranking titles through women affiliated with foreigners to their mixed blood offspring. This insistence on pure Samoan lineage reflects the deterioration of race relations between the Samoans and the foreign residents during the decade. Part-Samoans had little standing in either community and, without resources, they had to rely on their own ingenuity to maintain themselves.[20] As the expatriate populations grew, many of the positions once filled by part-island men were taken over by foreigners, while the part-island women found themselves excluded from mixed white society. Emma Coe, part-Samoan daughter of Jonas Coe, finally left Apia in 1878 determined to return only in such circumstances as would protect her from insults to which she had previously been subjected. In all port towns the general effect of European treatment of part-island inhabitants was similar. Without vital resources or services to offer they were forced to accept an inferior position in the communities. In Levuka when the Europeans established the Corporation of Fiji Settlers in 1870 the part-Fijians were expected to co-operate with the foreigners, but they were not considered fit to enjoy the protection of the foreigners' laws.[21] During the later years in the pre-colonial port towns, an ever-increasing number of Europeans pursued their goals without heed for community harmony or racial justice. The rights and needs of islanders and part-islanders alike were ignored in the interests of expatriate ascendancy.

To analyse the pattern of race relations only in terms of increasing competition masks certain prejudices that were deep-seated among the Europeans, and apparent from the first years of beach community development. One of the most sensitive areas between islander and foreigner was that of jurisdiction. In the earliest settlements, although the foreigners submitted to chiefly authority, it often caused tension and a great feeling of insecurity among the expatriates. However, except on the occasional visit of a naval vessel, the foreigners had no alterative source of authority to which to turn. White settlers in Fiji tried to avoid the problem by removing themselves to the island of Ovalau beyond the immediate sphere of Cakobau's power, but they found total isolation impossible. When roused, Cakobau still had the necessary influence to make his displeasure with the foreigners felt. With the arrival of the consular agents new patterns began to form. Anxious to be free from island jurisdiction the foreigners looked to their representatives to provide an alternative source of justice. But although the consuls were entitled to hear disputes between their own nationals, they had no authority to try cases in which islanders were involved or between foreigners of different nationalities. Even among their own nationals their punitive powers were minimal. These limitations, however, seldom restrained them from exercising illegal power and encouraging foreigners to demand extra-territorial status. In time white attitudes towards island law and the islanders' ability to dispense justice became increasingly vocal and prejudiced: 'Native evidence was said to be worth nothing',[22] their presence on juries was scorned, their ability to govern derided and their right to hold foreigners responsible to island laws denied. 'They [the Samoans] are but a degree removed from barbarism, and . . . not at all capable of acting as Judges or jurymen, or deciding right or wrong in civil cases. . . .'[23]

Two events in the early histories of Honolulu and Levuka reveal the emotions and tensions engendered by the conflict between island and foreign attitudes to jurisdiction. Following an incident in Honolulu in 1829, during which the British consul, Richard

Charlton, had arbitrarily and cruelly punished a Hawaiian for shooting one of his cows, Kamehameha III issued a proclamation which not only enumerated the laws in force in Hawaii, but also asserted quite emphatically that all foreigners resident in his territory, including the consuls, were subject to them.[24] The proposed publication of this proclamation caused such excitement and dissatisfaction in the town that gentlemen friendly with the missionaries warned them, without success, against printing it. The justice of Kamehameha's position as stated in the proclamation could not be refuted and Charlton, who had hoped to gain much from the incident, was left without a leg to stand on. The other English residents who had championed the consul's rights and demanded proper security for their property were similarly embarrassed. No British naval officer or home government would have accepted the consul's interpretation of events or his justification of his actions once they had read the Hawaiian decree. From that moment Charlton became an intransigent opponent of the Hawaiian government, sought any and every opportunity to hinder and embarrass it and claimed heavily for all British property stolen or damaged.

Only a week after the publication of Kamehameha's proclamation a statement from the United States government was issued concerning its citizens in Hawaii: 'Our Citizens who violate your [Hawaiian] laws, or interfere with your regulations, violate at the same time their duty to their own Government and Country, and merit censure and punishment'.[25] In almost hysterical terms several American merchants wrote to the Secretary of State in protest

> against this letter as containing parts which are unnecessary and improper, assertions which are false and unwarranted, and that the whole will have a powerful tendency to deceive the minds of the people of the Sandwich Islands, jeopardize the lives and property of Americans here residing, and erect the standard of fanaticism on the ruins of enterprise and industry.[26]

These incidents brought both the British and American settlers into sudden collision with the Hawaiian government, which they believed was exercising its judicial power in a deliberate attempt to control foreign property and business concerns. Every effort was made at this time to place all foreign activity beyond the Hawaiians' jurisdiction. It is not surprising that the Hawaiian chiefs complained to a visiting naval officer about the 'evil' deeds perpetrated against them by Charlton, Jones, the United States agent, and another American resident, French.[27] Extreme hostility was not lasting but the residual effects of these incidents were seen in the militant behaviour of the consular agents during the ensuing decade.

In Fiji until the 1850s the white residents had relied much upon the forbearance and protection of the chiefs for their personal security, and had enjoyed remarkably good relations with their hosts, despite exile and the occasional killing of a European. But on the foreigners' return from exile in Solevu in 1849 conditions in Levuka changed rapidly. In 1850 J. B. Williams made the first demand for compensation for goods stolen during a fire, and many Americans and a few English residents, who had suffered during exile, were not slow to follow his lead. Whippy, once the leader and focus of the community, soon joined their number. By 1852 the foreign population in Levuka had risen to fifty. This significant increase of thirty-five people since 1849, and the arrival of United States naval vessels, intransigently demanding the compensation mentioned above, gave rise to a strong feeling of white independence and intolerance.

Symptomatic of the resultant deterioration in community and race relations was the Europeans' reaction to the plundering of the wreck of the Levuka cutter *Wave* in September 1853. News of the event, which occurred on Malaki, an island under the authority of the chief of Viwa, reached Levuka within twenty-four hours, but instead of leaving the matter to the Viwa chief for settlement, as had been customary, the Levuka men took justice into their own hands and set out to revenge the attack. (It should be pointed out that at this stage the American commercial agent, J. B. Williams, was not resident in Levuka and he did not participate in this incident.) On the way they met the master and owner of the *Wave*, whom previously they had believed murdered. However, although he was unharmed by his experience, they determined to proceed. Later when the Europeans found that the Malaki Islanders had not returned all the plunder as they had demanded, they instituted a massacre.[28] No immediate punishment was inflicted upon the foreigners for this outrage since the chief of Viwa, fearing the unpredictable reactions of naval commanders to any action which he might take, decided to leave the matter to the judgment of the next man-of-war. By their behaviour the residents had made it clear that they refused any longer to bow to the jurisdiction of the Fijian chiefs. The determination shown on this occasion placed them on a new footing and gave them greater influence in Fijian affairs, but not without hazard. All pretence of European neutrality had been shattered and the Levuka settlers soon found involvement in Fijian politics highly injurious to their safety and economic prosperity. Two weeks after the Malaki massacre Levuka was fired and heavily plundered, despite desperate efforts on the foreigners' part to prevent it. The raid was made by the Lovoni hill tribe of Ovalau, who were almost certainly incited to do it by the chief of Viwa.[29] Later, in 1854-5, the foreigners became deeply involved in the civil wars that convulsed Fiji at that time.

The importance of these two sequences of events in Honolulu and Levuka was the opportunity they gave the foreigners to crystallise their ideas about the 'subordinate' island people and to sharpen their stereotypic group definition of them. The 'big event' plays a crucial role in developing a conception of the subordinate racial group:

> The event that seems momentous, that touches deep sentiments, that seems to raise fundamental questions about relations, and that awakens strong feelings of identification with one's racial group is the kind of event that is central in the formation of the racial image. Here, again, we note the relative unimportance of the huge bulk of experiences coming from daily contact with individuals of the subordinate group. It is the events seemingly loaded with great collective significance that are the focal points of the public discussion. The definition of these events is chiefly responsible for the development of a racial image and of the sense of group position.[30]

Both the 'cow' incident in Honolulu and the *Wave* incident in Levuka evoked such a response, although with differing degrees of intensity. The 1829 proclamation of laws and subsequent incidents caused a sudden, articulate outburst of prejudice, and a re-alignment of community loyalties which, however, lasted only as long as the residents believed that their interests were seriously endangered. The *Wave* incident, on the other hand, was the culmination of several trends which resulted in the foreigners taking a more determined stand against Fijian authority. Later events and attitudes were greatly influenced by the foreigners' forceful and unchallenged action during this crisis. Henceforth they endeavoured to keep Levuka and all foreign enterprises associated with it beyond Fijian interference, although often without success.

The establishment of protection societies was another method used by foreigners in Apia, Levuka and to a very limited extent in Kororareka, to frustrate the process of island law and to keep themselves and their concerns aloof from island authority. The sentiments and opinions that stimulated the rise of such societies were similar to those voiced by the Honolulu and Levuka residents during the two incidents analysed above, but in the case of protection associations the foreigners' fear and their refusal or inability to work with the islanders led to the formation of more 'permanent' alliances. Most foreigners settled in the islands for reasons of economic and social betterment. Thus, protection societies were not set up as a cover for political ambitions, except perhaps on the part of some consuls who used them to enlarge the scope of their authority, but were established because the expatriates fully believed their economic and social interests were being threatened.

In Apia a protection society appeared as early as 1848 (i.e. within the first ten years of foreign settlement there), created and led by the British consul, George Pritchard, who was also largely responsible for its later revival in 1854. On both occasions justification for the society in terms of disruptive Samoan civil wars masked the compelling foreign desire to isolate themselves from Samoan authority. Neither society lasted long, but the fears and prejudices that produced them were not eradicated, and again in the 1860s after the failure of an experimental Samoan government, the foreign residents sought the illusionary safety of a protection society, this time under the new title of the Association of Mutual Protection for The Life and Property. The 'supposed' arrogance of the Samoan police and their interference in foreign business affairs had proved the downfall of the experimental government, against which the foreigners quickly reacted. J. C. Williams, who had been largely responsible for initiating the

Samoan government, opposed it as loudly as the rest of the foreigners did, and revealed his deep-seated prejudices when he wrote to the Foreign Office to explain his reasons for taking up the judgeship of the new association: 'The steps taken by the Foreign Residents, I can recommend, for there is no dependance to be placed on the native authorities, there is so much jealousy existing amongst themselves they cannot act with any decision or impartiality'.[31] The Samoans resented Williams's rapid changes of interest and the powers assumed by the association, but like its fore-runners, the society's only authority derived from community co-operation, which never survived longer than the current crisis. Although these three protection societies were short-lived, they were symptomatic of the continual unrest in Apia and the foreigners' determination to control their own affairs. This aspira-tion was largely fulfilled by the Municipal Act of 1879, which established Apia as an independent foreign settlement, governed by consuls, who were in no way responsible to the Samoan chiefs.

In neither Kororareka nor early Levuka were race relations as tense as those in Apia, but in each of the former beach communi-ties one protection society appeared. The Kororareka Association, which was basically an alliance of propertied foreigners to protect themselves against the rabble white elements in the town, gained the co-operation of the small number of Maori in the area and so differed from the other protection societies, in as much as it was not usurping power from the island authority. This unusual toler-ance was extended by the foreigners only because the Maori made no attempt to interfere in the organisation of Kororareka or to impose their will upon the foreigners. Once the British consul, W. T. Pritchard, had been stripped of all his powers in July 1862, the foreign residents in Levuka suddenly found themselves power-less to prevent the Fijians from pillaging in the town. Faced with a situation in which no European had any ascendancy over the Fijians, the residents felt compelled to organise a self-protecting society 'to repel any aggressions on the part of the natives by force of arms'.[32] Like the Apia societies this one was short-lived, but its sudden creation revealed the fears and prejudices that immediately appeared among the foreigners as soon as they believed their security and independence were threatened.

Although the emphasis throughout this chapter has been placed on the many discordant elements in the port towns, at no time did they obliterate completely the basic harmony and community of interests that united the settlements and guaranteed their continued existence. The factors which fostered good community relations during this period were less obtrusive and dramatic than those productive of discord, but they were nonetheless effective. The fact that, despite moments of outspoken racial hostility, persistent consular campaigns to weaken island authority, and humiliating social exclusiveness imposed against both islanders and lower class foreigners, the beach communities never became divided by rigid social or racial barriers emphasises the centripetal forces operating within these communities.

Basic among the cohesive factors was the relative ease with which Europeans were able to establish good relations with the Polynesians and Fijians — people who satisfied their canons of beauty, grace and cleanliness and towards whose women they were attracted sexually. On the other hand, despite countless instances of foreign males' promiscuity, island men apparently never assumed that such conduct between them and white women would be condoned. In Hawaii there is no authenticated case of a consummated assault, and only one case of an attempted assault. Probably similar statistics would hold in the other islands but no study has been made. This sexual constraint among the island men was very important for the maintenance of good race relations. Furthermore the islanders' careful imitation of many aspects of Western social behaviour, particularly table etiquette, heightened foreign appreciation. Complementary to the foreigners' attraction was the islanders' tolerance of the Europeans' lack of knowledge of correct island behaviour. The islanders' acceptance of people of different cultural and racial origins and the facility with which they adopted new social habits and some new economic practices made informal contact within the multicultural settlements possible. Combined with this was their natural sense of dignity and their refusal to be considered as an inferior group in the community. Many Europeans, not untainted with racial prejudice, mistook this unwillingness to indulge in self-abasement or subservience as an indication of arrogance and contempt. D'Ewes, a visitor in Tonga in 1856, wrote: 'The prevailing vice of these islanders is the most inordinate pride; they consider themselves inferior to no native in the world, and do not think they can pay an European a greater compliment than by comparing him to a Tonga man'. Trood in Apia in 1857 found the Samoans 'excessively impudent and overbearing to foreigners'.[33] To expatriates convinced of their own superiority, such behaviour was most galling. But the islanders' self-confidence and dignity were essential for maintaining a position in the port towns which, even if it deviated at times from strict equality, never became servile.

The initial low intensity of foreign penetration and exploitation as compared with most other parts of the colonial world were also important factors in the maintenance of good race relations. The influence of this was, however, mitigated to some extent in the port towns, where foreign population was concentrated and competition most intense. Thus the greatest pressures put upon the islanders in the pre-colonial period originated in these centres. But only islanders willing to assimilate Western *mores* and eager to benefit from close association with foreign trade moved into beach communities. Those intimidated by, or resentful of, foreign settlement could easily isolate themselves from port town influences.

During their early development beach communities were open settlements in which islander and foreigner lived in a large degree of equality. Inter-racial liaisons were encouraged and a depth of mutual understanding was acquired through communal living and working patterns. In later years many foreigners believed that their numerical strength in the port towns was sufficient to crush island opposition to the expansion of plantations or to any particular development within the settlements themselves. Fortunately, however, tolerance prevailed and the good community relations established by the beachcombers, traders and missionaries were usually capable of restraining the more extravagant and arrogant attitudes of the incoming planters and speculators. At all times during the growth of the beach communities personal inter-racial relations played an important role in maintaining a background of community goodwill and sympathetic communication. In commercial and political spheres tensions multiplied but on individual social levels, except perhaps during the last years before annexation in Levuka, there was at least an appearance of equality and a desire to live in harmony.

In Honolulu between chiefs and commoners and foreigners of all classes personal contacts were numerous and friendly. From several journals kept in Honolulu throughout the period it is possible to build up a picture of inter-community social intercourse that extended from the most polite afternoon tea parties to long nights of gambling in the saloons. Friendships between leading foreigners and Kamehameha III or those of chiefly rank, particularly Boki, Kaahumanu and Kuakini, may be said to bear the taint of opportunism but, since contacts were long sustained and the exchange of gifts frequent, it is reasonable to assume that a depth of attachment was also involved. In 1834, over 100 foreign residents in Honolulu, which was at least one-third of the total foreign population, subscribed $800 to buy Kamehameha III a gift of clothing. All nationalities and classes were represented and few could have believed that they would benefit individually from the gift. However, it is highly probable that the foreigners hoped to maintain their popularity with Kamehameha III who had at this time broken loose from missionary restraint and was courting foreign favour. Liquor licences and many kinds of entertainment, previously prohibited, were permitted during the King's 'delinquent' period, and a gift of clothing might presumably help to prolong these conditions.[34] Even in the late 1830s, when the political and economic situation was becoming increasingly competitive, it was still the practice among the Honolulu merchants to send the King gifts of liquor and clothing: '2 bottles of wine for his Magesty's Dinner from Old H. Paty'.[35]

Relations in the port towns among the foreigners themselves were similar to those between islanders and foreigners — marked by a large degree of tolerance except in periods of crisis. As foreign populations grew the tendency towards cliquishness became manfest, but no expatriate was excluded from one clique or another because of his origin. Further, faced with island opposition, all foreigners would unite to protect their interests. Thus a few Negroes, Chinese, Malays and Europeans of minority groups, especially Jews, who settled in the beach communities were accepted without discrimination. The tavern of a Bensusan Jew in Levuka in the 1860s was well patronised by the local community who were certainly not forced by a scarcity of grog shops to frequent any one place. Similarly in Apia Black Bill's boarding house did not lack for customers.[36] In Honolulu the Negroes, Allen and Anderson, became wealthy and well respected citizens during the first two decades of the nineteenth century. The former engaged in black-smithing, raising animals, distilling liquor and even dabbling in medicine, while the latter was a sailor and helped maintain vessels. John King Bruce, a mildly eccentric Negro in Apia, was registered as a British subject and volunteered for special constable duties during the disturbances of early 1876.[37] Later developments in the beach communities, in particular the advent of planters, specula-tors and expatriate women, increased inter-community tensions and created social barriers, but for many years there had been such ease of contact between most residents that it was not completely undermined by growing friction and disharmony.

In the pre-colonial towns the pattern of race relations fluctu-ated, largely in response to the changing demands, aspirations and successes of the two major racial groups. The good relations which usually prevailed in the early beach communities, when the balance of power was still undecided and European economic interests were limited, were severely tested in later years. Racial wars or the creation of impenetrable racial barriers did not, however, occur. But on a less intense level bitter and sometimes implacable an-tagonism within the multi-cultural settlements became increasingly common. The growing number of foreigners in the beach com-munities with different commercial ambitions and social status created tensions and divisions among the Europeans, and between them and the island people. These were exacerbated and latent prejudice among many expatriates hardened as a result of the failure of their enterprises. On the other hand the intensity of change imposed upon the islanders in the port towns aroused feelings of resentment and fear. What once had been united multi-cultural communities faced disintegration into antagonistic racial groups, each seeing its hopes of survival and success thwarted by the demands of the other. The equality of early years was per-sistently undermined by the expatriates' rampant economic, poli-tical and social ambitions, which the islanders became increasingly unable to restrain or control.

nine

Epilogue

The predominantly egalitarian atmosphere which the islanders, beachcombers, traders and missionaries created and enjoyed in the early beach communities was largely undermined by later foreign development and population increase. Over a period of about forty years intensified foreign contact and activity in the port towns and their hinterlands resulted in European domination in political, economic and religious spheres and the slow Westernisation of these and many other aspects of life. The beach communities, once the sites of multi-cultural contact and development, were slowly transformed into port towns oriented exclusively to the demands of expatriate commerce and society. The period of about forty years during which this process occurred in Honolulu, Levuka and Apia did not effect the same degree of transformation in each town, nor was the economic and political control imposed by the foreigners uniform, but while there were variations, the fact of European dominance, at least in the towns, was undeniable. In two instances, Kororareka and Papeete, annexation formalised European control long before the resident foreign population had gained such a position. For the other beach communities forty years is only an approximate guideline to the length of time it took the expatriates to reach a position of power. There was, of course, no exact moment when a casual settlement of a few foreigners round a harbour developed into an unmistakable beach community. Similarly at the end of the period foreign control was not achieved suddenly.

For Honolulu the return of Kamehameha I with his island and foreign retinue to Oahu in 1804 consolidated earlier European contact with the harbour and established it as the port through which all future major commercial transactions would be channelled. Over the years the foreign and Hawaiian population of

Honolulu grew continuously, but always with the expatriates edging into influential positions. By the early 1840s, despite the formal recognition of Hawaii's independence by the Great Powers, American and English residents were firmly entrenched in the town, which many were to make their permanent home, and foreign-born representatives in the newly established Hawaiian parliament were able to introduce and pass legislation that was greatly to facilitate foreign development. In Fiji the bêche-de-mer traders first spoke of the aggregate of Europeans on Ovalau as the township of Levuka in 1831[1]. By the early 1870s the town was the centre of a burgeoning cotton boom which attracted to Fiji several hundred foreigners whose presence dramatically changed the character of previous community relations. With the collapse of cotton prices, conditions became so chaotic and racist prejudice so outspoken that the Fijian chiefs were left with no viable alternative but to cede their islands to Great Britain. Apia, which grew slowly from missionary beginnings in 1836, did not have a significant non-missionary population until the early 1840s. By 1879, however, the number of foreign residents had increased greatly and they had secured, through the consuls of Great Britain, America and Germany, complete control over the land and harbour of Apia and all their economic and social activities. Thus in these three port towns, over a span of about forty years, the foreigners had moved from a position of equality, sometimes even subordination, to one of controlling power. The islanders who moved into the towns gradually became second-class citizens, whose interests and rights were ignored or overridden in favour of foreign development. Only in Fiji, however, was this situation formally recognised by annexation.

Imperial intervention in Tahiti and New Zealand cut short independent foreign expansion in Papeete and Kororareka. The former did not become the major harbour in the Society Islands until the mid 1820s after which its foreign population grew slowly and numbered only seventy when French intervention occurred in 1842. Kororareka, whose earliest settlers arrived in the mid 1820s, was overrun by foreigners between 1836 and 1840, when New Zealand was annexed. But the residents in the township had little contact with the Maori population and certainly enjoyed no political ascendancy over them. British annexation was not a reflection of the power Kororareka settlers enjoyed in New Zealand but was rather the product of international rivalries and the activities of a large number of land speculators working south of the Bay of Islands area. Of the many diverse pressures brought to bear upon the British parliament the residents' lobby was only minor.

In Kororareka and Levuka the ceremonies of annexation proved later to have been their finest hours, which were followed by a loss of status as European centres of power, and the desertion of much of their population. On 29 February 1840, after New Zealand had been ceded to Britain, Lucett described the feverish activity in Kororareka:

> Such a rush has been made to New Zealand that the place is crowded with Europeans; . . . Every house has got more than three-fold its complement of inhabitants: tents pitched here and there supply with some the deficiency of house room. The market is glutted with goods. Auction bells are going all day long, and, notwithstanding the government proclamations, land is daily being bought and sold; a monomaniacal plague or land fever is abroad, and the whole atmosphere is infected with it.

Everyone believed that Kororareka would be the new capital, but in August 1840, after a bid to establish the capital at Okiato, Auckland was chosen as the seat of government. Despite bitter opposition from the Kororareka settlers the government removed to Auckland in February 1841; Kororareka was closed as a free port and with the rapid decrease in trade a large majority of the population was forced to move south. By November 1841, when Lucett returned, a very different scene prevailed:

> I walked over to Kororarika, and was struck with the apparent solitude of the place. Scarcely an individual was to be seen; the place seemed deserted, and business suspended; silence had usurped the place of noise, bustle, and activity, that prevailed the last time I was there; . . . No improvements had taken place; and works I had seen in progress had been abandoned.[2]

Levuka held tenuously to its title of the capital of Fiji for eight years after annexation in 1874, but indecision over the permanent site of the capital affected trade. In August 1879 Suva was chosen, and three years later the government offices were opened in the newly constructed township. The merchants maintained that Levuka would never lose its commercial predominance but insidiously the population ebbed to Suva and by 1886 even the *Fiji Times,* which had doggedly fought the government decision, was forced to admit that it could no longer afford not to follow suit.

[The *Fiji Times*] has vainly struggled against the deathly depression we have of late years experienced. But the strain still continues without the prospect of immediate relief; and having seen a population of 2,000, ninety per cent of whom were adult males, dwindle to fewer than 500, less than forty per cent of whom are wage-earners and bread-winners despite the force of old ties the admission is at length compelled that Levuka is no longer the place at which to publish the leading journal of the colony.[3]

Dual mercantile establishments were set up in Levuka and Suva by some merchants but those who could not afford to divide their businesses moved to the centre of European population. Opportunists, who had thrived in Levuka before annexation, were drawn to Apia rather than Suva. Otty Cudlip, who had been mayor of Levuka before annexation, died in December 1881 before the exodus and its effects were felt.[4] The fashionable days of Levuka were long past when the traveller Reginald Gallop reached the town in 1887: 'Since the seat of Government was shifted Levuka has been going down hill & the traces of this are sadly evident. There are more Tennis Courts than in Suva & not enough players. The Club has moved to Suva and Govt. Ho. is abandoned'.[5]

Suva became an outstanding example of a town built exclusively at the dictates of a colonial government. Its major functions were the organisation of trade between the island hinterlands and the metropolitan countries, and the dissemination of orders and regulations from the colonial government to the island people.[6] The latter, who visited or settled in the town, were never in doubt concerning their inferior status. But Honolulu, Apia and Papeete, despite their informal beginnings as beach communities with casual trading and political arrangements, were slowly moulded into functionally similar towns and have remained the capitals of their respective island groups. Levuka and Kororareka were not to become foci of European power, but they did not retain the characteristics of a beach community after annexation.

Although none of the beach communities of the early nineteenth century survived the intense foreign contact of later years, at Wainunu, in Vanua Levu, Fiji, far from the centre of colonial government, a settlement grew up that had many of the characteristics of the earlier beach communities. Here, a few miles from the one-time exile settlement of Solevu, David Whippy and several other Europeans and their part-Fijian families sought a final refuge in 1862. Land was divided among the extended Whippy family, the heirs of William Simpson who died on Wakaya Island, Isaac Driver, Isaac Hathaway, Jacob Andrews, James Stewart and Frank Johnson. Substantial houses were built and, on a communal basis, cotton and coconuts were cultivated, timber sawn for boat building and cattle raised. By 1878 no Fijian villages remained on the 9000 acres of land owned by the Wainunu inhabitants, but the Fijians and part-Fijians within the settlement formed a united community in which Fijian and European cultures were harmoniously blended. David Whippy died there in October 1871, probably the last full-blood European in the town, which has since become more and more Fijian in racial composition and culture.[7]

During the later years the long-established expatriate residents in all beach communities except Papeete were greatly outnumbered by new immigrant foreigners. The commercial enterprises built up by the pioneers made it possible for the later arrivals to settle in the port towns, without at any time having to establish significant contact with the islanders. Knowledge of their new environment and its inhabitants was thus usually minimal. European personnel, capital and techniques took over the commercial sphere and wielded great influence in politics. In keeping with these developments beach community society gradually assumed Western standards and conventions. Inevitably the islanders became second-class citizens in towns where social and economic opportunities had once been open to all. Between the foreign-dominated port settlements and the traditional villages a gulf appeared across which few islanders were encouraged to pass. In their villages the islanders still had recognised positions in the social hierarchy and the means of producing a livelihood, but the beach communities, where once both races lived and worked together in a great degree of harmony, had become alien enclaves in which the rights, interests and equality of the islanders were subordinated to the needs of expatriate development. Whether this situation was recognised by formal annexation or not, the period of the egalitarian, multi-cultural beach communities was over.

Appendix I

These are the names of the King of the Islands, and the Chiefs in Council:

KAUIKEAOULI, the King, GOV. BOKI,
KAAHUMANU, GOV. ADAMS KUAKINI,
MANUIA, KEKUANAOA, HINAU, AIKANAKA, PAKI,
KINAU, JOHN II, JAMES KAHUHU.

.   OAHU, Oct. 7, 1829.

This is my decision for you: we assent to the request of the English residents; we grant the protection of the laws; that is the sum of your petition.

This therefore is my proclamation, which I make known to you, all people from foreign countries:— The laws of my country prohibit Murder, Theft, Adultery, Fornication, Retailing Ardent Spirits at houses for selling spirits, Amusements on the Sabbath day, Gambling and Betting on the Sabbath day and at all times.

If any man shall transgress any of these laws, he is liable to the penalty, the same for every foreigner and for the people of these Islands, whoever shall violate these laws shall be punished.

This also I make known, — The Law of the Great God of heaven, that is the great thing by which we shall promote peace; let all men who remain here obey it.

Christian Marriage is proper for men and women. But if a woman regard her man as her only husband, and the man regard his woman as his only wife, they are legally husband and wife; but if the parties are not married, nor regard themselves as husband and wife, let them be forthwith entirely separate.

II. This is also our decision, which I now declare to you. We have seen your wickedness heretofore. You did not warn us that your dooryards and enclosed plantations were tabu before the time when our animals went into your enclosures; you unhesitatingly killed our animals. But we warned you of the tabu of our plantations before the time when the animals came into them, even yours; and then it was told again to you that have cattle; but for some days past we have known your cattle to come in to eat up what we had planted; on that account some of your cattle are dead.

This then is the way to obtain justice: if you judged the man guilty, you are not forthwith to punish him; wait till we have a consultation first: then, had we judged him guilty, we would have given you damages; but no you rashly and suddenly injured the man; that is one of the crimes of two of you. And we state to you all that the wounding of a beast is by no means equal to the wounding of a man, inasmuch as man is lord over all the beasts.

This is our communication to you all, ye parents from the countries whence originate the winds: have compassion on a nation of little children, very small and young, who are yet in mental darkness, and help us to do right and follow with us that which will be for the best good of this our country.

III. As to the recent death of the cow: she died for breaking a tabu for the protection of the plantation. The place was defended also by a fence built by the owner of the plantation. Having secured his field by a fence, what remained to be done was the duty of the owners of cattle, who were told by him who had charge of the plantation, to bring home their cattle at evening. He did tell them so; but they did not regard it: and in the night they came in, but not by day. On that account the owner of the plantation hoped to recover damage; for many were the cattle that were taken up before, but no damage was recovered for the crop they had devoured; the owners plead them off without paying damage, therefore he to whom belonged the crop determined that one of the cattle should die, for destroying the crop; for it had been said that if any of the cattle should come into the enclosure devouring the crop, such cattle would be forfeited and become the property of the owner of the crop. Many have been seized, but they were begged off and given up again; this has been done many times. Why then are you so quick to be angry? For within the enclosure was the place where the cow was wounded, after which she made her way out. What then means your declaration that the cow was wantonly shot in the common? The cow would not have been killed for simply grazing in the common pasture; her feeding upon the cultivated crop was well known by those who had the care of the plantation.

(Signed)   KAUIKEAOULI
[Original in Laws 1827-1829 in AH]

Preface

[1]A. A. Koskinen, *Missionary Influence as a Political Factor in the Pacific Islands;* W. P. Morrell, *Britain in the Pacific Islands;* H. E. Maude, 'Beachcombers and Castaways', in *Of Islands and Men: Studies in Pacific History* (article first published 1964); Deryck Scarr, *Fragments of Empire: A History of the Western Pacific High Commission 1877-1914;* W. H. Pearson, 'The Reception of European voyagers on Polynesian Islands, 1568-1797', *Journal de la Société des Océanistes,* 26 (1970), 121-53.

Chapter One

[1]Paul Ottino, *Ethno-histoire de Rangiroa,* 25-9; R. P. Gilson, *Samoa 1830 to 1900: The Politics of a Multi-cultural Community,* 65; John Martin, *An Account of the Natives of the Tonga Islands, in the South Pacific Ocean, . . . Comp. and arranged from the extensive communications of Mr William Mariner, several years resident in those islands . . . ,* I, 160-1; John Williams, *A Narrative of Missionary Enterprises in the South Sea Islands,* 90-1; A. W. Murray, *Forty Years' Mission Work in Polynesia and New Guinea, from 1835 to 1875,* 375-80.

[2]Samuel H. Elbert and Torben Monberg, *From the Two Canoes: Oral Traditions of Rennell and Bellona Islands;* Raymond Firth, *History and Traditions of Tikopia;* Kenneth Emory, *Kapingamarangi: Social and Religious Life of a Polynesian Atoll.*

[3]Firth, *History and Traditions,* 86.

[4]J. C. Beaglehole, *The Exploration of the Pacific.*

[5]Bolton G. Corney, *The Quest and Occupation of Tahiti by Emissaries of Spain during the years 1772-1776.*

[6]Pearson, 'The Reception of European Voyagers'; John

Turnbull, *A Voyage Round the World in the Years 1800, 1801, 1802, 1803 and 1804,* 133.

[7]*HRA,* Series I, I, 1.

[8]Maude, *Of Islands,* 178-232.

[9]J. M. R. Young, 'Australia's Pacific Frontier', *HS,* 12 (1966), 373-88; E. J. Tapp, *Early New Zealand: A Dependency of New South Wales 1788-1841,* 47-64, 178.

[10]Everard Im Thurn and Leonard C. Wharton, eds., *The Journal of William Lockerby, Sandalwood Trader in the Fijian Islands during the years 1808-1809;* Dorothy Shineberg, *They Came for Sandalwood: A Study of the Sandalwood Trade in the South-West Pacific 1830-1865.*

[11]Gordon Greenwood, *Early American-Australian Relations from the arrival of the Spaniards in America to the close of 1830.*

[12]Ernest S. Dodge, *New England and the South Seas,* 23, 60.

[13]Harold W. Bradley, *The American Frontier in Hawaii: The Pioneers 1789-1843,* 53-120; Richard A. Pierce, *Russia's Hawaiian Adventure, 1815-1817.*

[14]George G. Putnam, *Salem Vessels and their Voyages . . . ,* IV, 36, 94; Charles Wilkes, *Narrative of the United States Exploring Expedition during the years 1838, 1839, 1840, 1841, 1842,* III, 222; R. G. Ward, 'The Pacific Bêche-de-mer Trade with Special Reference to Fiji', in R. G. Ward, ed., *Man in the Pacific Islands,* 91-123.

[15]W. Patrick Strauss, *Americans in Polynesia 1783-1842,* 24; John Coulter, *Adventures on the Western Coast of South America . . . including a narrative of incidents at the Kingsmill Islands, New Ireland, New Britain, New Guinea, and other islands in the Pacific Ocean,* I, 186-288, II, 1-266; R. G. Ward, ed., *American Activities in the Central Pacific, 1790-1870 . . . taken from contemporary news-*

papers, III, 583.

16Michael Roe, 'Australia's Place in the Swing to the East 1788-1810', *HS*, 8 (1958), 202-13; A.B.C. Whipple, *Yankee Whalers in the South Seas*, 148-9.

17J.-A. Moerenhout, *Voyages aux îles du Grand Océan* . . .

18Maude, *Of Islands*, 233-83; H. Stonehewer Cooper, *Coral Lands* II, 51-2.

Chapter Two

1A. I. Hallowell, 'American Indians, White and Black: The Phenomenon of Transculturization', *Current Anthropology*, IV (December 1963), 519-31; for a succinct but comprehensive history of beachcombing in the Pacific, excluding New Zealand, see Maude, *Of Islands*, 134-77.

2Leonard Shaw, 'A Brief Sketch of the Sufferings of Leonard Shaw on Massacre Island', in Benjamin Morrell Jr, *A Narrative of Four Voyages to the South Sea, the North and South Pacific Ocean* . . . *From the Year 1822 to 1831*, 441-8; J. G. Marwick, comp., *The Adventures of John Renton*.

3Arthur S. Thomson, *The Story of New Zealand*, I, 297-304.

4[Anon.], 'A Cruise after and among the Cannibals', *Harper's New Monthly Magazine*, VII (1853), 455-75; John Marmon, 'Scenes from the Life of John Marmon,' *The New Zealand Herald*, 9 October 1880.

5[James Oliver], *Wreck of the Glide, with Recollections of the Fijiis, and of Wallis Island*, 110.

6John Williams, Journal, Cook Islands 1832-3; Horatio Hale, MS. of the Navigator Islands, 1835; H. B. Restarick, 'The First Clergyman Resident in Hawaii', *HHS Papers*, 1923, 54-61; [George Vason], *An Authentic Narrative of Four Years' Residence at Tongataboo one of the Friendly Islands, in the South Sea* . . . ; John P. Hockin, *A Supplement to the Account of*

the *Pelew Islands; compiled from the Journals of the Panther and Endeavour, . . . and the oral communications of Captain H. Wilson*; Martin, *An Account of the Natives*.

7J. D. Lang, Letter I—Origin and Commencement of Missionary Operations in the South Seas; Peter Bays, *A Narrative of the Wreck of the Minerva Whaler of Port Jackson on Nicholson's Shoal* . . . , 70-2.

8Henry Pease, 'Adventure on St Augustine Island', *The Dukes County Intelligencer*, III (May 1962), 3-13.

9E. H. Lamont, *Wild Life among the Pacific Islanders*, 120-5.

10Turnbull, *A Voyage round the World*, 272.

11Martin, *An Account of the Natives*, I, 65.

12James Morrison, *The Journal of James Morrison Boatswain's Mate of the Bounty describing the Mutiny* . . . *with an account of the Island of Tahiti*, 71.

13[Oliver], *Wreck of the Glide*, 103.

14William Diapea, pseud. [William Diaper], *Cannibal Jack: the true autobiography of a white man in the South Seas*, 43; John Jackson, pseud. [William Diaper], 'Jackson's Narrative' in John E. Erskine, *Journal of a Cruise among the Islands of the Western Pacific, including the Feejees* . . . *in Her Majesty's Ship Havannah*, 429, 441-2.

15Turnbull, *A Voyage round the World*, 292-8.

16Richard A. Cruise, *Journal of a Ten Months' Residence in New Zealand*, 120-1, 315.

17DLNR, Foreign Register, I, no. 60.

18E. J. Turpin, Diary and Narratives . . . 1870-c.1894; Archibald Menzies, *Hawaii Nei 128 Years Ago*, 150.

19[Vason], *An Authentic Narrative*, 154.

20James F. O'Connell, *A Resi-*

dence of Eleven Years in New Holland and the Caroline Islands, 191-2.

21Williams, *A Narrative*, 360; J. D. Freeman, 'The Joe Gimlet or Siovili Cult', in J. D. Freeman and W. R. Geddes, eds., *Anthropology in the South Seas*, 185-200.

22Mrs S. M. Smythe, *Ten Months in the Fiji Islands*, 66; Berthold Seemann, 'Foreign Correspondence', *The Athenaeum*, 26 January 1861; Bays, *A Narrative of the Wreck*, 118-19; DLNR, Foreign Register, III, no. 4887.

23John P. Twyning, *Shipwreck and Adventures of . . . among the South Sea Islanders: giving an account of their feasts, massacres . . .* , 62-73; A. M'L., 'A Trading Voyage among the South Sea Islands', newspaper cutting.

24Samuel M. Kamakau, *Ruling Chiefs of Hawaii*, 174; Basil Thomson, *South Sea Yarns*, 288-326; [William Cary], *Wrecked on the Feejees. Experiences of a Nantucket Man . . . sole survivor of whaleship Oeno and lived nine years among cannibals of South Sea Islands*, 43-56.

25Thomson, *South Sea Yarns*, 307-12; David Whippy, 'Account of a Fegee War' in Bêche-de-mer Records; Twyning, *Shipwreck and Adventures*, 93; Marmon, 'Scenes', *The New Zealand Herald*, 16 October 1880; Greg Dening, ed., *The Marquesan Journal of Edward Robarts 1797-1824*, 116.

26A. J. von Krusenstern, 'Extracts of two letters . . . July 19, and August 20, 1804', *The Philosophical Magazine*, XXII (1805), 11.

27J. Orlebar, *A Midshipman's Journal on board H.M.S. Seringapatam during the Year 1830; . . .* , 69.

28Archibald Campbell, *A Voyage Round the World from 1806 to 1812 . . . with an account of the present state of the Sandwich Islands . . .* , 134.

29J. Eagleston to David Whippy, 20 March 1833, Bêche-de-mer records.

30James Wilson, *A Missionary Voyage to the Southern Pacific Ocean, performed in the Years 1796, 1797, 1798, in the Ship Duff, . . .* , 58-81; *Transactions of the Missionary Society*, I, 24-6.

31Gilson, *Samoa 1830 to 1900*, 143; Murray, *Forty Years*, 173-6.

32[Cary], *Wrecked on the Feejees*, 14-18; James Drummond, ed., *John Rutherford the White Chief*, 126-7.

33Morrison, *The Journal*, 160-9.

34Twyning, *Shipwreck and Adventures*, 61-2.

35[Mrs M. D. Wallis], *Life in Feejee, or, Five Years among the Cannibals*, 107.

36Campbell, *A Voyage round the World*, 146.

37Gabriel Franchère, *A Voyage to the North West Coast of America*, 38.

38Turnbull, *A Voyage Round the World*, 236.

Chapter Three

1Douglas L. Oliver, 'Papeete, Tahiti' in Alexander Spoehr, ed., *Pacific Port Towns and Cities: A Symposium*, 43.

2Campbell, *A Voyage*, 200; Morrison, *The Journal*, 201; R. A. Derrick, *A History of Fiji*, 39.

3The model for this argument is based on H. E. Maude and Edwin Doran Jr, 'The Precedence of Tarawa Atoll', *Annals of the Association of American Geographers*, LVI (June 1966), 269-89.

4Alexander M'Konochie, *A Summary View of the Statistics and Existing Commerce of the Principal Shores of the Pacific Ocean, . . .* , 340-1.

5Alexander Spoehr, 'Port Town and Hinterland in the Pacific Islands', *American Anthropologist*, LXII (1960),

588 (my emphasis).

6Laura Thompson, *The Native Culture of the Mariannas Islands*, 12; Cyril Belshaw, 'Pacific Island Towns and the Theory of Growth', in Spoehr, *Pacific Port Towns*, 17.

7Alfred Tetens, *Among the Savages of the South Seas; Memoirs of Micronesia, 1862-1868 . . . ;* Saul H. Riesenberg, *The Native Polity of Ponape,* 4-5; Ward, *American Activities,* III, 534-622.

8A. I. Andreyev, ed., *Russian Discoveries in the Pacific and in North America in the Eighteenth and Nineteenth Centuries,* 163-4; Bradley, *The American Frontier,* 23-4; Ralph S. Kuykendall, *The Hawaiian Kingdom 1778-1854 : Foundation and Transformation,* 49.

9Peter Corney, *Voyages in the Northern Pacific: Narrative of several trading voyages from 1813 to 1818, between the Northwest Coast of America, the Hawaiian Islands and China . . .* 96; Adelbert von Chamisso, Chamisso's Account of the Voyage Around the World on the Rurick 1815-1818, typescript translation.

10Thomas Brown to Marshall and Wildes, Canton 1822, Marshall MSS.

11*HRA,* Series I, VIII, 102; John Davies, Journal, 22 January 1809; Frank Debenham, ed., *The Voyage of Captain Bellingshausen to the Antarctic Seas 1819-1821,* II, 261-2.

12Kathleen Shawcross, The Maoris of the Bay of Islands, 1769-1840, 328-9.

13[Cary], *Wrecked in the Feejees,* 27-30, 43, 51; Ward, 'The Pacific Bêche-de-mer Trade', 91-123.

14George Platt, 'Raiatea to Hervey and Samoan Groups 1835-1836', Journal; Gilson, *Samoa 1830-1900,* 176; John Williams and Charles Barff, 'A Journal of a Voyage . . . '; Petition to Commander Bayley, 18 September 1855, USNR Pacific

Squadron.

15H. E. Maude, 'Baiteke and Binoka of Abemama: arbiters of change in the Gilbert Islands', in J. W. Davidson and Deryck Scarr, eds., *Pacific Islands Portraits,* 201-24; Maude, *Of Islands,* 148; Ernest Beaglehole, *Social Change in the South Pacific: Rarotanga and Aitutaki,* 101.

16J. H. Eagleston, Journal, Bêche-de-mer Records.

17Quoted by W. W. Bolton, 'The Beginnings of Papeete and its founding as the Capital of Tahiti', *Société des Etudes Océaniennes,* V, no. 12 (1935), 437-42.

18Bolton, 'The Beginnings of Papeete'.

19Elisha Loomis, Journal, 11 September 1820.

20J. W. Davidson, *Samoa mo Samoa: The Emergence of the Independent State of Western Samoa,* 43.

21Erskine, *Journal of a Cruise,* 174.

22R. G. Ward, *Land Use and Population in Fiji: A Geograhical Study,* 21.

23Cooper, *Coral Lands,* II, 51-2.

24Spoehr, 'Port Town and Hinterland', 586-92.

25R. P. Gilson, Administration of the Cook Islands (Rarotonga), 111-12; H. B. Sterndale, 'Memoranda . . . on some of the South Sea Islands', in *Papers relating to the South Sea Islands, Their Natural Products, Trade Resources, etc.,* 6.

26Augustus Earle, *A Narrative of a nine months' residence in New Zealand in 1827 . . .,* 12-28; Harrison M. Wright, *New Zealand 1769-1840: Early Years of Western Contact,* 34; Ernest Dieffenbach, *Travels in New Zealand: with contributions to the Geography, Geology, Botany and Natural History of that Country,* I, 241.

27LCC, R 314; Berthold Seemann, *Viti: An Account of a Government Mission to the*

Vitian or Fijian Islands in the Years 1860-61, 65-72; Alastair D. Couper, The Island Trade: An Analysis of the Environment and Operation of a Seaborne Trade among three Island Groups in the Pacific, 30-1, 65-6.

[28]Gavan Daws, 'Honolulu in the 19th Century: Notes on the Emergence of Urban Society in Hawaii', *JPH*, II (1967), 77-96.

Chapter Four

[1]Campbell, *A Voyage Round the World*, 165; C. S. Stewart, *The Hawaiian Islands in 1822*, 12-15; Otto von Kotzebue, *A New Voyage Round the World in the Years 1823, 24, 25 and 26*, I, 146; Shawcross, The Maoris, 328-9 and population table, 254; The Report of the Work of God in the Bau circuit . . . June 1843, MMS 6; Hunt to Miller, 23 May 1847, BCT 24/3; Erskine, *Journal of a Cruise*, 173; Home to Stafford, 20 December 1852, Adm. 1/5617; John D'Ewes, *China, Australia and the Pacific Islands in the Years 1855-56*, 170.

[2]Rev. J. Crook to Burder, 3 October 1823, LMS SSL 4/2B.

[3]Fremantle to Osborne, 15 November 1855, Adm. 1/5672.

[4]Captain Golovnin, *Tour Around the World . . . in 1817, 1818, 1819;* Solid Men of Boston in the North West, 13; Agnes C. Conrad, ed., *The Letters and Journal of Francisco de Paula Marin*, 207-14; Pierce, *Russia's Hawaiian Adventure*, 47, 53-4, 163, 166, 172.

[5]Hunnewell to Chamberlain, 25 April 1832, in KC (Hunnewell's underlining).

[6]Conrad, *Marin Letters*, 213, 215; Otto von Kotzebue, *Voyage of Discovery in the South Sea . . . undertaken in the Years 1815, 16, 17 and 18*, I, 94; Golovnin, *Journal.*

[7]Pierce, *Russia's Hawaiian Adventure*, 172.

[8]Wilkes, *Narrative*, III, 69.

[9]Eagleston, Journals; John B. Knights, 'A Journal of a voyage

in the brig Spy . . . ' , in *The Sea, the Ship and the Sailor; tales of adventure from log books and original narratives,* introduced by Captain Eliot Snow, 186-7; Derrick, *A History*, 59-60.

[10]Erskine, *Journal of a Cruise,* 173.

[11]James Calvert, Journal, 31 July 1861, MMS 36.

[12]Whippy's role in Levuka will be discussed further in Chapter 6.

[13]Wildes to Marshall, 27 March 1825, Marshall MSS.

[14]J. S. C. Dumont d'Urville, *Voyage de l' Astrolabe*, IV. Le *Voyage au Pole Sud,* Chapter 33.

[15]Alexander Adams, Journal, 1816-1819; Wilkes to His Majesty, 7 December 1840, FO and EX 1840; J. C. Williams to J. M. Coe, 15 February 1864, BCS 5/1.

[16]*The Friend,* 15 August 1846.

[17]Conrad, *Marin Letters,* 216; J. W. Davidson, European Penetration of the South Pacific 1779-1842, 113-14.

[18]Crook to Burder, 21 August 1822, LMS SSL 3/8A.

[19]Home to Stafford, 20 December 1852, Adm. 1/5617.

[20]Thos C. Dunn to George West, 13 November 184[9], Bêche-de-mer Records; Vewa Record, 7 August 1851, MMS 38.

[21]Bays, *A Narrative,* 167.

[22]Kotzebue, *Voyage of Discovery,* I, 94; Conrad, *Marin Letters,* 200.

[23]Shawcross, The Maoris, 351-2 .

[24]Stephen Reynolds, Journal, 11 July 1839; John Colcord, Journal; Bradley, *The American Frontier,* 234; *Hawaiian Gazette,* 13 September 1876.

[25]James Hunnewell, 'Honolulu in 1817 and 1818', *HHS Papers,* VIII (1895), 3-19; William French, Account Book . . . 1818-1819.

[26]Hunnewell, 'Honolulu', 3-

19.

27French, Account Book.

28Davidson, European Penetration, 146, 162; George F. J. Bergman, 'Solomon Levey in Sydney', *Royal Australian Historical Society Journal,* XLIX (March 1964), 401-22; S. P. Henry to Captain Laws, 6 January 1829, Pacific Islands, 1822-75.

29Kotzebue, *A New Voyage,* I, 171.

30Lawrence M. Rogers, ed., *The Early Journals of Henry Williams . . . 1826-40,* 245, 261, 269; John R. Lee, Southseaman, The Story of the Bay of Islands, 154-7; Ruth M. Ross, *New Zealand's First Capital,* 11-12.

31Jos. Winn to Mr David Whippy, August 1834, Bêche-de-mer Records; Eagleston Journals; Ward, 'The Pacific Bêche-de-mer Trade', 91-123.

32Eagleston to Phillips, 17 July 1834, Bêche-de-mer Records.

33R. B. Lyth, Journals II, V, VI; J. Calvert, Journal, 12 December 1839, MMS 35; Thos. C. Dunn to George West, 1 January 1850 and Thos. C. Dunn to West brothers, 5 October 1851, Bêche-de-mer Records.

34[E. Lucett], *Rovings in the Pacific, from 1837 to 1849; with a Glance at California,* II, 153-8; *Samoan Reporter,* March 1847; Thomas Trood, *Island Reminiscences; a graphic detailed romance of life spent in the South Sea Islands,* 30-3; Gilson, *Samoa 1830-1900,* 172-5, 182-5.

35DLNR, Foreign Testimony II, no. 364; Foreign Register I, no. 32, no. 248.

36Pierce, *Russia's Hawaiian Adventure,* 167.

37DLNR, Foreign Testimony II, no. 576.

38LCC R87.

39LCC R525.

40Pritchard to Aberdeen, 31 December 1845, FO 58/38.

41J. S. Polack, Title Deeds of Land in Kororareka.

42R. G. Jameson, *New Zealand, South Australia, and New South Wales: A record of recent travels in these colonies . . . ,* 198; Olive Wright, *The Voyage of the Astrolabe — 1840. An English rendering of the journals of Dumont d'Urville and his officers of their visit to New Zealand in 1840 . . . ,* 70.

43S. P. Henry to Nicholas, 24 March 1843, BCT 24/24; [Joseph Smith], Tahiti 1824-1857.

44Conrad, *Marin Letters,* 222.

45Earle, *A Narrative,* 90-6, 112-21; Hugh Carleton, *The Life of Henry Williams . . . ,* 116-23, 246; J. S. Polack, *New Zealand; being a narrative of travels and adventure during a residence in that country between the years 1831 and 1837,* II, 240-3.

46Kotzebue, *A New Voyage,* I, 195; Elley to Canning, 28 February 1827, FO 58/14.

47Maxwell to Pritchard, 4 February 1848, BCS 2/1.

48Pritchard to Admiral Bruce, May 1856, BCS 3/1; USCD-A, I.

49Fremantle to Osborne, 15 November 1855, Adm. 1/5672.

50Mervine to Secretary of Navy, 30 June 1856, USNR Pacific Squadron, 1841-1886.

51Conrad, *Marin Letters,* 214-15.

52Hunnewell, 'Honolulu', 3-19.

53Jackson, pseud. [Diaper], 'Jackson's Narrative', 453.

54 G. C. Henderson, ed., *The Journal of Thomas Williams Missionary in Fiji 1840-1853,* II, 285, 472-4; Wallis, *Life in Feejee,* 24, 234-5; Hunt to Miller, 23 May 1847, BCT 24/3.

55Enclosure 6 in Home to Stafford, 20 December 1852, Adm. 1/5617.

56Pierce, *Russia's Hawaiian Adventure;* Conrad, *Marin Letters;* Kotzebue, *Voyage of Discovery,* I, 94-7.

57High Court of Appeals, 29

March 1822, Edward Eager *v.*
S. P. Henry, in Pacific Islands,
1822-75; Paul E. LeRoy, 'The
Emancipists, Edward Eager, and
the Struggle for Civil Liberties',
*Royal Australian Historical
Society Journal,* XLVIII
(1962), 276-7.

58Fremantle to Osborne, 15
November 1855, FO 58/84B;
Golovnin, *Tour Around the
World.*

Chapter Five

1*The Friend,* 1 May 1850;
Samuel Parker, *Journal of an
Exploring Tour Beyond the
Rocky Mountains, under the
direction of the ABCFM performed in the years 1835, '36
and '37,* 347.

2Pritchard to Bidwell, 30
March 1842, BCT 24/8.

3Ross, *New Zealand's First
Capital,* 14; Jameson, *New
Zealand,* 188.

4Julius N. Brenchley, *Jottings
during the Cruise of H.M.S.
Curaçoa among the South Sea
Islands,* 145; Trade Report
1866, Extracts from Consular
Letter Books, Levuka.

5T. H. Hood, *Notes of a
Cruise in H.M.S. Fawn in the
Western Pacific in the Year
1862,* 70.

6Bryant and Sturgis to Bul-
lard, 12 October 1820, in KC;
Jean I. Brookes, *International
Rivalry in the Pacific Islands
1800-1875,* 49-50.

7Crocker to Secretary of
State, 9 November 1825, in KC.

8Williams to Secretary of
State, 5 January 1869, BCS
3/3; H. M. Jones to Secretary
of State, 12 May 1865, FO
58/105.

9W. B. Churchward, *Black-
birding in the South Pacific or,
The First White Man on the
Beach,* 15.

10Conway Shipley, *Sketches
in the Pacific,* 23.

11Jones to Marshall and
Wildes, December 1822, Marshall MSS.

12Carleton, *Life of Henry*

Williams, 249-54; Lee, Southseaman, 193.

13Williams to Coe, 18 June
1866, USCD-A, II, and following.

14Levi Chamberlain, Journal,
22 August-3 September 1825;
Reynolds, Journal, 24 July, 10
September 1826, 27 June 1828,
24-26 April 1831.

15USCD-T, I-II; FO 58/15-
16; John Davies, *The History
of the Tahitian Mission 1799-
1830,* 337.

16Williams to Secretary of
State, 1 April 1864, 27 February
1865, BCS 3/3; Gilson, *Samoa
1830 to 1900,* 246-54.

17W. T. Pritchard, *Polynesian
Reminiscences; or Life in the
South Pacific Islands,* 349-50.

18Marie M. King, *Port in the
North: A Short History of Rus-
sell, New Zealand,* 31-3; Lee,
Southseaman, 205-6.

19Jenkins to Secretary of
State, 15 August 1856,
USCD-A, I.

20USCD-L, II; Derrick, *A
History of Fiji,* 133-6, 177-82.

21T. ap Catesby Jones to
Kamehameha III, October 1826,
FO and EX 1826; To Kame-
hameha III, 20 January 1829,
FO and EX 1829; Bradley, *The
American Frontier,* 105-13,
178-9, 193-5. Captain Finch's
visit will be discussed in detail
in Chapter 8.

22Rogers, *The Early Journals,*
320, 331, 368.

23Whippy to Williams, 28
June 1858, USCD-L, III.

24Maria Loomis, Journal, 8
August, 19, 20 November 1820;
Reynolds, Journal, 11 November
1823.

25Proclamation of Kauikeaouli [Kamehameha III], 7
October 1829, FO and EX,
1829. This incident will be discussed further in Chapter 8.

26Calvert to Hebblewhite, 7
October 1853, Pacific Islands,
1822-1875; J. B. Williams to
Secretary of State, 2 August
1858, USCD-L, III.

27Rufus Newburgh, A Narrative of Voyage, FO and EX, 28 April 1835.

[28]W. T. Pritchard to Secretary of State, 30 September 1857, BCS 3/2.

[29]Bartley to Coe, 26 July 1866, USCD-A, II.

[30]Unsigned Memorandum to Admiralty, 20 September 1836, FO 58/8.

[31]Aulick to Navy Department, 13 October 1841, USCD-T, II.

[32]Petition of British Residents to His Majesty's Government, 10 May 1834, Despatches from Governor of New South Wales, A1267-13; Petition of British Residents to the King's Most Excellent Majesty, 1837, reprinted in Polack, *New Zealand*, II, 431-7.

[33]Colcord, Journal.

[34]Dirickson to Secretary of State, 25 November 1859, USCD-A, II.

[35]Jones to Marshall and Wildes, 20 November 1821, Marshall MSS.

[36]J. M. Orsmond to July 1829, LMS SSL 7/3A.

[37]M. Loomis, Journal, 25 July-13 September 1821.

[38]E. Loomis, Journal, 1 October-12 December 1825; Chamberlain, Journal, 28 February 1826; Report of the ABCFM for the Eighteenth General Meeting, 1827.

[39]W. Colenso, *The Authentic and Genuine History of the Signing of the Treaty of Waitangi, New Zealand, February 5 and 6, 1840*, 18-34; [F. J. Moss], *A Month in Fiji*, 8; Vewa Record, 16 September 1851, MMS 38.

[40]Brookes, *International Rivalry*, 82-5, 106-10; Kuykendall, *The Hawaiian Kingdom*, 137-47, 163-7.

[41]Wilkes, *Narrative*, IV, 14; Jarves *v.* Dudoit, August 1839, FO and EX 1839; Colcord, Journal.

[42]Wilkes, *Narrative*, II, 19-20; W. W. Bolton, Old Time Tahiti, Vol. I, Chapter 10, MS; Colin Newbury, 'Aspects of Cultural Change in French Polynesia ...', *JPS*, 76 (1967), 7-26.

[43]Lee, Southseaman, 216-17.

[44]*Sailors Magazine*, October 1834.

[45]Trade Report 1864, Extracts from Consular Letter Books, Levuka.

Chapter Six

[1]Fremantle to Osborne, 12 December 1855, Adm. 122/12.

[2]Reynolds, Journal, 6 May 1829.

[3]Reynolds, Journal, 11 August-17 September 1829; Polack, *New Zealand*, II, 154-7.

[4]E. Alison Kay, ed., 'The Sandwich Islands from Richard Brinsley Hinds' Journal ...', *The Hawaiian Journal of History*, II (1968), 109.

[5]R. B. Lyth, Journal IV, 3 June 1848.

[6]LCC R369.

[7]Hood, *Notes of a Cruise*, 104.

[8]J. W. Boddam - Whetham, *Pearls of the Pacific*, 146.

[9]George Simpson, *Narrative of a Journey Round the World during the years 1841 and 1842*, I, 427; Wilkes, *Narrative*, II, 47-8.

[10]Hugh Cuming, Journal of a Voyage from Valparaiso to the Society and the adjacent Islands . . . in the Years 1827 and 1828, 43-4.

[11]W. K. Bull, *A Trip to Tahiti, and other islands in the South Seas*, 28.

[12]Butler to Kamehameha III, 9 February 1838, FO and EX 1838; Butler to Kamehameha III, 16 April 1838, Interior Department Miscellaneous 1838; Fayerweather Letters, 1831-5.

[13]John Coulter, *Adventures in the Pacific; with observations on the natural productions, manners and customs of the natives of the various islands*, 270, 280-1.

[14]R. W. Robson, *Queen Emma: The Samoan-American Girl who founded an Empire in*

19th Century New Guinea,
16-33. The family Bible is held
in NLA.

15Lilian Overell, *A Woman's
Impressions of German New
Guinea,* 147.

16Robert Coffin, *The Last of
the Logan,* 80-1; LCC R588.

17Ross Cox, *The Columbia
River,* 30-2; E. Loomis, Journal,
6 August 1825; Kaahumanu II
to United States President, 12
January 1839, FO and EX,
1839.

18Cox, *The Columbia River,*
31.

19Conrad, *Marin Letters,* 216.

20Quoted in Reginald Yzendoorn, *History of the Catholic
Mission in the Hawaiian Islands,*
41.

21Colcord, Journal; d'Urville,
Voyage; Fayerweather Letters,
1831-5.

22Jones to Wildes, 30 September 1827, Marshall MSS.

23*Pacific Commercial Advertiser,* 10 July 1856.

24Isaac Iselin, *Journal of a
Trading Voyage Around the
World, 1805-1808,* 78.

25Reynolds, Journal, 4 July
1829, 4 July 1834.

26*Fiji Times,* 27 May 1871;
Fiji Gazette, 9 November 1872,
31 May 1873.

27Reynolds, Journal, 5 January 1828.

28Colcord, Journal.

29Ephraim W. Clark, Private
Journal, 13 September 1828;
Reynolds, Journal, 13 Septem-
ber 1828, 27 April 1831.

30Binner to Eggleston, 3
October 1860, Missionary Correspondence.

31Frederick Debell Bennett,
*Narrative of a Whaling Voyage
Round the Globe From the Year
1833 to 1836,* I, 81.

32Quoted by Wright, *New
Zealand,* 31.

33Robert McNab, ed., *Historical Records of New Zealand,* II,
608-11.

34M. Loomis, Journal, May-
September 1820; Reynolds,
Journal, 10 January 1833.

35*Samoan Reporter,* March
1860; Henry to Ellis, 2 November 1840, LMS SSL 13/2D;
Ross, *New Zealand's First Capital,* 38.

36*Sailors Magazine,* November 1833.

37A. Gavan Daws, Honolulu
—The First Century: Influences
in the Development of the Town
to 1876, 454.

38*Samoan Reporter,* September 1846, March 1849; Pritchard to Ellis, 5 February 1834,
LMS SSL 9/5A.

39Earle, *A Narrative,* 146;
Rogers, *The Early Journals,* 89,
125, 139; A. G. Bagnall and G.
C. Petersen, *William Colenso:
Printer, Missionary, Botanist,
Explorer, Politician. His Life
and Journeys,* 45-8.

40The Report of the work of
God in the Bau Circuit for . . .
June 1843, MMS 6.

41John Hunt, Private Journal,
II, 269.

42Hunt to Miller, 23 May
1847, BCT 24/3.

43Eric Ramsden, *Busby of
Waitangi; H.M's Resident at
New Zealand, 1833-40,* 73; Wil-
son to Pritchard, 27 May 1841,
BCT 24/8.

44Chamberlain, Journal, 7
August 1825.

45Colcord, Journal; Reynolds,
Journal, May 1841-December
1843; Chamberlain, Journal,
May 1841-December 1843.

46Trood, *Island Reminis-
cences,* 43-4.

47Murray, *Forty Years,* 321,
336-7, 350-2; *Samoan Reporter,*
March 1860.

48Binner to Eggleston, 21
February 1859, Missionary Correspondence.

49Maurice Lennard, *Motuarohia, An Island in the Bay of
Islands,* 46-7; King, *Port in the
North,* 34-5; Ross, *New Zealand's First Capital,* 11.

50Churchward, *Blackbirding,*
9-12.

51Karl Van Damme, 'In the
South Seas', *Australasian,* 17
November 1866; Reynolds, Jour-

nal; G. B. Rieman, *Papalangee; or, Uncle Sam in Samoa*, 32-3.

52Petition, 12 May 1868, BCS 3/3.

53Sterndale, 'Memoranda', 9.

54LCC R975.

55Cox, *The Columbia River*, 29.

56Cuming, Journal, 37.

57Kotzebue, *A New Voyage*, II, 218.

58Chamberlain, Journal, 25 December 1827.

59Bennett, *Narrative*, I, 64; Bull, *A Trip*, 23.

Chapter Seven

1Simpson, *Narrative of a Journey*, I, 434; Bradley, *The American Frontier*, 239-50.

2*Samoa Times*, 27 October 1877; J. C. Williams, Trade Reports, 2 January 1867 and 1 January 1868, BCS 3/3; Trood, *Island Reminiscenses*, 70.

3*Fiji Times*, 9 October, 18 December 1869, 24 December 1870.

4Wilkes, *Narrative*, III, 394.

5Bradley, *The American Frontier*, 397; Francis A. Olmsted, *Incidents of a Whaling Voyage, to which are added, observations on the Scenery, Manners and Customs, and Missionary Stations of the Sandwich and Society Islands*, 64.

6Kamehameha III to Charlton, 30 June 1840, FO and EX 1840; Skinner/Dominis case, 13 October 1841, FO and EX 1841.

7Bradley, *The American Frontier*, 402-66.

8H. Britton, *Fiji in 1870*, 40; *Fiji Times*, 21 December 1870, 7 January 1871.

9*Town and Country Journal*, 8 July 1871.

10*Fiji Times*, 19, 22 June 1872.

11Peter France, *The Charter of the Land: Custom and Colonization in Fiji*, 73-91.

12G. C. Henderson, History of Government in Fiji 1760-1875, II, 196-470; Derrick, *A History*, 195-241.

13Richard Philp, Diary.

14J. C. Williams, Trade Report, 1 January 1873, BCS 3/3; J. M. Coe, Trade Report, 2 January 1873, USCD-A, III; Gilson, *Samoa 1830 to 1900*, 276-86.

15BCS 3/3, 1875-76; USCD-A, III, 1875 and IV, 1876; James Lyle Young, Private Journal, 3 June 1875-15 February 1876.

16C. F. Gordon Cumming, *A Lady's Cruise in a French Man-of-War*, 75.

17Petition to E. Liardet, 29 June 1877, BCS 2/2; Davidson, *Samoa*, 60.

18Wilkes, *Narrative*, IV, 58; Kekuanaoa v. Wilkes, FO and EX 1840.

19*Fiji Times*, 21 October 1871; Litton Forbes, *Two Years in Fiji*, 314-18.

20*Fiji Times*, 28 October 1871, 5 February 1873.

21Forbes, *Two Years*, 277.

22Forbes, *Two Years*, 279-80; John Gaggin, *Among the Man-Eaters*, 22-30.

23Boddam-Whetham, *Pearls*, 293.

24Great Britain Foreign Office Confidential Print, No. 3846 (1878); Petition to Liardet, 29 June 1877, BCS 2/2.

25*Samoa Times*, 10 November 1877; Griffin to Secretary of State, 10 November 1877, USCD-A, V.

26Liardet to the Earl of Derby, 20 December 1877, Confidential Print, No. 3846.

27Kay, 'The Sandwich Islands', 125.

28Mrs Lydia Nye, Journal, 30 December 1842.

29*Fiji Gazette*, 30 November 1872.

30*Fiji Times*, 6 August 1870, 3 April 1872.

31Hinckley to Hunnewell, 26 November 1833, Hunnewell MSS.

32Philp, Diary.

33C. F. Gordon Cumming, *At Home in Fiji*, 28.

34Hinckley to Hunnewell, 26 November 1833, Hunnewell

MSS.
35Fayerweather to his sisters, 2 August 1833.
36G. H. W. Markham, Diary, 27 February 1870, 15 March 1871; *Town and Country Journal*, 8 July 1871.
37Faxon D. Atherton, *The California Diary of . . . 1836-1839*, 122.
38Kay, 'The Sandwich Islands', 117.
39*Fiji Times,* 6 January 1872.
40Nye, Journal, 25 November 1842.
41Edward H. Harrison, Journal, 15 June, 4 August 1834; Reynolds, Journal, 1834-6; *Fiji Times,* 13 May 1871, 17 January 1872 ; *Fiji Gazette,* 29 March, 11 April 1873.
42Fayerweather to his father, 2 March 1838; *Hawaiian Spectator,* I, April 1838; *Polynesian,* 10 July 1841; *Fiji Times,* 21 August 1872, 30 April 1873, 14 January 1874; Amy Williams, Journal, 29 October 1873.
43Reynolds, Journal, 7, 11 April 1843; William Paty, Journal, 11 April 1843; *Samoa Times,* 1 December 1877.
44*Fiji Times,* 6 December 1871.
45Wilkes, *Narrative,* III, 375.
46*Fiji Times,* 18 January 1873.
47*Fiji Times,* 21 January 1871.

Chapter Eight
1The substance of this chapter was first published as an article in *JPH*, 6 (1971), 39-59.
2Edward B. Reuter, 'Impersonal Aspects of Race Relations', in Edgar T. Thompson and Everett C. Hughes, eds., *Race: Individual and Collective Behaviour*, 184-6.
3Written for Cakanauto to J. B. Williams, 20 June 1848, USCD-L,I.
4J. B. Williams to Henry Williams, 1846-50, J. B. Williams MSS.
5J. C. Jones to Marshall, 20 November 1821, Marshall MSS.

6Cruise, *Journal,* 241.
7*Fiji Times,* 6 December 1871, also 19 July 1871.
8Deryck Scarr, 'John Bates Thurston, Commodore J. G. Goodenough, a n d Rampant Anglo-Saxons in Fiji', *HS*, XI (1964), 361-82.
9*Fiji Times,* 18 December 1872.
10Dawson to Secretary of State, 13 September 1879, USCD-A, VII.
11Proponents of this theory include T. G. P. Spear, *The Nabobs. A Study of the Social Life of the English in eighteenth century India;* O. Mannoni, *Prospero and Caliban: The Psychology of Colonization;* Philip Mason, *Prospero's Magic: Some thoughts on Class and Race.*
12Amy Williams, Journal, 24 December 1873; Article, 'Fiji from a Woman's Point of View', *Fiji Times,* 9 October 1872.
13*Fiji Times,* 6 August 1870.
14*Fiji Times,* 8 January 1870.
15Reynolds, Journal, 24 July 1840.
16Mason, *Prospero's Magic,* 2.
17Mrs Hooper to Mr Hooper, 12 March 1840, Hooper MSS.
18Amy Williams, Journal, 13 September 1864.
19Reynolds, Journal, 30 November 1836.
20Gilson, *Samoa 1830-1900,* 342.
21*Fiji Times,* 18 June 1870.
22Jarves-D u d o i t C a s e, 8 August 1839, FO and EX 1839.
23Foster to Secretary of State, 3 October 1875, USCD-A, IV.
24See Chapter 5, p. 219-20 and also Appendix pp. 219-21, for the full text of the proclamation.
25To Kamehameha III, 20 January 1829, FO and EX 1829.
26Petition to Secretary of State, 10 November 1829, copy from USNR in KC.
27Petition to Captain Finch, 30 October 1829, copy from USNR in KC.
28Calvert to Hebblewhite, 7

October 1853, Pacific Islands, 1822-1875.

[29]Smythe, *Ten Months,* 103.

[30]Herbert Blumer, 'Race Prejudice as a Sense of Group Position', in J. Masuoka and P. Valien, eds., *Race Relations: Problems and Theory, Essays in Honor of Robert E. Park,* 225.

[31]Williams to Secretary of State, 1 April 1864, BCS 3/3.

[32]Pritchard, *Polynesian Reminiscences,* 350.

[33]D'Ewes, *China, Australia,* 145; Trood, *Island Reminiscences,* 37.

[34]To his Majesty Kauikeaouli, 19 March 1834, FO and EX 1834.

[35]H. Paty to Kamehameha III, 13 May 1839, Interior Department Miscellaneous 1839 (his emphasis).

[36]Binner to Eggleston, 3 October 1860, Missionary Correspondence; Damme, 'South Seas', *Australasian,* 8 December 1866; Trood, *Island Reminiscences,* 33.

[37]M. Loomis, Journal, 23 June 1820; Daniel Tyerman and George Bennet, *Journal of Voyages and Travels,* I, 425; *The Friend,* 1 January 1845; 6 March 1876, BCS, Miscellaneous Documents.

Chapter Nine

[1]Eagleston, Journal, 6 June 1831.

[2]Lucett, *Rovings,* I, 66-7, 213.

[3]*Fiji Times,* 29 December 1886.

[4]Gilson, *Samoa 1830 to 1900,* 341-8; *The Cyclopedia of Samoa,* 96; *Fiji Times,* 21 December 1881.

[5]Reginald Gallop, Letters from the Pacific, IX, 31 July 1887.

[6]Belshaw, 'Pacific Island Towns', 17-24.

[7]LCC R588; *Fiji Times,* 8 November 1871.

Bibliography

I MANUSCRIPT RECORDS
1. *Official MSS.*
General

Foreign Office Pacific Islands: FO 58/3-17 (AJCP 1509-13); 27 (AJCP 1515); 38 (AJCP 1519); 84B (AJCP 1534-5); 88 (AJCP 1536); 90 (AJCP 1537); 92 (AJCP 1538). The following FO 58 were read in the Mitchell Library microfilm series: 58/94, 96, 98, 102, 105, 109, 111, 113, 115, 118, 120, 131, 135, 142, 147, 150.

Admiralty Records.

Adm. 1/218 Bethune to Maitland, H.M.S. Conway, Port Jackson, 9 February 1838. (Tahiti & Samoa) (AJCP 3262).

Adm. 1/5548 Home to Cochrane, H.M.S. North Star, Auckland, 15 October 1844. (Samoa) (AJCP 3298).

Adm. 1/5577 Blake to Seymour, H.M.S. Juno off Tongataboo, 30 March 1847. (Samoa) (AJCP 3301).

Adm. 1/5590 Maxwell to Secy. of Adm., H.M.S. Dido, Auckland, 18 March 1848. (Samoa) (AJCP 3302).

Adm. 1/5593 Pritchard to Palmerston, British Consulate, Samoa, 12 August 1848. (Samoa & Fiji) (AJCP 3302).

Adm. 1/5617 Home to Secy. of Adm., H.M.S. Calliope, Sydney, 20 December 1852. (Samoa & Fiji) (AJCP 3303).

Adm. 1/5672 Fremantle to Secy. of Adm., H.M.S. Juno, At Sea, 15 November 1855. (Samoa) (AJCP 3304).

Adm. 1/5969 Hope to Wiseman, H.M.S. Brisk, Hawaii, 5 September 1866. (Samoa) (AJCP 3319).

Adm. 1/6096 Lambert to Secy. of Adm., H.M.S. Challenger, Sydney, 8 September 1869. (Samoa) (AJCP 3325).

Adm. 1/6192 Montgomerie to Stirling, H.M.S. Blanche, Sydney, 1 July 1871. (Samoa) (AJCP 3329).

Adm. 1/6303 Goodenough to Secy. of Adm., H.M.S. Pearl, Levuka, 16 March 1874. (Samoa) (AJCP 3338).

Adm. 1/6345 Goodenough to Secy. of Adm., H.M.S. Pearl, Sydney, 15 March 1875. (Samoa) (AJCP 3342).

Adm. 122/12 Fremantle to Secy. of Adm., H.M.S. Juno, At Sea, 12 December 1855. (Fiji) (AJCP 2705).

Adm. 125/135 Fremantle to Secy. of Adm., H.M.S. Juno, At Sea, 4 October 1856. (Samoa) (AJCP 2712).

United States Naval Records, Pacific Squadron 1841-86, microfilm copies in NLA of originals held in National Archives, Washington.

Royal Navy Commander-in-Chief, Australian Station:
Pacific Islands 1857-79, RNAS 13-14; Fiji 1868-75, RNAS 28-31, microfilm copies in NLA of originals held in National Archives, Wellington.

Hawaii

British Consulate Papers (incoming and outgoing), 1825-43, typescript of
originals in AH.

Admiralty Records — Reports of Lord Byron, Lord Paulet and Rear
Admiral Thomas, MS. copies in AH.

Navy Department Archives — Extracts from United States Naval Records,
typescript copies in Kuykendall Collection in UH.

Despatches from United States Consuls in Honolulu [USCD-H], Vols.
I-II, October 1820-December 1847, microfilm copies in ML of
originals held in National Archives, Washington.

Original Records in the Archives of Hawaii (AH)

Foreign Office and Executive [FO and EX], documents dated 1794-1843
(including flat file) and undated items 1-208.

Historical and Miscellaneous Manuscripts, documents dated 1810-43 and
undated items 1-165.

Immigration and Naturalization, Naturalization records 1838-46; Deniza-
tion 1846-59.

Interior Department, Miscellaneous, n.d.-1843; Licences n.d.-1843.

Land File, Records from the Department of Land and Natural Resources,
Foreign Testimony Vols. I-XVI and Foreign Register Vols. I-III.

Laws 1827-9.

Vital Statistics, Marriage, Birth and Death Certificates.

Tahiti

Great Britain and Ireland, Foreign Office, Consular Despatches and
Papers: Vol. I Tahiti and Society Islands . . . 1822-7, FO 58/14;
Vol. IV Tahiti and Society Islands . . . 1837-9, FO 58/15, MSS.
23/1 & 4 in ML.

British Consulate Papers Tahiti, MSS. 24/1-24 in ML.

Despatches from United States Consuls in Tahiti [USCD-T], Vols. I-II,
January 1836-December 1850, microfilm copies in ML of originals
held in National Archives, Washington.

New Zealand

New South Wales, Governor's Despatches, Vols. 28-34, 1837-40, MSS.
A1217-A1223 in ML.

Transcripts of Missing Despatches from Governor of New South Wales
(typescript copies), 1833-41, A1267-5 & 6 in ML.

Despatches from Governor of New South Wales, Enclosures etc., typescript copies from Public Record Office, 1832-40, A1267-13-19 in ML.

Despatches to Governor of New South Wales, Secretary of State Despatches 1833-9 & 1845, MSS. A1270-A1281 & A1296 in ML.

Despatches from United States Consuls in Auckland and the Bay of
Islands [USCD-B. of I.], Vol. I, 27 May 1839-30 November 1846,
microfilm copies in ML of originals held in National Archives,
Washington.

Fiji

Extracts from Letter Books of H.B.M. Consular Office, Levuka, Fiji,
1863-9, originals in Central Archives of Fiji, typescript copies A3167

in ML. (Compiled by R. A. Derrick, 1949.)

Colonial Office 83, Original Correspondence Fiji, 1860-72, CO 83/1-2. (AJCP 2202-3).

Despatches from United States Consuls in Lauthala [USCD-L], Vols. I-V, November 1844-December 1876, microfilm copies in ML of originals held in National Archives, Washington.

Records in the National Archives of Fiji
Cakobau Government

Inwards Correspondence General 1871-3.

Executive Council — Inwards Correspondence General, January-December 1873.

Chief Secretary — Inwards Correspondence General, 1871-4.

Chief Secretary — Levuka Council By-laws.

Chief Secretary — Naval and Consular Correspondence Inwards, 1872-4.

Miscellaneous Papers 1873.

Secretariat — Cakobau, Ad Interim and Provisional Governments. Papers relating to Censuses of Population 1872-5.

Royal Commission to Quiet Land Titles, Claim Files 1872-3.

Land Claims Commission [LCC] 1875-87 and Executive Council sitting for the Rehearing of Claims to Land 1879-87. (Reports of original claims are referred to thus: LCCR-. Original claims that became subjects of subsequent appeals are referred to thus: LCCP-.)

Samoa

British Consulate Samoa [BCS] Series 2, General Inwards Correspondence, 1847-1911, 2/1-4, microfilm copies in ML of originals held in National Archives, Wellington.

British Consulate Samoa [BCS] Series 3, Despatches to the Foreign Office, 1848-98, 3/1-4, microfilm copies in ML of originals held in National Archives, Wellington.

British Consulate Samoa [BCS] Series 5, General Outwards Correspondence, 1859-1913, 5/1-2, microfilm copies in ML of originals in National Archives, Wellington.

British Consulate Samoa [BCS] Miscellaneous Documents in the Department of Justice, Apia — Register of Marriages Non Consular possibly/probably Valid ; Register of Marriages pursuant to Act 12 and 13 Vict. C. 68; Index to Register of Half Castes; Miscellaneous Lists and Registers from 1875; List of British Subjects from 1808.

Despatches from the United States Consuls in Apia [USCD-A], 1843-1906, Vols. I-VII, December 1843-January 1880, microfilm copies in ML of originals held in National Archives, Washington.

Samoa — Estate and Probate Files, Supreme Court and Public Trust Office, Apia.

Samoan Land Commission 1891-4, Land Claims 1-3857, Lands and Survey Department, Apia.

Great Britain Foreign Office Confidential Print, No. 3846, Part II. Further

Correspondence respecting Affairs in the Navigators' Islands, 1877-8. [This is a printed document.]

2. *Non-Official MSS.*

Account of Navigator Island, February 2nd 1823, Vol. IV, 38-51, Papers of William Elyard [there is some doubt whether Elyard was the author of the account] MS. A2884 in ML.

Adams, Alexander. Journal, MS. M1 in AH.

———— Miscellaneous MSS. 1840-50, in AH.

American Protestant Mission Material relating to 1826, MS. and printed M105 in AH.

Anon. Journal kept aboard H.M.S. *Thunder*, 1836-7, MS. 091 in WTu.

Banks, Joseph. Banks Papers, Brabourne Collection, Vol. IV, Australia 1801-20. MS. A78-3 in ML.

Bateman, Thomas. Logbook and Letters of Thomas Bateman, NZ 656 MSS., in Auckland Public Library.

Bêche-de-mer Records Salem, a selection of letters, journals and extracts from logs from the PMS. (Two reels of microfilm in the Department of Pacific History, ANU.)

Belcher, Edward. Private Journal: Remarks: H.M. Ship Blossom on Discovery during the years 1825, -6, -7. Capt. F. W. Beechey Comdr., MS. in WTu.

Bell, Edward. Journal of Voyage in *Chatham* 1791-4, 2 vols., qMS-1791-94 p in WTu.

Bingham, Hiram. Bingham Letters, February 1829-February 1832 and Correspondence between Bingham and the foreign residents, November 1831, Xerox copies of MSS. in Houghton Library, in HMCS.

Bishop, Francis T. Narrative of a Voyage in the North and South Pacific Oceans with Recollections of the Society, Sandwich and other Islands visited during the years 1832-35, 3 vols., MSS. in UH.

Boit, John. The Journal of a Voyage Round the Globe 1795 and 1796, Vol. 2 only, photocopies of original MSS. in BPBM.

Bolton, W. W. Tahitian Vignettes, 2 vols., A3359-60. Old Time Tahiti, 3 vols., A3373-5. Inter Alia Bolton Papers, MSS. A3377 in ML.

Brewster Papers. Harry the Jew (J. H. Danford) Doc. No. 24, Doc. File No. 24 in Fiji Museum.

Brinsmade, Peter Allen. Collection of Letters, M15 in AH.

Brown, George. Journal 1867-71, Vol. 2 only, MS. A1686-8/10 in ML.

———— 'Old Hands and Old Times in the South Seas', typescript, MSS. 1119 in ML.

Browning, George. Journal of a Trip to the South Sea Islands in the Schooner Caledonia, Belonging to Sydney, N.S.Wales, MS. in Auckland Public Library.

Bryant and Sturgis. Letter Books, copies of MSS. in Harvard College Library, in the Kuykendall Collection in UH.

Cargill, David. Journal, Vol. 2, MS. A1818 in ML.

Chamberlain, Levi. Journals I-XXIV, November 11 1822-December 23

1843, MSS. in HMCS.

———— Letter to J. Evarts, Honolulu, September 11 1826, Missionary Letters, II, 471-5, typescript in HMCS.

Clark, B. F. Logbook of H.M.S. *Esk,* June 1863-September 1867, MS. 67 in Auckland Museum.

Clark, Ephraim W. Private Journal, 4 April 1828-2 August 1834, MS. in HMCS.

Coe Family Bible, MS. 2385 in NLA.

Colcord, John. Journal and Account Book, MS. M12 in AH.

Conditions and Prospects of the Children of the Missionaries. Unsigned to the Prudential Committee of the Sandwich Island Mission, n.d., MS. in HMCS.

Cuming, Hugh. Journal of a Voyage from Valparaiso to the Society and the adjacent Islands . . . in the years 1827 and 1828, MS. A1336 in ML.

Davies, John. Journal, LMS, South Sea Journals, Box 3, 1808-10, microfilm copy in ML of original held in LMS Archives, London.

Dimond, Henry and Ann Marie. Letters 1835-65, MS. M42 in AH.

Davis, Robert G. Letters, photocopies of original MSS. in California State Library, in Kuykendall Collection in UH.

Dimsdell, J. L. Account of the Death and Remains of Capt. Cook at Owhyhee recd. by J. Le Dimsdell, Quarter Master of the Gunjara, Capt. James Barbor, MS. Q209 in DL.

Drafts on Australian Merchants 1867-71, qMS — 1867-71 — p in WTu.

Eagleston, J. H. Journals and Letters, Bêche-de-mer Records, Salem, selection from PMS. (2 reels of microfilm in Department of Pacific History, ANU.)

Fayerweather, A. H. Fayerweather Letters 1831-55, in AH.

French, William. Account book of William French [?] 1818-19, MS. 657 F88 in HHS.

Fitch Documents, originals in Bancroft Library, MS. and typescript copies in Kuykendall Collection in UH.

Gallop, Reginald. Letters from the Pacific 1877, item G, uncat. MSS.; set 488 in ML.

Hale, Horatio. Hale's MS. of the Navigator Islands 1835, A321 in ML.

Hamond, A. S. Letter Books of Capt. Hamond, H.M.S. *Salamander,* April 1844-June 1853, 5 vols., MSS. A2050-2054 in ML.

Hankey, Frederick B. A Journal of the Cruizes and Remarkable Events occurring on board H.M.S. *The Collingwood,* May 1844-February 1846, MSS. A430-431 in ML.

Harrison, Edward H. Journal of a voyage from Warren to Oahu, 1833-4, MS. 091 — 1833-34, in WTu.

Hoare, H. J. My Journal of H.M. Ships *Dido, Clio,* and *Pearl;* . . . and the Fiji Islands; between the 20 April 1871 and the 16 June 1874, 2 vols., MSS. A1761-1762 in ML.

Holmes, Oliver. Papers, 2 items, MS. M66 in AH.

Hooper Papers, 1832-43, MSS. in UH.

Hope, Charles W. Letter Journals of Captain Charles W. Hope of HMS. *Brisk* 1865-8, 4 vols., MSS., q091 — 1865-68, in WTu.

Howell, W. H. W. H. Howell Collection — Trading agreements for flax 1815, MS. Ah 47 in ML.

Hudson, John T. Journal of the Schooner *Tamana* from Woahao (Sandwich Islands) to the Coast of America, MS. H.M. 30491 in Huntington Library, San Marino, California.

Hunnewell, James. Papers, Vol. I, 1820-4 'Ventures in Ships, Thaddeus, Rover, Pearl', and Vol. II, 1826-34, 'The Beginning of C. Brewer & Co. Ltd.', MSS. in Harvard College Library, Xerox copies in Carter Collection in BPBM.

Hunt, John. Private Journal, 2 vols., typescript of MSS. A3349-50 in ML.

Im Thurn, Everard. Im Thurn Papers Fiji 1870-1919, MSS. in National Archives of Fiji.

Ingraham, Joseph. Journal of the Voyage of the Brigantine *Hope* from Boston to the North West Coast of America, 1790-1792, qMS — 1790-92 — p in WTu.

King, Philip. Captain King's Visit to New Zealand and Norfolk 1838-9, MS. C 764-2 in ML.

Kuykendall, R. S. Kuykendall Collection. Copies of documents housed in repositories in the United States, in UH.

Lang, J. D. Letter I. Origin and Commencement of Missionary operations in the South Seas, n.d., MS. fragment in Ferguson Collection in NLA.

Larkin documents, originals in Bancroft Library, MS. and typescript copies in Kuykendall Collection in UH.

Lomberg, E. W. G. Diary of E. W. Lomberg, Bureta, Fiji, 1862-9, 2 vols., MSS. B519/1-2 in ML.

London Missionary Society South Sea Journals and South Sea Letters, microfilm copies in ML of originals in London Missionary Society Archives, London.

Loomis, Elisha. Journal 1824-6, MS. in HMCS.

Loomis, Maria. Journal 1819-24, MS. in HMCS.

Lowther, Asia James. A Petition to the Right Honarable his Excellency the Resident Governer of the Crown Colony Fee-Jee, MS. in National Archives of Fiji.

Lyth, R. B. A History of Fiji, MS. B552 in ML.

————— Journals I-VII, October 1842-December 1851, MSS. B535-546 in ML.

————— Tongan and Fijian Reminiscences, MS. B549 in ML.

————— Voyaging Journals, I, III and IV, 1848-52, MSS. B537 in ML.

McLaren, Jas. A Journal of the Barque *Cheviot* from London, Whaling November 1831-1838, typescript of original in WTu.

Marin, Don Francisco de Paula. Extracts from the Journals of Don

Francisco de Paula Marin, typescript of a copy of the original in AH.

———— Marin Collection, 67 items, MSS. M102 in AH.

Markham, G. H. W. Diary, Fiji, 1869-74, MS. A1462 in ML.

Marsden, Samuel. Reverend Samuel Marsden Papers, Vol. 3, New Zealand Missions 1816-1837, MSS. A1994 in ML.

Marshall, Josiah. Marshall and Wildes MSS., originals in Houghton Library, Harvard, copies in Kuykendall Collection in UH.

Methodist Missionary Society Papers 1812-89, originals in the Methodist Missionary Society, London, microfilm copies (55 reels) in NLA.

Missionary Correspondence, Fiji-Rewa, Rotuma and Ovalau, Bau and Miscellaneous, typescript, MS. 205 in DL.

Newburgh, Rufus. A Narrative of Voyage etc., MS. dated 28 April 1835, FO and EX 1835 in AH.

Nye, Lydia R. (Mrs). Journal, Honolulu, 1841-2 and Miscellaneous Letters 1842-9, MSS. in AH.

Pacific Islands, 1822-75 and 1833-51. Two collections of papers about the South Sea Islands, SP 194-195 in DL.

Paty, William. Journal 1842-3, MS. in AH.

Paty Collection. Five Letters, William Paty to Henry Paty 1837-40, MSS. M119 in AH.

Petigru, T. Petigru Letter to Chief Tui Viti of Bau — 1851, MS. q091-1851 in WTu.

Philp, Richard. Diary 19 August-13 December 1872, MS. in National Archives of Fiji.

Platt, George. Journal — Raiatea to Hervey and Samoan Groups 1835-1836, LMS, South Sea Journals, Box 8, Item 110, microfilm copy in ML of original held in LMS Archives, London.

Polack, J. S. Title Deeds of Land in Kororareka, August 1833, MS. An 57/5 in ML.

Puget, Peter. Journal Log of the *Chatham* — Extracts — Hawaii, 1792-4, photocopies of original in HHS.

Restieaux, Alfred. Manuscripts Part 2 Pacific Islands, in WTu.

Reynolds, Stephen. Journal, November 1823-December 1843, original in PMS, microfilm copy in HMCS.

Ryder, A. P. Remarks on Hawaii, Tahiti and other Islands, MS. B195 in ML.

Ryder, G. L. Ryder Papers, originals in the possession of Miss Ryder, microfilm copy FM 3/241 in ML.

Simpkinson, F. G. Diary of F. G. Simpkinson on board the H.M.S. *Sulphur* 1837. MS. A3343 in ML.

[Smith, Joseph.] Tahiti 1824-1857, Ross MSS. in BPBM.

Solid Men of Boston in the North West, MS. in Bancroft Library, California.

Steinberger, A. B. Papers in Roman Catholic Mission, Samoa, microfilm FM 4/200 in ML.

Stevenson, Robert Louis. Missions in the South Seas, Stevenson Papers AS 25-2 in ML.

Swainson, H. G. Journal 1850-1 (on board H.M.S. *Bramble*), MS. 1850-51 — p in WTu.

Swanston, R. S. Journals 1857-66 and 1874-85, 6 vols., MSS. in National Archives of Fiji.

Thierry, Charles P. H. Letters and Papers, MSS. in Auckland Public Library.

Thomas, John. Journal of a Visit to the Navigators Islands 1855, MS. 336 in DL.

Turner, Peter. Journals 1835-9, MSS. B302-305 in ML.

Turpin, E. J. Diary and Narratives of E. J. Turpin 1870-*c*.1894, MSS. in National Archives of Fiji.

Vallejo Documents, originals in Bancroft Library, MS. and typescript copies in Kuykendall Collection in UH.

Whippy, David. Letters of, and relating to David Whippy, MSS. in National Archives of Fiji.

Williams, J. B. Manuscript Collection, originals in PMS, microfilm copy, 1864, and (2) Journals to J. C. Williams, September 1873-January 1874, 3 vols. in PMB 24.

Williams, John. Cook Islands 1832-3. Rarotonga to Navigators, Tongataboo etc. in the Olive Branch, London Missionary Society, South Seas Journals, Item 101, microfilm copy in ML of original held in LMS Archives, London.

Williams, John and Charles Barff. A Journal of a voyage undertaken chiefly for the purpose of introducing Christianity among the Fegees and Hamoas . . . in 1830, MS. A1636 in ML.

Williams, J. B. Manuscript Collection, originals in PMS, microfilm copy, Micro MS. 418 in WTu.

————— Miscellaneous manuscript dealing with the history of Fiji 1843-57, MS. G11 in WTu.

Williams, John Chauner. Journal of Events, February 1868-March 1872, in PMB 37.

————— Journals II and III to Amy Williams, October 1873-February 1874. in PMB 24.

Young, James Lyle. Private Journal, January 1875-December 1877 in PMB 21.

Young, John. Journal 1801-8, FO and EX 1801 in AH.

————— Letter from Captain Magee to John Young, 10 February 1804, FO and EX 1804 in AH.

————— Letter from Thomas Meek to John Young, n.d., FO and EX. item 87 in AH.

II CONTEMPORARY PUBLISHED MATERIAL
Books, Articles and Newspapers

Adams, Alexander. 'Extracts from an Ancient Log, Selections from the log book of Captain Alexr. Adams in connection with the early history of Hawaii', *The Hawaiian Annual,* 1906, 66-74.

Alexander, W. D. 'Early Trading in Hawaii', *Hawaiian Historical Society Papers,* XI (1904), 22-4. [Papers of French & Co.]

Andreyev, A. I., ed., *Russian Discoveries in the Pacific and in North America in the Eighteenth and Nineteenth Centuries,* translated by Carl Ginsburg, Michigan, Ann Arbor, 1952.

[Anon.] 'A Cruise after and among the Cannibals', *Harpers New Monthly Magazine,* VII (1853), 455-75.

Arago, Jacques. *Narrative of a Voyage Round the World in the Uranie and Physicienne Corvettes commanded by Captain Freycinet during the Years 1817, 1818, 1819 and 1820,* London, Treuttel and Wurtz, Treuttel, Jnr and Richter, 1823.

Atherton, Faxon D. *The California Diary of Faxon Dean Atherton 1836-1839,* edited by Doyce B. Nunis Jr, San Francisco, California Historical Society, 1964.

Barlow, Nora, ed. *Charles Darwin's Diary of the Voyage of H.M.S. Beagle,* Cambridge, At the University Press, 1933.

Barnard, Charles. 'A Narrative of the Adventures of Capt. Charles H. Barnard of New York during a Voyage Round the World (1812-1816) with an Account of his Abandonment and Solitary Life on one of the Falkland Islands', in *The Sea, The Ship and The Sailor,* introduced by Captain Eliot Snow, Salem, Marine Research Society, 1925.

Barrot, Adolphe. 'Visit of the French sloop of war Bonite to the Sandwich Islands in 1836', *The Friend,* 4 January-1 June 1850 (6 instalments translated from French).

Bayly, George. *Sea-Life Sixty Years Ago: A record of adventure which led up to the discovery of the relics of the long-missing expedition commanded by the Comte de la Pérouse,* London, Kegan Paul, Trench & Co., 1885.

Bays, Peter. *A Narrative of the Wreck of the Minerva Whaler of Port Jackson, New South Wales on Nicholson's Shoal, 24°S. 179°W . . . . ,* Cambridge, Bridges, 1831.

Beechey, F. W. *Narrative of a Voyage to the Pacific and Beering's Strait . . . in the years 1825, 1826, 1827, 1828,* 2 vols., London, Henry Colburn & Richard Bentley, 1831.

Belcher, Edward. *Narrative of a Voyage round the World, performed in H.M.S. Sulphur during the years 1836-1842,* 2 vols., London, Henry Colburn, 1843.

Bennett, Frederick Debell. *Narrative of a Whaling Voyage Round the Globe From the Year 1833 to 1836,* 2 vols., London, Richard Bentley, 1840.

Bensusan, M. 'The Fiji Islands', *The Royal Geographical Society of London Journal,* XXXII (1862), 42-50.

Bingham, Hiram. *A Residence of Twenty-One Years in the Sandwich*

Islands, New York, Sherman Converse, 1847.

Bligh, William. *The Log of the Bounty* . . . , 2 vols., London, The Golden Cockerel Press, 1937.

Boddam-Whetham, J. W. *Pearls of the Pacific,* London, Hurst and Blackett, 1876.

Brenchley, Julius L. *Jottings during the Cruise of the H.M.S. Curaçoa among the South Sea Islands in 1865,* London, Longmans, Green, 1873.

Britton, H. *Fiji in 1870,* Melbourne, Samuel Mullen, 1870.

Bull, W. K. *A Trip to Tahiti, and other islands in the South Seas,* Melbourne, Edgar Ray & Co., 1858.

Buller, James. *Forty Years in New Zealand,* London, Hodder & Stoughton, 1878.

Burns, Barnet. *A Brief Narrative of the Remarkable History of Barnet Burns, an English sailor; . . . with a faithful account of the way in which he became a Chief of One of the Tribes of the New Zealanders* . . . , Coventry, Printed for the author, by John Turner, 1835.

Campbell, Archibald. *A Voyage Round the World from 1806 to 1812 . . . with an account of the present state of the Sandwich Islands, and a vocabulary of their language,* Edinburgh, Archibald Constable & Co., 1816.

[Cary, William]. *Wrecked on the Feejees. Experience of a Nantucket man, a century ago, who was sole survivor of whaleship 'Oeno' and lived nine years among cannibals of South Sea Islands,* Nantucket, The Inquirer & Mirror Press, 1928.

Catlin, George. *Episodes from Life among the Indians and Last Rambles, with 152 scenes and portraits by the Artist,* edited by M. C. Ross, Norman, University of Oklahoma, 1959.

'Ceres'. *The Fiji Islands, with maps; Commercially Considered as a Field for Emigration,* Melbourne, Printed by Sands & McDougall, 1869.

Chamisso, Adelbert von. 'Chamisso's Account of the Voyage Around the World on the "Rurick" 1815-1818', typescript translation from the German 1836 edition, in AH.

Churchward, W. B. *Blackbirding in the South Pacific; or, The First White Man on the Beach,* London, Swan Sonnenschein & Co., 1888.

Coffin, Robert. *The Last of the Logan,* edited by Harold W. Thompson, New York, Cornell University Press, 1941.

Colenso, William. *The Authentic and Genuine History of the Signing of the Treaty of Waitangi, New Zealand, February 5 and 6, 1840* . . . , Wellington, Government Printer, 1890.

Conrad, Agnes C., ed. *The Letters and Journal of Francisco de Paula Marin,* in *Don Francisco de Paula Marin: A Biography,* by Ross H. Gast. *The Letters and Journal of Francisco de Paula Marin,* edited by Agnes C. Conrad, Honolulu, The University of Hawaii Press, 1973.

Constitution and By-laws of the Sandwich Island Institute, 1838.

Cook, James. *The Journals of Captain James Cook on his Voyages. of Discovery,* edited from the original manuscripts by J. C. Beaglehole, 4 vols. & a Portfolio, Cambridge, Published for the Hakluyt Society, At the University Press, 1955-67.

Cooper, H. Stonehewer. *Coral Lands,* 2 vols., London, Richard Bentley & Son, 1880.

Corney, Bolton G. *The Quest and Occupation of Tahiti by Emissaries of Spain during the years 1772-1776,* 3 vols., London, Printed for the Hakluyt Society, 1913.

Corney, Peter. *Voyages in the Northern Pacific: Narrative of several trading voyages from 1813 to 1818, between the Northwest Coast of America, the Hawaiian Islands and China, with a description of the Russian Establishments on the Northwest Coast,* Honolulu, Thos. G. Thrum, 1896.

Coulter, John. *Adventures in the Pacific: with observations on the natural productions, manners and customs of the natives of the various islands* . . . , Dublin, William Curry, Jun. & Company, 1845.

———— *Adventures on the Western Coast of South America, and the interior of California: including a narrative of incidents at the Kingsmill Islands, New Ireland, New Britain, New Guinea, and other islands in the Pacific Ocean* . . . , 2 vols., London, Longman, Brown, Green & Longmans, 1847.

Cox, Ross. *The Columbia River,* edited and with an introduction by Edgar I. Stewart and Jane R. Stewart, Norman, University of Oklahoma Press, 1957.

Crocombe, R. G. and Marjorie. *The Works of Ta'unga. Records of a Polynesian Traveller in the South Seas, 1833-1896,* Canberra, Australian National University Press, 1968.

Cruise, Richard A. *Journal of a Ten Months' Residence in New Zealand,* London, Longman, Hurst, Rees, Orme, Brown & Green, 1824.

Cumming, C. F. Gordon. *At Home in Fiji,* Edinburgh, William Blackwood & Sons, 1885.

———— *A Lady's Cruise in a French Man-of-War,* Edinburgh, William Blackwood & Sons, 1882.

Damme, Karl van. 'In the South Seas', *Australasian,* October-December 1866.

Davies, John. *The History of the Tahitian Mission, 1799-1830,* edited by C. Newbury, Cambridge, Published for the Hakluyt Society, At the University Press, 1961.

Davis, William Heath. *Seventy Five Years in California,* San Francisco, John Howell, 1929.

Debenham, Frank, ed. *The Voyage of Captain Bellingshausen to the Antarctic Seas 1819-1821,* 2 vols., London, Hakluyt Society Press, 1945.

Delano, Amasa. *A Narrative of Voyages and Travels, in the Northern and Southern Hemispheres: comprising three Voyages round the*

World: together with a voyage of survey and discovery in the Pacific Ocean and Oriental Islands, Boston, Privately printed for the author by E. G. House, 1817.

Dening, Greg, ed. *The Marquesan Journal of Edward Robarts 1797-1824,* Canberra, Australian National University Press, 1974.

De Ricci, James H. *Fiji: Our New Province in the South Seas,* London, Edward Stanford, 1875.

D'Ewes, John. *China, Australia and the Pacific Islands, in the years 1855-56,* London, Bentley, 1857.

Diapea, William, pseud. [William Diaper]. *Cannibal Jack: the true autobiography of a white man in the South Seas,* London, Faber & Gwyer Limited, 1928.

Dieffenbach, Ernest. *Travels in New Zealand: with contributions to the Geography, Geology, Botany, and Natural History of that Country,* 2 vols., London, John Murray, 1843.

Dillon, Peter. *Narrative and Successful Result of a Voyage in the South Seas . . . to Ascertain the Actual Fate of La Pérouse's Expedition, interspersed with Accounts of the Religion, Manners, Customs, and Cannibal Practices of the South Sea Islanders,* 2 vols., London, Hurst Chance & Co., 1829.

Dumont d'Urville, J. S. C. *Voyage de l'Astrolabe,* Vol. IV, *Le Voyage au Pole Sud,* translated by Olive Wright, typescript in WTu.

Earle, Augustus. *A Narrative of a nine months' residence in New Zealand in 1827; together with a Journal of a residence in Tristan D'Acunha . . . ,* London, Longman, Rees, Orme, Brown, Green & Longman, 1832.

Elder, John R., ed. *The Letters and Journals of Samuel Marsden 1765-1838,* Dunedin, Coulls, Somerville, Wilkie Ltd & A. H. Reed, 1932.

———— *Marsden's Lieutenants,* Dunedin, Coulls, Somerville, Wilkie Ltd & A. H. Reed, 1934.

Ellis, William. *A Narrative of a Tour through Hawaii, or Owhyhee; with remarks on the History, Traditions, Manners, Customs and Language of the Inhabitants of the Sandwich Islands,* Reprint of the London 1827 edition, Honolulu, Hawaiian Gazette Co. Ltd, 1917.

———— *Polynesian Researches, during a residence of nearly eight years in the Society and Sandwich Islands,* 4 vols., London, Fisher, Son & Jackson, 1831.

Endicott, William. *Wrecked among Cannibals in the Fijis: a narrative of shipwreck and adventure in the South Seas,* Salem, Marine Research Society, 1923.

Erskine, John E. *Journal of a Cruise among the Islands of the Western Pacific, including the Feejees and others inhabited by the Polynesian Negro races, in Her Majesty's Ship 'Havannah',* London, John Murray, 1853.

Events in Feejee: Narrated in recent letters from several Wesleyan Missionaries. With additions by the Rev. James Calvert and Professor

Harvey, London, John Mason, 1856.

Fiji Gazette & Central Polynesian, January 1871-April 1874. In October 1872 the paper became incorporated as the *Fiji Gazette.*

Fiji Times, September 1869-December 1887.

Fijian Weekly News & Planters' Journal, August-November 1868 (thirteen issues only).

Fitzroy, Robert. *Narrative of the Surveying Voyages of his Majesty's ships Adventure and Beagle between the years 1826 & 1836 . . . ,* 3 vols., London, Henry Colburn, 1839.

Forbes, Litton. *Two Years in Fiji,* London, Longmans, Green & Co., 1875.

Franchère, Gabriel. *A Voyage to the North West Coast of America,* Chicago, The Lakeside Press, 1954.

The Friend, 1843-6. The title of the paper changed from *Temperance Advocate & Seamen's Friend* to *The Friend, of Temperance and Seamen.* It was always, and still is, referred to as *The Friend.*

Gaggin, John. *Among the Man-Eaters,* London, T. Fisher Unwin, 1900.

Golovnin, V. M. Tour Around the World performed by the Command of His Majesty the Emperor on the Sloop of War Kamchatka in 1817, 1818, 1819, typescript translation of 1822 Russian edition, in Kuykendall Collection.

Goodenough, J. G. *Journal of Commodore Goodenough, during his Last Command as Senior Officer on the Australian Station 1873-1875,* edited with a Memoir by his widow, London, S. King & Co., 1876.

Hawaiian Gazette, 13 September 1876. [Obituary of James Robinson.]

Hawaiian Spectator, 1838-9. Two, four-part volumes published by an Association of Gentlemen.

Henderson, G. C., ed. *Fijian Documents; Political and Constitutional 1858-1875,* Sydney, Angus & Robertson, 1938.

————— *The Journal of Thomas Williams Missionary in Fiji 1840-1853,* 2 vols., Sydney, Angus & Robertson, 1931.

Henry, Teuira. *Ancient Tahiti,* Honolulu, Bishop Museum Press, 1928.

Historical Records of Australia, Series 1, Vols. I, VIII, XVIII, XX; Series 3, IV [Sydney], Library Committee of the Commonwealth Parliament, 1914-25.

Hockin, John P. *A Supplement to the Account of the Pelew Islands; compiled from the Journals of the Panther and Endeavour, two vessels sent by the Honourable East India Company to those Islands in the year 1790; and from the oral communications of Captain H. Wilson,* London, Printed for Captain H. Wilson, 1803. [Bound with the fifth edition of Keate q.v.]

Holden, Horace. *A Narrative of the Shipwreck, Captivity and sufferings of Horace Holden and Benj. H. Nute; who were cast away in the American ship 'Mentor', on the Pelew Islands, in the year 1832 . . . ,* Boston, Russell Shattuck & Co., 1836.

Hood, T. H. *Notes of a Cruise in H.M.S. Fawn in the Western Pacific in the Year 1862*, Edinburgh, Edmonston & Douglas, 1863.

Hübner, Joseph Alexander. *Through the British Empire*, 2 vols., London, John Murray, 1886.

Hunnewell, James. 'Honolulu in 1817 and 1818', edited by James F. Hunnewell, *Hawaiian Historical Society Papers*, VIII (1895), 3-19.

Hunt, John. *Memoir of the Rev. William Cross, Wesleyan Missionary to the Friendly and Feejee Islands*, London, John Mason, 1846.

Ii, John Papa. *Fragments of Hawaiian History as recorded by John Papa Ii*, translated by Mary Kawena Pukui, edited by Dorothy B. Barrère, Honolulu, Bishop Museum Press, 1959.

Im Thurn, Sir Everard and Leonard C. Wharton, eds. *The Journal of William Lockerby, Sandalwood Trader in the Fijian Islands during the years 1808-1809*, London, Printed for Hakluyt Society, 1925.

Iselin, Isaac. *Journal of a Trading Voyage Around the World, 1805-1808*, New York, McIlroy & Emmet Press, n.d.

Jackson, John, pseud. [William Diaper]. 'Jackson's Narrative', in John E. Erskine, *Journal of a Cruise among the Islands of the Western Pacific, including the Feejees and others inhabited by the Polynesian Negro races, in Her Majesty's Ship 'Havannah'*, London, John Murray, 1853.

Jameson, R. G. *New Zealand, South Australia and New South Wales: A record of recent travels in these colonies . . .* , London, Smith, Elder & Co., 1842.

Judd, Laura Fish. *Honolulu: Sketches of Life Social, Political, and Religious, in the Hawaiian Islands, From 1828 to 1861*, New York, Anson D. F. Randolph & Co., 1880.

Kay, E. Alison, ed. 'The Sandwich Islands From Richard Brinsley Hinds' Journal of the Voyage of the Sulphur (1836-1842)', *The Hawaiian Journal of History*, II (1968), 102-35.

Keate, George. *An account of the Pelew Islands, situated in the western part of the Pacific Ocean; composed from the journals and communications of Captain Henry Wilson, and some of his officers, who, in August, 1783, were there shipwrecked in the Antelope . . .* London, Printed for Captain Wilson, 1789.

Kenny, Robert W., ed. *The New Zealand Journal 1842-1844 of John B. Williams of Salem, Massachusetts*, Salem, Peabody Museum, 1956.

Knights, John B. 'A Journal of a voyage in the brig Spy of Salem (1832-1834), John B. Knights, Master', in *The Sea, The Ship and The Sailor*, introduced by Captain Eliot Snow, Salem, Marine Research Society, 1925.

Kotzebue, Otto von. *A New Voyage Round the World in the Years 1823, 24, 25 and 26*, 2 vols., London, Henry Colburn & Richard Bentley 1830.

———— *Voyage of Discovery in the South Sea and to Behring's Straits, in search of a North-East Passage; undertaken in the Years 1815, 16, 17 and 18*, 2 vols., London, Printed for Sir Richard Phillips & Co., 1821.

Krusenstern, A. J. von. 'Extracts from two letters from Captain von Krusenstern . . . July 19, and August 20, 1804', *The Philosophical Magazine,* XXII (1805), 3-13 and 115-23.

———— *Voyage Round the World, in the Years 1803, 1804, 1805 and 1806,* translated from German, 2 vols., London, John Murray, 1813.

Lamont, E. H. *Wild Life Among the Pacific Islanders,* London, Hurst & Blackett, 1867.

Lang, John Dunmore. *New Zealand in 1839: or Four Letters, to the Right Hon. Earl Durham, Governor of the New Zealand Land Company . . . ,* London, Smith, Elder & Co., 1839.

Langsdorff, G. H. von. *Voyages and Travels in Various Parts of the World During the Years 1803, 1804, 1805, 1806 and 1807,* 2 vols., London, Henry Colburn, 1813.

La Pérouse, J. F. G. de. *A Voyage round the World, performed in the Years 1785, 1786, 1787 and 1788, by the Boussole and Astrolabe . . . ,* 2 vols., London, G. G. & J. Robinson, 1799.

Lay, William and C. M. Hussey. *A Narrative of the Mutiny, on board the Ship Globe . . . and the Journal of a Residence of Two Years on the Mulgrave Islands: . . . ,* New London, Published by the Authors, 1828.

Lisiansky, Urey. *A Voyage Round the World in the Years 1803, 4, 5 & 6,* London, John Booth, 1814.

Little, George. *Life on the Ocean, or Twenty Years at Sea, being the personal adventures of the author,* Aberdeen, George Clark & Son, 1847.

[Liverpool, Cecil George S. Foljambe, 4th Earl of]. *Three Years on the Australian Station,* London, Hatchard & Co., 1868.

[Lucett, E.]. *Rovings in the Pacific, from 1837 to 1849; with a Glance at California,* 2 vols., London, Longman, Brown, Green and Longmans, 1851.

M'Donnell, Thomas. *Extracts from Mr. M'Donnell's MS. Journal, containing observations on New Zealand,* London, John Moyes, 1834.

M'Konochie, Alexander. *A Summary View of the Statistics and Existing Commerce of the Principal Shores of the Pacific Ocean: With a Sketch of the Advantages, political and commercial, which would result from the establishment of a central free port within its limits,* London, James M. Richardson & William Blackwood, 1818.

M'L., A. 'A Trading Voyage among the South Sea Islands', South Sea Islands Newspaper Cuttings, Q988/S in ML.

McNab, Robert, ed. *Historical Records of New Zealand,* 2 vols., Wellington, Government Printer, 1908, 1914.

Macrae, James. *With Lord Byron at the Sandwich Islands in 1825, Being extracts from the MS. diary of James Macrea Scottish Botanist,* arranged by W. F. Wilson, Honolulu, —, 1922.

Markham, Edward. *New Zealand, or recollections of it,* edited with an introduction by E. H. McCormick, Wellington, Government Printer, 1963.

Marmon, John. 'Scenes from the Life of John Marmon', *The New Zealand Herald*, 9, 16 October, 6, 13, 27 November, 11 December 1880.

Marshall, William B. *A Personal Narrative of Two Visits to New Zealand in His Majesty's Ship Alligator A.D. 1834*, London, James Nisbet, 1836.

Martin, John. *An Account of the Natives of the Tonga Islands, in the South Pacific Ocean . . . Comp. and arranged from the extensive communications of Mr. William Mariner*, 2 vols., London, John Murray, 1817.

Mathison, Gilbert F. *Narrative of a Visit to Brazil, Chile, Peru and the Sandwich Islands 1821 and 1822*, London, Charles Knight, 1825.

Melville, Herman. *Omoo: A Narrative of Adventures in the South Seas; a sequel to 'Typee or the Marquesas Islanders'*, London, John Murray, 1893.

————— *Typee: A Peep at Polynesian Life, during a four months' residence in a Valley of the Marquesas*, London, George Routledge & Co., 1850.

Menzies, Archibald. *Hawaii Nei 128 Years Ago*, edited by W. F. Wilson, Honolulu, —, 1920.

Moerenhout, J-A. *Voyages aux îles du grand océan, contenant des documens nouveaux sur la géographie physique et politique, . . . et des considérations générales sur leur commerce, leur histoire et leur gouvernment, depuis les temps les plus reculés jusqu'à nos jours*, 2 vols., Paris, Adrien Maisonneuve, 1837.

Morison, S. E. 'Boston Traders in the Hawaiian Islands, 1789-1823', *Massachusetts Historical Society*, LIV (1920-1), 9-47.

Morgan, John. *The Life and Adventures of William Buckley: thirty-two years a wanderer amongst the Aborigines of the then unexplored country round Port Phillip now the Province of Victoria*, Hobart, Archibald MacDougall, 1852.

Morrell, Benjamin, Jr. *A Narrative of Four Voyages to the South Sea, North and South Pacific Ocean, Chinese Sea, Ethiopic and South Atlantic Ocean, Indian and Antarctic Ocean From the year 1822 to 1831 . . .*, New York, J. & J. Harper, 1832.

Morrison, James. *The Journal of James Morrison Boatswain's Mate of the Bounty, describing the Mutiny and subsequent misfortunes of the mutineers together with an account of the Island of Tahiti*, London, The Golden Cockerel Press, 1935.

[Moss, F. J.] *A Month in Fiji*, Melbourne, Samuel Mullen, 1868.

Murray, A. W. *Forty Years' Mission Work in Polynesia and New Guinea, from 1835 to 1875*, London, James Nisbet & Co., 1876.

Nautical Magazine, 1833, 1852, 1853, 1868.

Nicholas, John Liddiard. *Narrative of a Voyage to New Zealand in the years 1814 and 1815 . . .*, 2 vols., London, James Black & Son, 1817.

Nightingale, Thomas. *Oceanic Sketches,* London, James Cochrane & Co., 1835.

O'Connell, James F. *A Residence of Eleven Years in New Holland and the Caroline Islands,* Boston, B. B. Mussey, 1836.

[Oliver, James]. *Wreck of the Glide with Recollections of the Fijiis, and of Wallis Island,* New York, Wiley and Putnam, 1848.

Olmsted, Francis A. *Incidents of a Whaling Voyage, to which are added, observations on the Scenery, Manners and Customs, and Missionary Stations of the Sandwich and Society Islands,* London, John Neale, 1844.

Orlebar, J. *A Midshipman's Journal, on board H.M.S. Seringapatam during the year 1830; . . .* London, Whittaker, Treacher and Co., 1833.

Pacific Commercial Advertiser, 10 July 1856. [Alexander Adams's reminiscences of 4 July 1812.]

Parker, Rev. Samuel. *Journal of an Exploring Tour Beyond the Rocky Mountains, under the direction of the ABCFM performed in the Years 1835, '36 and '37,* Minneapolis, Ross and Haines, 1967.

Patterson, Samuel. *Narrative of the Adventures and Sufferings of Samuel Patterson, experienced in the Pacific Ocean, and many other parts of the world, with an account of the Feegee, and Sandwich Islands,* Rhode Island, From the Press in Palmer, 1817.

Pease, Henry. 'Adventure on St. Augustine Island', *The Dukes County Intelligencer,* III (May 1962), 3-13.

Pechey, W. C. *Fijian Cotton Culture, and Planters' Guide to the Islands,* London, Jarrold & Sons, 1870.

Pembroke, George R. C. H., 13th Earl of. 'The Fiji Islands with a few remarks on the Labour Trade', *Temple Bar,* XXXVI (November 1872), 22-31.

————— and G. H. Kingsley, *South Sea Bubbles: by the earl and the doctor,* London, Richard Bentley & Son, 1872.

Perkins, Edward T. *Na Motu: or Reef-Rovings in the South Seas,* New York, Pudney & Russell, 1854.

Pierce, Richard A. *Russia's Hawaiian Adventure, 1815-1817,* Berkeley, University of California Press, 1965.

Polack, J. S. *Manners and Customs of the New Zealanders; with notes corroborative of their habits, usages, etc., . . . ,* 2 vols., London, James Madden & Co., 1840.

————— *New Zealand: being a narrative of travels and adventures during a residence in that country between the years 1831 and 1837,* 2 vols., London, Richard Bentley, 1839.

Polynesian, June 1840-December 1841. In 1844 it recommenced publication under the same name and became the official government paper.

Porter, David. *Journal of a cruise made to the Pacific Ocean, by Captain David Porter in the United States Frigate Essex in the years 1812, 1813 and 1814,* 2 vols., Philadelphia, Bradford and Inskeep, 1815.

Porter, Robert Ker. *Travelling Sketches in Russia and Sweden, during the years 1805, 1806, 1807, 1808,* 2 vols., London, Richard Phillips, 1809. [Vol. II contains a description of the Marquesan beach-comber, Jean Cabri, in Moscow.]

Pritchard, W. T. *Polynesian Reminiscences; or, Life in the South Pacific Islands,* London, Chapman & Hall, 1866.

Reynolds, J. N. *Voyage of United States Frigate Potomac . . . during the circumnavigation of the Globe in the years 1831, 1832, 1833 and 1834 . . .* New York, Harper and Brothers, 1835.

Reynolds, Stephen. *The Voyage of the New Hazard to the Northwest Coast, Hawaii and China, 1810-1813,* edited by F. W. Howay, Salem, Peabody Museum, 1938.

Rieman, G. B. *Papalangee; or, Uncle Sam in Samoa,* Oakland, Butter & Stilwell, 1874.

Roe, Michael, ed. *The Journal and Letters of Captain Charles Bishop on the North-West Coast of America, in the Pacific and in New South Wales 1794-1799,* Cambridge, Published for the Hakluyt Society, At the University Press, 1967.

Rogers, Lawrence M., ed. *The Early Journals of Henry Williams Senior Missionary in New Zealand of the Church Mission Society 1826-40,* Christchurch, Pegasus Press, 1961.

Roquefeuil, M. Camille de. *A Voyage Round the World Between the years 1816-1819,* London, Richard Phillips & Co., 1823.

Ross, Alexander. *Adventures of the First Settlers on the Oregon or Columbia River,* London, Smith, Elder & Co., 1849.

Sailors Magazine, 1833-6.

St Julian, Charles. *Notes on the Latent Resources of Polynesia,* Sydney, Printed by Kemp & Fairfax, 1851.

Samoa Times, 1877-81.

Samoan Reporter, 1845-70. A missionary publication concerned largely with their own activities.

Sandwich Island Gazette, and Journal of Commerce, 1836-9.

Sandwich Island Mirror and Commercial Gazette, 1839-40 (twelve issues only including a supplement in January 1840).

Savage, John. *Some Account of New Zealand,* Dunedin, Hocken Library, 1966.

Seed, W. 'Area, Population, Trade etc. of the Principal Groups of Islands', in *Papers relating to the South Sea Islands, Their Natural Products, Trade Resources, etc., etc.,* 1-17, Wellington, 1874.

Seemann, Berthold. 'Foreign Correspondence', *The Athenaeum,* 26 January 1861.

———— *Viti: An Account of a Government Mission to the Vitian or Fijian Islands in the years 1860-61,* Cambridge, Macmillan & Co., 1862.

[Shaler, William]. 'Journal of a Voyage Between China and the North-West Coast of America made in 1804', *American Register,* III (1808), 137-75.

Shaw, Leonard. 'A Brief Sketch of the Sufferings of Leonard Shaw on Massacre Island', in Benjamin Morrell Jr, *A Narrative of Four Voyages to the South Sea, the North and South Pacific Ocean, Chinese Sea, Ethiopic and South Atlantic Ocean, Indian and Antarctic Ocean From the Year 1822 to 1831,* New York, J. & J. Harper, 1832.

Shaw, William. *Golden Dreams and Waking Realities; being the Adventures of a Gold-Seeker in California and the Pacific Islands,* London, Smith, Elder & Co., 1851.

Shipley, Conway. *Sketches in the Pacific: The South Sea Islands,* London, T. McLean, 1851.

Simpson, Alexander. *The Sandwich Islands: Progress of Events since their Discovery by Captain Cook. Their Occupation by Lord George Paulet. Their Value and Importance,* London, Smith, Elder & Co., 1843.

Simpson, George. *Narrative of a Journey Round the World, During the Years 1841 and 1842,* 2 vols., London, Henry Colburn, 1847.

Smythe, Mrs S. M. *Ten Months in the Fiji Islands,* Oxford, John Henry & James Parker, 1864.

Stanmore, Arthur C. Hamilton Gordon. *Fiji: Records of Private and of Public Life 1875-1880,* 4 vols., Edinburgh, Printed by R. & R. Clark Ltd, 1897-1912.

Sterndale, H. B. 'Memoranda . . . on some of the South Sea Islands', in *Papers relating to the South Sea Islands, Their Natural Products, Trade Resources, etc., etc.,* 1-55, Wellington, 1874.

Stewart, C. S. *The Hawaiian Islands in 1822,* Boston, The Old South Association, Old South Leaflet No. 221, n.d.

Tetens, Alfred. *Among the Savages of the South Seas; Memoirs of Micronesia, 1862-1868 by Captain Alfred Tetens,* translated by Florence M. Spoehr, Stanford, Stanford University Press, 1958.

Thurston, Lucy G. *Life and Times of Mrs. Lucy G. Thurston, wife of Rev. Asa Thurston, Pioneer Missionary to the Sandwich Islands, . . . over a period of more than Fifty Years,* Michigan, S. C. Andrews, 1882.

Torrey, William. *Torrey's Narrative: or, the Life and Adventures of William Torrey. Who for the space of 25 months, . . . was held a captive by the cannibals of the Marquesas . . . ,* Boston, A. J. Wright, 1848.

Townsend, Ebenezer Jr. 'Extract from The Diary of Ebenezer Townsend Jr., Supercargo on the Sealing Ship "Neptune" on her voyage to the South Pacific and Canton', *Hawaiian Historical Society Reprints,* No. 4, n.d.

Transactions of the Missionary Society, vol. I, London, The Missionary Society, 1804.

Trood, Thomas. *Island Reminiscences; a graphic detailed romance of life spent in the South Sea Islands,* Sydney, McCarron, Stewart

& Co., 1912.

Turnbull, John. *A Voyage round the World in the Years 1800, 1801, 1802, 1803 and 1804* . . . London, A. Maxwell, 1813.

Turner, George. *Nineteen Years in Polynesia: missionary life, travels, and researches in the islands of the Pacific,* London, John Snow, 1861.

Turpin, Edwin. *Turpin's Fijian Nautical and Commercial Almanac and Fiji Directory, 1873 & 1874,* Levuka, printed by William Cook, 1873 and 1874.

Twyning, John P. *Shipwreck and Adventures of John P. Twyning among the South Sea Islanders: giving an account of their feasts, massacres, etc., etc.* . . . , London, Printed for the benefit of the author, 1849.

Tyerman, Daniel and George Bennet. *Journal of Voyages and Travels,* compiled from original documents by James Montgomery, 2 vols., London, Frederick Westley & A. H. Davis, 1831.

Vancouver, George. 'A Letter from Vancouver, March 2, 1794', *Hawaiian Historical Society Annual Report,* 1908, 18-19.

————— *A Voyage of Discovery to the North Pacific Ocean and Round the World* . . . *1790* . . . *1795,* 6 vols., London, John Stockdale, 1801.

[Vason, George]. *An Authentic Narrative of Four Years' Residence at Tongataboo one of the Friendly Islands, in the South Sea, by* ————— *who went thither in the 'Duff', under Captain Wilson, in 1796,* London, Longman, Hurst, Rees, Orme, L. B. Seeley and Hatchard, 1810.

Vox Populi. *British Despotism in the South Seas Islands, and the Persecution of Mr. W. J. Hunt by Sir Arthur Gordon, High Commissioner,* Wellington, Printed at the New Zealand Times Office, 1883.

Wallis, Mrs M. D. *Life in Feejee, or, Five Years among the Cannibals,* Boston, William Heath, 1851.

Walpole, Frederick. *Four Years in the Pacific in her Majesty's Ship 'Collingwood' from 1844 to 1848,* 2 vols., London, Richard Bentley, 1849.

Ward, R. G., ed. *American Activities in the Central Pacific, 1790-1870. A history, geography and ethnography pertaining to American involvement and Americans in the Pacific taken from contemporary Newspapers, etc.,* 8 vols., Ridgewood, N.J., The Gregg Press, 1967.

Waterhouse, Joseph. *The King and the People of Fiji: containing a life of Thakombau* . . . , London, Wesleyan Conference Office, 1866.

Wilkes, Charles. *Narrative of the United States Exploring Expedition during the years 1838, 1839, 1840, 1841, 1842,* 5 vols., London, Wiley & Putman, 1845.

Williams, John. *A Narrative of Missionary Enterprises in the South Sea Islands* . . . , London, John Snow, 1846.

Williams, Thomas and James Calvert. *Fiji and the Fijians,* edited by G. S. Rowe, 2 vols., London, Alexander Heylin, 1858.

Wilson, James. *A Missionary Voyage to the Southern Pacific Ocean, performed in the years 1796, 1797, 1798, in the Ship 'Duff', Commanded by Captain James Wilson,* . . . , London, Printed for T. Chapman, 1799.

Wright, Olive. *The Voyage of the Astrolabe — 1840. An English render-ing of the journals of Dumont d'Urville and his officers of their visit to New Zealand in 1840* . . . Wellington, A. H. & A. W. Reed, 1955.

III SECONDARY MATERIAL
Books, Articles and Unpublished Works
Alexander, W. D. 'The Oahu Charity School', *Hawaiian Historical Society Annual Report*, 1908, 20-38.
Andersen, J. C. and G. C. Petersen. *The Mair Family*, Wellington, A. H. & A. W. Reed, 1956.
Australian Dictionary of Biography 1788-1850, general editor, Douglas Pike, 2 vols., Melbourne, Melbourne University Press, 1966-7.
Bagnall, A. G. and G. C. Petersen. *William Colenso: Printer, Missionary, Botanist, Explorer, Politician. His Life and Journeys*, Wellington, A. H. & A. W. Reed, 1948.
Beaglehole, Ernest. *Social Change in the South Pacific: Rarotonga and Aitutaki*, London, G. Allen & Unwin, 1957.
Beaglehole, J. C. *The Exploration of the Pacific*, London, Black, 1966.
Belshaw, Cyril. 'Pacific Island Towns and the Theory of Growth', in Alexander Spoehr, ed., *Pacific Port Towns and Cities: A Symposium*, 17-24, Honolulu, Bishop Museum Press, 1963.
Bergman, George F. J. 'Solomon Levey in Sydney, from convict to mer-chant prince', *Royal Australian Historical Society Journal*, XLIX (March 1964), 401-22.
Billington, R. A. *The American Frontiersman*, Oxford, Clarendon Press, 1954.
Binney, Judith. *The Legacy of Guilt: A Life of Thomas Kendall*, Uni-versity of Auckland, Oxford University Press, 1968.
Blumer, Herbert. 'The Nature of Race Prejudice', in Edgar T. Thompson and Everett C. Hughes, eds., *Race: Individual and Collective Behaviour*, 484-92, Glencoe, The Free Press, 1958.
———— 'Race Prejudice as a Sense of Group Position', in J. Masuoka and P. Valien, eds., *Race Relations: Problems and Theory, Essays in Honor of Robert E. Park*, 217-27, Chapel Hill, University of North Carolina Press, 1961.
Bolton, W. W. 'The Beginnings of Papeete and its Founding as the Capital of Tahiti', *Société des Etudes Océaniennes*, V, No. 12, (1935), 437-42.
Bradley, Harold W. *The American Frontier in Hawaii: The Pioneers 1789-1843*, Stanford, Stanford University Press, 1942.
British Admiralty, Naval Intelligence Division, *Geographical Handbook Pacific Islands*, 4 vols., London, 1945.
Brookes, Jean I. *International Rivalry in the Pacific Islands 1800-1875*, Berkeley, University of California Press, 1941.
Carleton, Hugh. *The Life of Henry Williams Archdeacon of Waimate*, Wellington, A. H. & A. W. Reed, 1948.

Cartwright, Bruce. 'Place Names in Old Honolulu', *Paradise of the Pacific*, L (January 1938), 18-20.

Cochrane, D. G. 'Racialism in the Pacific: A descriptive analysis', *Oceania*, XL (1969), 1-12.

Cottez, J. 'Jean-Baptiste Rives, de Bordeaux aventurier hawaien (1793-1833)', *Société des Etudes Océaniennes*, X (June and September 1958), 792-812, 819-46.

Couper, Alastair D. The Island Trade: An Analysis of the Environment and Operation of Seaborne Trade among three Island Groups in the Pacific (Ph.D. thesis, Australian National University, 1967).

Cowan, James. *A Trader in Cannibal Land, The Life and Adventures of Captain Tapsell*, Dunedin, A. H. & A. W. Reed, 1935.

Cumpston, J. S. *Shipping Arrivals and Departures, Sydney, 1788-1825*, Canberra, —, 1963.

The Cyclopedia of Fiji, Sydney, The Cyclopedia Company of Fiji, 1907.

The Cyclopedia of Samoa, Tonga, Tahiti and the Cook Islands, Sydney, McCarron, Stewart & Co., 1907.

Davidson, J. W. European Penetration of the South Pacific 1779-1842 (Ph.D. thesis, Cambridge University, 1942).

————— 'Peter Dillon: the voyages of the *Calder* and *St Patrick*', in J. W. Davidson and Deryck Scarr, eds., *Pacific Islands Portraits*, Canberra, Australian National University Press, 1970.

————— *Samoa mo Samoa: The Emergence of the Independent State of Western Samoa*, Melbourne, Oxford University Press, 1967.

Daws, Gavan. 'The Decline of Puritanism at Honolulu in the Nineteenth Century', *The Hawaiian Journal of History*, I (1967), 31-42.

————— 'The High Chief Boki — A Biographical Study in Early Nineteenth Century Hawaiian History', *Journal of the Polynesian Society*, LXXV (March 1966), 65-83.

————— Honolulu — The First Century: Influences in the Development of the Town to 1876 (Ph.D. thesis, University of Hawaii, 1966).

————— 'Honolulu in the 19th Century: Notes on the Emergence of Urban Society in Hawaii', *The Journal of Pacific History*, II (1967), 77-96.

————— *Shoal of Time*, New York, Macmillan & Co., 1968.

Deighton, H. S. 'History and the Study of Race Relations', *Race*, I (1959), 15-25.

Dening, Gregory. 'Ethnohistory in Polynesia: The Value of Ethnohistorical Evidence', *The Journal of Pacific History*, I (1966), 23-42.

Derrick, R. A. 'The Early Days of Levuka', *Transactions of the Fiji Society*, II (1940-4), 49-58.

————— *A History of Fiji*, Suva, Printing & Stationery Dept, 1946.

Dodge, Ernest S. 'Captain Benjamin Vanderford of Salem', *Essex Institute Historical Collections*, LXXIX (October 1943), 315-29.

————— 'Fiji Trader', *Proceedings of the Massachusetts Historical Society*, LXXVIII (1966), 3-19.

————— *New England and the South Seas,* Cambridge, Mass., Harvard University Press, 1965.

Dorrance, John C. John Brown Williams and the American Claims in Fiji (A Study), Microfilm — Pacific Manuscripts Bureau, 27.

Doumenge, François. 'Development of Papeete — Capital of French Polynesia', *South Pacific Bulletin,* XVII, No. 3 (1967), 47-51.

Drummond, James, ed. *John Rutherford the White Chief,* Christchurch, Whitcombe and Tombs Ltd, 1908.

Elbert, Samuel H. and Torben Monberg. *From the Two Canoes: Oral Traditions of Rennell and Bellona Islands,* Honolulu, Copenhagen, University of Hawaii Press in co-operation with the Danish National Museum, 1965.

Emory, Kenneth P. *Kapingamarangi: Social and Religious Life of a Polynesian Atoll,* Honolulu, Bishop Museum Bulletin 228, 1965.

Firth, Raymond. *History and Traditions of Tikopia,* Wellington, The Polynesian Society, 1961.

Fornander, Abraham. *An Account of the Polynesian Race Its Origins and Migrations and the Ancient History of the Hawaiian People to the Times of Kamehameha I,* 2 vols., London, Trübner, 1878.

France, Peter. *The Charter of the Land: Custom and Colonization in Fiji,* Melbourne, Oxford University Press, 1969.

Freeman, J. D. 'The Joe Gimlet or Siovili Cult', in J. D. Freeman and W. D. Geddes, eds., *Anthropology in the South Seas,* 185-200, New Plymouth, N.Z., Thomas Avery & Sons, 1959.

Gibbons, Peter. Some thoughts on the Pre-1840 Paheka-Maori, Term Paper, Massey University, Palmerston North, N.Z., 1969.

Gilman, Gorman D. 'Streets of Honolulu in the Early Forties', *The Hawaiian Almanac,* 1904, 74-101.

Gilson, R. P. Administration of the Cook Islands (Rarotonga) (M.Sc. thesis, University of London, 1952).

————— *Samoa 1830 to 1900: The Politics of a Multi-cultural Community,* Melbourne, Oxford University Press, 1970.

Greenwood, Gordon. *Early American-Australian Relations from the arrival of the Spaniards in America to the close of 1830,* Melbourne, Melbourne University Press, 1944.

Greer, Richard A. 'Here Lies History: Oahu Cemetery, A Mirror of Old Honolulu', *The Hawaiian Journal of History,* I (1967), 53-71.

Gunson, Niel. 'The Deviations of a Missionary Family: the Henrys of Tahiti', in J. W. Davidson and Deryck Scarr, eds., *Pacific Islands Portraits,* Canberra, Australian National University Press, 1970.

————— Evangelical Missionaries in the South Seas 1797-1860 (Ph.D. thesis, Australian National University, 1959).

Hainsworth, D. R. 'In Search of a Staple: The Sydney Sandalwood Trade 1804-09', *Business Archives and History,* V (1965), 1-20.

Hallowell, A. I. 'American Indians, White and Black: The Phenomenon of Transculturization', *Current. Anthropology,* IV (December 1963),

519-31.

Handy, E. S. C. *History and Culture in the Society Islands,* Honolulu, Bishop Museum Press, 1930.

Henderson, G. C. History of Government in Fiji 1760-1875, 2 vols., typescript on microfilm in ML.

Henderson, G. M., ed. *The Antecedents and Early Life of Valentine Savage, Known as Taina,* Wellington, The Wingfield Press, 1948.

Horton, Donald. 'The Functions of Alcohol in Primitive Societies: A Cross Cultural Study', in Clyde Kluckhohn and Henry A. Murray, eds., *Personality in Nature, Society and Culture,* New York, Alfred A. Knopf, 1948.

Hughes, Everett C. 'The Nature of Racial Frontiers', in J. Masuoka and P. Valien, eds., *Race Relations: Problems and Theory, Essays in Honor of Robert E. Park,* Chapel Hill, The University of North Carolina Press, 1961.

Jore, Léonce A. 'Captain Jules Dudoit, the First French Consul in the Hawaiian Islands 1837-1867 and his Brig Schooner, the Clementine', Translated by Dorothy B. Aspinwall, *Hawaiian Historical Society Annual Report,* 1955, 21-36.

————— 'Le Capitaine Irlandais Thomas Ebrill', *Société des Etudes Océaniennes,* XI (June 1961), 261-80.

Kamakau, Samuel M. *Ruling Chiefs of Hawaii,* Honolulu, The Kamehameha Schools Press, 1961.

Kelly, D. L. The Part Europeans of Fiji (M.Sc. thesis, Victoria University, Wellington, 1966).

King, Marie M. *Port in the North: A Short History of Russell, New Zealand,* Russell, Published by Russell Centennial Committee, n.d. [1949].

Knight, Oliver. 'The *Owyhee Avalanche*: The Frontier Newspaper as a Catalyst in Social Change', *Pacific Northwest Quarterly,* LVIII (April 1967), 74-81.

Koskinen, A. A. *Missionary Influence as a Political Factor in the Pacific Islands,* Helsinki, Suomalaisen Tiedeakatemian Toimituksia, 1953.

Kuykendall, Ralph S. *The Hawaiian Kingdom 1778-1854: Foundation and Transformation,* Honolulu, University of Hawaii Press, 1968.

Lee, John R. Southseaman. The Story of the Bay of Islands, typescript in Turnbull Library, Wellington, 1952.

Legge, Christopher. 'William Diaper: A Biographical Sketch', *The Journal of Pacific History,* I (1966), 79-90.

Legge, John D. *Britain in Fiji 1858-1880,* London, Macmillan & Co., 1958.

Lennard, Maurice. *Motuarohia, An Island in the Bay of Islands,* Auckland, Pelorus Press, 1959.

Leroy, Paul E. 'The Emancipists, Edward Eagar, and the Struggle for Civil Liberties', *Royal Australian Historical Society Journal,* XLVIII (1962), 270-301.

Lind, Andrew W. 'Race Relations Frontiers in Hawaii', in J. Masuoka and P. Valien, eds., *Race Relations: Problems and Theory, Essays in Honor of Robert E. Park,* Chapel Hill, University of North Carolina Press, 1961.

Lips, J. E. *The Savage Hits Back; or, The White Man through Native Eyes,* translated by Vincent Benson, London, Lovat Dickson, 1937.

McArthur, Norma. 'Essays in Multiplication: European Seafarers in Polynesia', *The Journal of Pacific History,* I (1966), 91-105.

[Maning, F. E.]. *Old New Zealand; a tale of the good old times; . . . ,* London, R. Bentley, 1876.

Mannoni, O. *Prospero and Caliban: The Psychology of Colonization,* translated by Pamela Powesland, London, Methuen & Co. Ltd, 1956.

Martin, K. L. P. *Missionaries and Annexation in the Pacific,* London, Oxford University Press, 1924.

Marwick, J. G., compiler. *The Adventures of John Renton,* Kirkwall, Kirkwall Press, 1935.

Mason, Philip. *An Essay on Racial Tension,* London, Royal Institute of International Affairs, 1954.

—————— *Prospero's Magic: Some Thoughts on Class and Race,* London, Oxford University Press, 1962.

Masterman, Sylvia. *The Origins of International Rivalry in Samoa 1845-1884,* London, George Allen & Unwin Ltd, 1934.

Maude, H. E. 'Baiteke and Binoka of Abemama: Arbiters of Change in the Gilbert Islands', in J. W. Davidson and Deryck Scarr, eds., *Pacific Islands Portraits,* Canberra, Australian National University Press, 1970.

—————— *Of Islands and Men: Studies in Pacific History,* Melbourne, Oxford University Press, 1968.

—————— and Edwin Doran Jr. 'The Precedence of Tarawa Atoll', *Annals of the Association of American Geographers,* LVI (June 1966), 269-89.

Millar, David P. *Whalers, flax traders and Maoris of the Cook Strait area: an historical study in cultural confrontation,* Wellington, Dominion Museum, 1971.

Moorehead, Alan. *The Fatal Impact: an account of the invasion of the South Pacific 1767-1840,* London, Hamish Hamilton, 1966.

Morrell, W. P. *Britain in the Pacific Islands,* Oxford, Clarendon Press, 1960.

Newbury, Colin. 'Aspects of Cultural Change in French Polynesia: The Decline of the Arii', *Journal of the Polynesian Society,* 76 (1967), 7-26.

Oliver, Douglas L. 'Papeete, Tahiti', in Alexander Spoehr, ed., *Pacific Port Towns and Cities: A Symposium,* Honolulu, Bishop Museum Press, 1963.

O'Reilly, Patrick. *Tahitiens supplément Répertoire bio-bibliographique de la Polynésie Française,* Paris, Publications de la Société des

Océanistes, 1966.

————— and Raoul Teissier. *Tahitiens. Répertoire bio-bibliographique de la Polynésie Française,* Paris, Publications de la Société des Océanistes, 1962.

Ottino, Paul. *Ethno-histoire de Rangiroa,* Papeete, Centre Ostrom, n.d.

Overell, Lilian. *A Woman's Impressions of German New Guinea,* London, John Lane, The Bodley Head Ltd, 1923.

Paske-Smith, M. *Early British Consuls in Hawaii,* Honolulu, Star Bulletin Ltd, 1936.

Pearson, W. H. 'The Reception of European Voyagers on Polynesian Islands 1568-1797', *Journal de la Société des Océanistes,* 26 (1970), 121-53.

Porter, Kenneth W. 'Notes on Negroes in Early Hawaii', *Journal of Negro History,* XIX (April 1934), 193-7.

Putnam, George G. *Salem Vessels and their Voyages: A History of . . . South Pacific Islands Trade as carried on by Salem Merchants, particularly the firm of N. L. Rogers & Brothers,* Vol. IV, Salem, Massachusetts, The Essex Institute, 1930.

Ralston, Caroline. 'The Pattern of Race Relations in 19th Century Pacific Port Towns', *The Journal of Pacific History,* 6 (1971), 39-59.

Ramsden, Eric. *Busby of Waitangi; H.M's Resident at New Zealand, 1833-40,* Wellington, A. H. & A. W. Reed, 1942.

Rappaport, Roy A. 'Aspects of Man's Influence upon Island Ecosystems: Alteration and Control', in F. R. Fosberg, ed., *Man's Place in the Island Ecosystem,* H. E. Maude, discussant, Honolulu, Bishop Museum Press, 1963.

Restarick, H. B. 'The First Clergyman Resident in Hawaii', *Hawaiian Historical Society Papers,* 1923, 54-61.

Reuter, Edward B. 'Impersonal Aspects of Race Relations', in Edgar T. Thompson and Everett C. Hughes, eds., *Race: Individual and Collective Behaviour,* Glencoe, The Free Press, 1958.

Riesenberg, Saul H. *The Native Polity of Ponape,* Washington, Smithsonian Institution Press, 1968.

Robson, R. W. *Queen Emma: The Samoan-American Girl who founded an Empire in 19th Century New Guinea,* Sydney, Pacific Publications, 1965.

Roe, Michael. 'Australia's Place in the Swing to the East 1788-1810', *Historical Studies, Australia and New Zealand,* 8 (1958), 202-13.

Ross, Ruth M. *New Zealand's First Capital,* Wellington, Department of Internal Affairs, 1946.

Sahlins, Marshall D. 'Poor Man, Rich Man, Big-Man, Chief: Political Types in Melanesia and Polynesia', in Ian Hogbin and L. R. Hiatt, eds., *Readings in Australian and Pacific Anthropology,* Melbourne, Melbourne University Press, 1966.

Scarr, Deryck. *Fragments of Empire: A History of the Western Pacific*

High Commission 1877-1914, Canberra, Australian National University Press, 1967.

———— 'John Bates Thurston, Commodore J. G. Goodenough, and Rampant Anglo-Saxons in Fiji', *Historical Studies, Australia and New Zealand,* 11 (1964), 361-82.

Schmitt, Robert C. 'Early Crime Statistics of Hawaii'. *Hawaiian Historical Review,* II (July 1966), 325-31.

Scholefield, G. H., ed. *A Dictionary of New Zealand Biography,* 2 vols., Wellington, Department of Internal Affairs, 1940.

Schwimmer, E. G. 'The Mediator', *Journal of the Polynesian Society,* LXVII (1958), 335-50.

Shawcross, Kathleen. The Maoris of the Bay of Islands, 1769-1840: A Study of Changing Maori Responses to European Contact (M.A. thesis, University of Auckland, 1967).

Sherrin, R. A. A. *Early History of New Zealand. From Earliest Times to 1840,* Auckland, H. Brett, 1890.

Sherwood, L. M. 'An Account of Freemasonry in Fiji', *Transactions of the United Masters Lodge, No. 167, N.Z.C.* (n.d.), 249-52.

Shineberg, Dorothy. *They came for Sandalwood: A Study of the Sandalwood Trade in the South-West Pacific 1830-1865,* Melbourne, Melbourne University Press, 1967.

Sinclair, Keith. *A History of New Zealand,* Harmondsworth, Middlesex, Penguin Books, 1959.

Smith, Bernard W. *European Vision and the South Pacific, 1768-1850: A Study in the History of Art and Ideas,* Oxford, Clarendon Press, 1960.

Spate, O. H. K. 'The Nature of Historical Geography', *The Geographical Society of New South Wales Monthly Bulletin,* VII (November 1962), new series.

———— 'Toynbee and Huntington: A Study in Determinism', *Geographical Journal,* CXVIII (1952), 406-28.

Spear, T. G. P. *The Nabobs. A Study of the Social Life of the English in eighteenth century India,* London, Oxford University Press, 1932.

Spoehr, Alexander, ed. *Pacific Port Towns and Cities: A Symposium,* Honolulu, Bishop Museum Press, 1963.

———— 'Port Town and Hinterland in the Pacific Islands', *American Anthropologist,* LXII (1960), 586-92.

Spoehr, Florence M. *White Falcon: The House of Godeffroy and its Commercial and Scientific Role in the Pacific,* California, Pacific Books, 1963.

Stackpole, Edouard A. *The Seahunters: The New England Whalemen During Two Centuries 1635-1835,* Philadelphia, J. B. Lippincott, 1953.

Strauss, W. Patrick. *Americans in Polynesia 1783-1842,* East Lansing, Michigan State University Press, 1962.

Tapp, E. J. *Early New Zealand: A Dependency of New South Wales*

1788-1841, Melbourne, Melbourne University Press, 1958.

Thompson, Laura. *The Native Culture of the Marianas Islands,* Honolulu, Bishop Museum Bulletin 185, 1945.

Thomson, Arthur S. *The Story of New Zealand: Past and Present — Savage and Civilized,* 2 vols., London, John Murray, 1859.

Thomson, Basil. *South Sea Yarns,* Edinburgh, William Blackwood & Son, 1894.

Ward, John M. *British Policy in the South Pacific (1786-1893): A study in British policy towards the South Pacific islands prior to the establishment of Governments by the Great Powers,* Sydney, Australasian Publishing Co. Pty Ltd, 1948.

Ward, R. G. *Land Use and Population in Fiji: A Geographical Study,* London, Her Majesty's Stationery Office, 1965.

———— 'The Pacific Bêche-de-mer Trade with Special Reference to Fiji, in R. G. Ward, ed., *Man in the Pacific Islands,* Oxford, Clarendon Press, 1972.

Washburn, Wilcombe E., ed. *The Indian and the White Man,* New York, Anchor Books, Doubleday & Co. Inc., 1964.

Webb, M. C. 'The Abolition of the Taboo System in Hawaii', *Journal of the Polynesian Society,* LXXIV (March 1965), 21-39.

Wedgwood, Camilla H. 'Some Aspects of Warfare in Melanesia', *Oceania,* I (1930-1), 5-33.

Whipple, A. B. C. *Yankee Whalers in the South Seas,* London, Victor Gollancz, 1954.

Wright, Harrison M. *New Zealand, 1769-1840: Early Years of Western Contact,* Cambridge, Mass., Harvard University Press, 1959.

Wyman, W. D. and C. B. Kroeber, eds. *The Frontier in Perspective,* Madison, University of Wisconsin Press, 1957.

Young, John M. R. 'Australia's Pacific Frontier', *Historical Studies, Australia and New Zealand,* 12 (1966), 373-88.

———— Frontier Society in Fiji 1858-1873 (Ph.D. thesis, University of Adelaide, 1968).

Yzendoorn, Reginald, *History of the Catholic Mission in the Hawaiian Islands,* Honolulu, Honolulu Star Bulletin Ltd, 1927.

Index

Caroline Ralston is a graduate of The University of Adelaide and has a Ph.D. from The Australian National University. She is now Lecturer in History at Macquarie University, Sydney. In the course of research for her thesis on which this book is based she spent some time in the Pacific islands working in archives and libraries and gaining first-hand knowledge of the island world. Typesetting by TypoGraphics Communications, 234 Sussex Street, Sydney, 2000.

First published in Australia 1977

Printed in Australia for The Australian National University Press, Canberra